THE ECONOMICS OF THE GOA JESUITS, 1542-1759

About the Author

Charles Julius Borges is a Jesuit priest of the Goa Province of the Society of Jesus since 1967. Educated at Pune, Bombay, Belgaum, Baroda and Goa, he has had a fine academic career and obtained a doctorate in history from the University of Bombay in 1989. He had been Administrator of the Xavier Centre of Historical Research (Goa) since 1981 and most recently is its Associate Director. His field of research being Jesuit history in India, he has contributed many papers to national and international seminars on the above theme.

The Economics of the Goa Jesuits, 1542-1759 is his first book.

The Economics of the Goa Jesuits, 1542-1759

An Explanation of Their Rise and Fall

CHARLES J. BORGES

CONCEPT PUBLISHING COMPANY, NEW DELHI-110059

ISBN 81-7022-505-1

First Published 1994

Published and Printed by
Ashok Kumar Mittal
Concept Publishing Company
A/15-16, Commercial Block, Mohan Garden
NEW DELHI 110059 (India)

Lasertypeset by
Printing Express
H-13, Bali Nagar
NEW DELHI 110015

To
All the Jesuits of the Goa Province past and present with my admiration and respect

CONTENTS

LIST OF ABBREVIATIONS

ACE	*Assentos do Conselho do Estado, ed.* P.S.S. Pissurlencar
AGS	*Archivo General de Simancas,* Spain
AHNM	*Archivo Historico Nacional,* Madrid
AHSI	*Archivum Historicum Societatis Iesu,* Rome
AHU	*Arquivo Historico Ultramarino,* Lisbon
ANTT	*Arquivo Nacional da Torre do Tombo,* Lisbon
ARSI	*Archivum Romanum Societatis Iesu,* Rome
ASPR	*Anuario do Seminario-Patriarcal de Rachol*
Baz.	*bazaruco*
BEAG	*Boletim Eclesiastico da Arquidiocese de Goa*
BFUP	*Boletim da Filmoteca Ultramarina Portuguesa*
BG	*Boletim do Governo,* Panjim
BIVG	*Boletim do Instituto Vasco da Gama,* Bastora
BML	British Museum Library, London
BNM	Biblioteca Nacional, Madrid
Bro.	Brother
BVE	Biblioteca Nazionale Centrale Vittore Emmanuele II, Rome
DAAM	Directorate of Archives, Archaeology and Museum, Goa
DI	*Documenta Indica,* ed. J. Wicki
DRI	*Documentos Remetidos da India ou Livros das Monções,* ed. R.A. Bulhão Pato
DUP	*Documentação Ultramarina Portuguesa*
FG	*Fondo Gesuitico*, Rome
Fr.	Father
ICHR	*Indian Church History Review,* Bangalore
IOL	India Office Library, London
JBHS	*Journal of the Bombay Historical Society*
JIH	*Journal of Indian History,* University of Trivandrum, Kerala
JPHS	*Journal of Punjab Historical Society*
JRASB	*Journal of Royal Asiatic Society of Bengal*
MASB	*Memoirs of the Asiatic Society of Bengal*
MR	*Monções do Reino*
RF	*Relação das Fazendas*
rs.	*réis*
SASJ	Shembaganur Archives of the Society of Jesus, Kodaikanal
tga.	*tanga*
tgs.	*tangas*
xe.	*xerafim*
xs.	*xerafins*

LIST OF MAPS AND APPENDICES

APPENDICES

MAPS

ACKNOWLEDGEMENTS

My interest in the lives of the Jesuits in India and the world has grown ever since my entry into the Society of Jesus in June 1967. The exploits, travels and achievements of its members, the Jesuits, have struck me and have excited a deeper study into their lives ever since.

In this study, I have written mainly about the Goa Jesuits. Goa was the centre of activity of the Portuguese Province since 1542. Many have chronicled their lives and labours, and these accounts have ranged from pure admiration on the one hand to total condemnation on the other. I have dwelt here more on their economic background, on the material avenues they explored to keep their missions and works going.

I am grateful to all who have helped me while I set about this work. I would like to thank for his encouragement and insights, my research guide, the late Prof. B.S. Shastry. Dr. Teotonio de Souza, Director, XCHR, has always been generous with his information, personal direction and involvement, all of which have been inestimable. He helped me decipher many documents and brought many more to my knowledge.

Dr. Jose Blanco of the Fundação Calouste Gulbenkian (FCG, Lisbon), made it possible for me to consult archival documentation in Europe during the latter half of 1987. I am much indebted to him personally and also to Mrs. Maria Clara Farinha of the International Services at the FCG. The Jesuit communities at Sacred Heart College (Shembaganur), Rua da Lapa (Lisbon), Jesuit Missions (London), Via dei Penitenzieri and Borgo Santo Spirito (Rome) were cordial and generous in their attention while I stayed in their midst during my time of research.

The management of the Directorate of Archives, Archaeology and Museum, Goa, and Mrs. T. Almeida, in particular, were most helpful in offering volumes of importance. Mrs. Lilia D'Souza, librarian, XCHR, and Fr. Timoteo Lobo brought much relevant material to my notice with their customary kindness and graciousness. Dr. S.K. Mhamai and Mr. R.N. Naik were kind enough to get ready for me some of the maps included in this volume. I recall the help accorded to me by Mrs. Pia Rodrigues and Mrs. Lourdes Costa Rodrigues of the Central Library, Panjim. I am indebted to Brig. Kevin F. D'Lima (Retd.) for preparing the delightful colour painting for the cover.

I am grateful to many others, Jesuits and friends, who in various ways had been interested in and supported my work. I am especially grateful to my former Provincials Frs. Romuald D'Souza (for the kind words, too, that he has written in the foreword to this book), to Leslie Almeida, the late Matthew Lederle, Edwin D'Souza and the present Provincial Superior Gregory Naik. Fr. Josef Ubelmesser (Nurenberg) and Fr. Hubert Hanggi (Zurich) took a keen interest in my research during my visit to Europe. I thank the members of my Jesuit community, past and present, Frs. Moreno de Souza, Antonio Pereira, Teotonio de Souza, Matthew Almeida, Pratap Naik, Edwin Sequeira, George N.K., Reinhold Kiess, Cajetan Coelho and Delio Mendonça for their brotherly support. I recall with deep gratitude all the encouragement and love I received from my late father Mr Peter Borges and from my mother Mrs. Anne Borges while in this field of research.

Fellow historians in Goa and elsewhere have been always generous with their suggestions and insights into Jesuit history and I thank most especially the renowned Prof. Charles Boxer, and Dr. J.S. Cummins, Dr. M.N. Pearson, Dr. Anthony Disney, Dr. George Winius, Fr. John Correia-Afonso, S.J., Dr. Carmo Azevedo, Dr. P.P. Shirodkar, Dr. K.M. Matthew, Prof. Daniel D'Souza, Dr. Joseph de Barros, Dr. Mariano Dias and Prof. Sharmila Veloso.

There are many others to whom I owe much in different ways and I am sure they will understand should I have failed to mention them personally. I trust that what I have presented will add in some small measure to the knowledge of the Society of Jesus in India.

FOREWORD

Right from its inception in 1540, the history of the Society of Jesus shows an impressive record of achievements with Goa as the centre of activity which extended from the Arabian Gulf to China and Japan. The towering personality of Francis Xavier dominates the early part of that record, but there are others, hundreds of them, whose clear sense of purpose and an extra level of commitment and enthusiasm got them involved in such varied endeavours as diplomacy, trade and commerce, the study of indigenous languages and the production of literary works, printing and publishing, together with evangelization and the practice of prayer.

The present work by Dr. Charles Borges gives us a deeper insight into the activities of the Goa Province of the Society of Jesus until its suppression in 1759, how it was able to attain a level of achievement that could not be ignored even by those who were unfavourably disposed. With ample documentation drawn from archives in India and abroad, the author has compiled a study which is a valuable contribution to the understanding of Jesuit motivation and performance in the first two centuries of its activities in India. The reader who wants to know more about the Jesuits will find this work very rewarding.

It has been my privilege to have known Fr. Borges right from his school days, and I am delighted that he has chosen to research the history of the Goa Jesuit Province with the intention that the achievements of the past will challenge us to like efforts. I wish him and the Xavier Centre of Historical Research to which he belongs every success in the mission assigned to them. May the achievements of St. Francis Xavier the first Jesuit to the Goa Province and the dedication of those who followed him continue to inspire us today.

Feast of St. Ignatius
31 July 1993

FR. ROMUALD D'SOUZA, S.J.
Jesuit House, Panaji, Goa

PREFACE

1542: Francis Xavier and his band of Jesuits arrived in Goa with the financial and moral backing of the Portuguese empire. 1759: that is a little over two hundred years later, the Jesuits returned home in disgrace, penniless and as unsung criminals. How did the scene change? How did the well-organized Society of Jesus collapse so helplessly to regal regulations?

This study has sought to trace the growth and collapse of the Jesuits of Goa during their stay in India. The emphasis has been on the economic aspects, on the means they used to gather resources, the extent of them, and the use they put them to.

The method is not quantitative. Relevant statistical and quantifiable data on the subject and for the period 1542-1759 are fragmentary. Yet a reconstruction is possible from these and other largely "literary" or descriptive sources. One discovers the inventive ability of these religious in gathering funds apart from the Crown bounty to build up their missions in India, Africa and Asia.

The Jesuits were among the many religious Orders that came to India under the Portuguese patronage in the sixteenth century. They raced ahead of the others, and turned out the most powerful. Goa was the centre of their activities, spiritual and temporal, and these took them to other parts of India and the world.

There have been many studies on the Jesuits, but they do not touch sufficiently on the economic aspects. One does not discover, as a result, how they came across their wealth, and how they involved themselves in political and economic affairs of the State.

The Directorate of Archives, Archaeology and Museum, Goa contains references to Jesuit houses, to the money received, earned and spent, and to the gains the State made as a result of events in 1759. Annual letters and correspondence between the Jesuits in India and their centre in Rome, are available at the Archives of the Society of Jesus in Rome. One can find references to them also at the British Museum, London, at the National Archives and at the Overseas Archives, Lisbon, and at the Archives at Simancas, Spain.

I have concentrated on the Jesuits of the Province of Goa as distinct from the Provinces of Malabar and Japan and the Vice-Province of China. Some have attempted similar studies for other fields. One can single out for mention Fr. William F. Rea's work for the Zambezi Missions (*The Economics of the Zambezi Missions: 1580-1759*), and Prof. Dauril Alden for his economic analysis of the Jesuit missions in South America.

The present work studies the role of the Society Jesus in India and outside, and its reliance on economic resources (ch. 1); the means it took to gather them and the extent of them (ch. 2); the objections the Superiors in Rome had to certain practices and customs (ch. 3); the perennial grievances of the villages of Ambelim, Velim and Assolná in Salcete (ch. 4); resentment which the State, the Crown and the people had against these religious (ch. 5); similar economic activities in Jesuit-missions of Asia and America (ch. 6); and the tough policy of the Marquis of Pombal in suppressing the Society of Jesus in the Portuguese domains and the aftermath of the suppression in Goa (ch. 7).

The thesis raises some questions which I have attempted to study in the following pages. Among them are: Did the Jesuits run a parallel economy which became the envy of others? Was their economic set-up multi-national in its implications? Why were the Jesuits in other parts of the world unable to help their colleagues in Goa? Did pride of their own successes and disdain for the others, lead to their ruin? And what parallels were there between Jesuit and other religious economic endeavours in Goa and India?

The Society of Jesus blazed a new trail in India. Other religious Orders either only followed them or reacted to its operations. Perhaps, in its absence, the State would have faltered much earlier than it did, or come up a worse tyrant and usurper. The Society's impress in other fields such as religion, culture, education and health, have been long-lasting. They caused their own problems of racism, cultural alienation and economic impoverishment, which hastened the events in 1759.

The hunt for financial resources, although aided with cautions from their constitutional and spiritual writings, brought the Jesuits into involvements and alliances with many, and made them victims of the objections and hatred of others. The pages ahead have probed their story, a story that had its flashes of brilliance, yet one that ended in failure.

1

THE SOCIETY OF JESUS

The Society of Jesus was a religious Order of the sixteenth century. It came to Goa under the Portuguese patronage in 1542. Some financial help from the Crown and private fund-raising led to a vast network which the Order divided into the Provinces of Goa, Malabar, Japan and the Vice-Province of China. Goa continued as the centre where men came to study and to rest, to work and to move. They belonged to various European nationalities and their individual rivalries surfaced at times. A fine centralised set-up was at the heart of their structure. They wrote regularly to Rome, and Visitors and briefs from their Superiors-General kept matters and activities in check when needed.

The men who could be as many as five hundred in certain years, manned parishes alongside native clerics and other religious, served in hospitals, taught in the seminaries, and converted where they could. Travellers met and stayed with them and described their experiences. They impressed many, including the State and the Church, with their performance. But their life-style and fund-raising excited the passions and the envy of many.

The Beginnings of the Society of Jesus

Ignatius of Loyola, a Spanish soldier turned ascetic, founded the religious Order, the Society of Jesus in the sixteenth century. After a period of spiritual conversion, he gathered around him a group that shared his ideals and vision. They had been fellow students with him at the Universities of Alcalá , Salamanca and Paris.

His book, *The Spiritual Exercises*, captured through a series of meditations and exercises, the methods and dispositions necessary to establish the Kingdom of God on earth. "Three Classes of Men, Three Degrees of Humility, and Rules for Thinking with the Church" formed part of a strategy to rid a person of overpowering personal desires and to work solely at holiness and the conversion of souls.

His group withstood the assaults and taunts of the clergy and the laity and later impressed all by its zeal and freshness of approach. They spread all over Europe in answer to Papal summons and engaged in such diverse activities as preaching in churches or nursing the sick, assisting at Council meetings or drawing up treatises.

They moved all over Europe, and even further afield. One of them, a former Spanish nobleman, Francis Xavier stood in for the then ailing India-bound Nicholas Bobadilla, and in 1542 sailed for the Indies instead. Along with two others, a priest and a brother, he launched the Society of Jesus in Goa. His zeal and personal sanctity inspired his men and colleagues during the ten years of his labours in the East. The others who followed played their part and stamped on the Order their individual plans and orientation. They flourished, clashed but never withdrew, till events in the fading months of 1759, saw them no more.

For the Jesuits who came from Europe in regular groups on Portuguese vessels, Goa was the centre of their activities.[1] They came there as priests and brothers, but did not remain long if they were not part of the Goa Province. They went instead to the separate Jesuit missions of Malabar, Japan and China.

The Structure of the Order

It had at the head a Superior-General whom the General Congregation consisting of Provincials, the elected representatives of each Province, and the Frs. Assistant, elected for life. The Vicar-General took over in cases of his death or illness. Every third year the Provinces had their own reunions known as the Provincial Congregations.

During these, the Jesuits with the right to active vote, chose their representatives for Rome. Known as Procurators, they would debate on various issues including the need or not for a General Congregation. Except for the year 1606, they always voted in the negative. The Provinces in India and in the East, held a Provincial Congregation every sixth year, and after 1628 one every ninth. They had fifteen informal meetings too, between 1575 and 1664.

The Goa Province

It comprised from 1542 till 1601, of the Goa islands, of certain areas in the North and the South of India, of Japan and of China. In them the Jesuits had their colleges, their churches and their residences. At Goa, they had the College of St. Paul's, the Church of Bom Jesus, the Professed House, the Novitiate of Chorão, and the Colleges of Rachol and Margão. There were colleges or residences too, in the Mughal empire and at Bengãl, at Srinagar and in Tibet, at Madurai, Calicut and Vaipikotta.

There were eleven residences in Salcete of Goa, the College of Jesus and two residences at Bassein, the College of the Mother of God with five residences at Thane, the College of Eleven Thousand Virgins at Daman, a residence at Diu, and a house of the Apostles Peter and Paul at Chaul. The Province also had missions in Ethiopia and in Persia. The Province headquarters were at St. Paul's, the Japan Province had its centre at the College of Macao, and Malabar had its at the College of Cochin.[2]

By 1594 there were sixty-nine houses, seventeen of them in the category of 'major' in the Province of Goa. Four hundred and sixty-four Jesuits worked in it, three hundred and ten in India (Malacca, the Moluccas and Ethiopia included), and a hundred and fifty-four in Japan and China. Of these, twenty-five were professed priests with four vows, fourteen in India and eleven in China and Japan.

Malabar Province

The houses of the Malabar Province functioned independently of the Goa Province after 1601. The College of the Mother of God at Cochin turned into a major College in 1663, and the Seminary for priests formed part of it. The Province had the College of Malacca (1576), the Seminary of Santa Cruz of Vaipikotta (1584), which shifted to Ambalacata in 1663 after the Dutch invasion, the Colleges and the Seminaries of Quilon, of Tuticorin and of Mylapore, respectively. The Dutch destroyed the College of Tuticorin, but the College carried out its activities after 1663 at the Fishery Coast.

Colleges were set up at Ternate, at Cranganore, and at Colombo in 1656; at Jaffnapatam which the Dutch destroyed in 1658; at Bengal (later closed in 1740); at Nagapattanam (also one which the Dutch destroyed in 1660; at Ambalacata along with a Seminary in the same place (both in 1663), and the College of Topo. There were houses of the Jesuits at Talai in 1743 and at Manapad in 1746.[3]

The Province had five priests and a brother to look after some of its interests in Goa. One was the Fr. Procurator with a Brother companion. Another was the Fr. Administrator at Assolná. The rest were aged and too old for mission work.[4]

Japan Province

The Japan Province came into being in 1611. Fr. Visitor, Alessandro Valignano spoke of the generosity of Viceroy Dom Duarte de Menezes who had given the Province 2,000 *cruzados*, and the use of four Arab horses.[5] King Dom Sebastian gifted 1,000 *cruzados* to the College of St. Paul de Funay, while 500 *cruzados* came from the rents of the villages of Ponvem and Kondoti in Bassein and from Mulgão for the Novitiate of Usuqui. The Province had two houses in the port of China yielding 200 *cruzados* which the Patriarch-Bishop Melchior Carneiro had gifted to the Seminary of Arima.[6]

The Goa Province: St. Paul's

King John III by an *alvará* of 10 March 1554 had handed over to the College of St. Paul's the rents of the temples of Goa and its adjacent islands. His nephew, Dom Sebastian in his *alvará* of 22 February 1570 gave it the ownership of the villages of Bandra, Corlem, Sargy and Mori. Dom John IV later confirmed these donations.

The College had an annual royal income of 8,00,000 *rs*. from the rents of the city of Goa.[7] The Jesuit Visitor, Fr. Gonçàlo Alvarez in his letter to Fr. General Francis Borgia in December 1568 mentioned the income of the College as an annual sum of 1,000 *cruzados*. It came in from the temple-properties, and from the gifts which the King received from the local chiefs but which he did not retain for himself. The Jesuits had complained that the Governor Fernão Teles de Menezes had not given them the money equivalent to the gifts offered by the State. The Crown ordered Viceroy Duarte de Menezes to honour the practice.[8]

Seminary of the Holy Faith

The secular clergy had managed the Seminary of the Holy Faith and its revenues. Later, Fr. Francis Xavier and his companions took over its spiritual and temporal charge, and in 1549 at Governor Jorge Cabral's request, the financial and administrative maintenance, too.[9]

Miguel Vaz and Fr. Diogo Borba started the Seminary in 1541. They handed over the charge temporarily to the Jesuits a year later. The Jesuits renamed it the College of St. Paul's and it served as their principal home.

From 1556 onwards the activities included public debates in philosophy, which were later printed.

St. Paul's

The College had classes in grammar and in rhetoric, and lectures for a study of Ovid, Virgil and Cicero.[10] There was a school attached to the College for 450 students who were taught to read and to write. There was besides a hospital for the sick Christians.[11]

Fr. Aires Brandão in his letter to Fr. Balthasar Dias, the Vice-Provincial in Portugal, discussed St. Paul's and the instruction imparted. The students included Malayalees, Kanarese, Parsees and Goans. Their teachers were full of hope for their charges and looked forward to their future with much expectation.[12]

Books

Jesuit communities needed to have the *Summa* of Navarro, the *Bible and the notes for preachers*, as part of their reading material. The list also included *Manual de Confessores e penitentes* (Manual for Confessors and Penitents) by Martin de Azpilcueta y Jaureguizar.[13]

The Jesuits in Goa put the printing press to much use for their catechetical work. The printed works included the *Doutrina Cristã* (Christian Doctrine - 1556), and *Doutrina* by Francis Xavier (1557); Thomas Stephens' *O Purana* (The Epic - 1616) and *A Doutrina (1634); Diogo Ribeiro's, A Declaração da Doutrina* (A Declaration of the Faith); Stephen da Cruz's *O Purana* (1634); and Thomas Stephens' *Gramatica Concani* (Konkani Grammar - 1640).[14]

The College Properties

Francisco Barretto, the Crown attorney, had asked Loupo Pinto, the chief *thanadar* (native police chief) to draw up an inventory of the plots, orchards, palm-groves and other properties of St. Paul's on the Goa islands, Divar and Chorão. The adjacent islands had also offered gifts from their temples and their associations, in accordance with the dictates of the King and his Governors. The inventory was similar to the one undertaken by his predecessor, Antonio Ferrão, containing the affidavits of the royal estates. The *ganvkars* of the villages had to make the declarations on oath. They were aware that they would forfeit their lands and be exiled to Diu for a term of five years if they had wilfully withheld any information expected of them.[15]

Loupo Pinto after the Chorão meeting on 12 February 1556, went to Divar and summoned all the *ganvkars* and secretaries of Navelim, and the residents for a meeting. They held it under a large mango-tree at Javarnak during which he informed them of the statutes of the King and of the Governor. St. Paul's could from then on own property belonging to the temples, or to the Portuguese, Hindus or native Christians.[16]

He invited the *ganvkars* on 13 February 1556, and nine among these donated their properties. Two days later, at Malar and at Divar, sixteen members handed over their lands. At Vanxim, he summoned the *ganvkars* of Goltim, tenants of Vanxim, to make over the lands of the temples, since there were neither *ganvkars* nor residents at Vanxim. A similar meeting took place at Jua on 20 February 1556.[17]

King Sebastian confirmed the donation of Bandra, Kurla, Sabi and Mohili in favour of this College.[18] The College owned the village of Bandra from about 1568 though the Jesuits came there only in 1573. They built a chapel on the Mount (where the present day Church of Mount Mary stands), and had a mass said every Saturday. There were two other churches, that of St. Andrew and of St. Anne. Two Fathers and two brothers looked after the properties belonging either to this College or to the Provinces of Malabar, Japan and China. The Jesuit house at Bandra was first under the jurisdiction of the Rector of Bassein until Thane separated from that College. In 1620 Bandra was independent of Thane, while St. Andrew's, Holy Cross (Kurla) and later Kondoti and Parel came under the supervision of the Fr. Superior of Bandra.

Till 1665, Bandra was a peaceful place and prospered agriculturally under the brothers. The income from the lands were used to support the many Jesuit-undertakings in Asia. But after the arrival of the English on 8 February 1665, Bandra became a military outpost, and many labourers came into Bombay in search of better-paid jobs.[19]

The Professed House

The Provincial stayed at the Professed House along with the Professed Fathers, the Administrators of the Royal Hospital, the various Province Procurators and the Father of Christians (*Pai dos Cristãos*). The house was the centre of the Province's apostolic activity, a place of rest for the elderly, and a model home for the members of the Province. The members who lived therein did so solely on alms.

The house had two important benefactors, Jeronimo Mascarenhas and Antonio Moreno. In his instructions to the Visitor, Fr. Gonçalo Alvares, the General Fr. Francis Borgia, in 1567, had suggested the foundation of a Professed House. The Provincial Fr. Antonio Quadros, had wished to establish in Goa one such house where the practice of the Institute of the Society of Jesus could show itself. Thus it was till 1759 a centre of evangelization for the East, for the works in India, China and Japan.[20]

Originally known as the *Casa de Jesus* (House of Jesus) it later changed its name to *Bom Jesus* (Infant Jesus) in the seventeenth century. It was built on the *Terreiro dos Gallos* (The Cocks' Field) near the church of Our Lady of Mercy and the Convent of St. Francis in Old Goa. Bro. Domingos Fernandes and a Goan engineer, Julio Simão helped in its construction which commenced in 1593.

Fr. General Acquaviva wanted this new Professed House to have a maximum of fourteen Jesuits who would work exclusively among the natives. He believed the other Religious Orders could attend to the spiritual needs of the Portuguese. The Province maintained the number in the seventeenth century. There were nine in 1706, seven in 1716, eight in 1724, fourteen in 1735, and twelve in 1752. The Constitution of the Society of Jesus had decreed that it had to concentrate purely on spiritual ministries and had not to receive any regular income.[21]

João Dias Ribeiro had gifted 50,000 *xs.* towards the foundation of the house. The amount which Jeronimo Mascarenhas had given had been insufficient for its foundation.[22]

The house had an infirmary with a Prefect of Health at its head. The sick remained in the house during their period of treatment and convalescence. If for some reason they had to go to another house of the Society, the Professed House met their medical expenses there. The Province promised help whenever necessary. The house could own real estate. The members could sell or exchange the fruits of their garden, but could not maintain any beast of burden since it would be against their vow of poverty.[23] The Jesuits had wisely joined the sewage drain of the house to the one from the Viceroy's palace that ran alongside it. But the objections of many others put an end to the practice.[24]

Rachol

The Province started the Seminary and the College of St. Ignatius at Rachol in 1574, and the College of Holy Spirit at Margão in 1668. It moved this latter College to Rachol in 1580 but transferred it once again to Margão in 1597. It moved its location yet again to Rachol in 1606 under the new name of All Saints. It finally came to be known as the College of St. Ignatius.

King Dom Sebastian had gifted two temple lands to the College of the Holy Spirit on 21 March 1569. An ordinance of 9 March 1579 by Dom Henriques granted it an additional 1,000 *cruzados* from the temple lands of ten villages.

There were other benefactors too. On 30 May 1607, Agostinho Dinis and his mother, Izabel de Souza donated a plot close to the College. The *ganvkars* of Margão on 22 May 1606 offered a plot in Navelim for the Church of Our Lady of the Rosary, and Maria de Aguiar, wife of Domingos Afonço on 11 October 1606 donated the plot (*Tontem Cumbarbatta*). The *ganvkars* of Benaulim offered a plot (*Dongaçim*) on 19 October 1596, while those of Raia on 20 September 1669 did likewise. A certain Antonio de Goes gifted to the College a salt-pan in his possession at Talaulim.[25]

Chorão

The Novitiate at Chorão came up in 1584 and functioned for many years under the College of St. Paul's. Later, it received a grant from Gaspar Viegas. On entering the Society of Jesus he had gifted much of his wealth to it. His 2,000 *ducats* helped buy properties in Carmoná, Taleigão and Panjim. Before his death he had bequeathed a further 12,000 *pardaus* to the Society.[26]

The Jesuits had done much on the island of Chorão. But Viceroy Dom Afonso de Noronha during his visit to the island, expressed the need for more. As a sign of his appreciation he gifted a huge plot of ground to the Church. This helped to house nearer the Church the Christians from far-flung areas. They were then more frequent in their attendance at the religious services.

The Royal Treasury had confiscated the rents of Assolná, Velim and Ambelim from their owners and had leased the villages instead to Dom Pedro de Castro. He had been unable to pay the required rent and had donated the villages to the Jesuits. They had managed a yield of 5,000 *xs*. They paid 1,343 *xs*. to the Crown in two equal instalments from the College of Cochin and the Novitiate of Chorão respectively.

The Novitiate had a palmgrove in Carmoná, lands and salt-pans gifted by Bro. Gaspar Viegas, yielding 1,000 *xs*. but which doubled under its care. It owned the island of Luvary in the parish of S. André of Goa

Velha. There were forty novices along with seven priests in charge of them. Two of the Frs. Procurator stayed at Assolná and at Zuari respectively.[27]

The North Province: Bassein, Thane, Daman and Chaul

The Viceroy, Dom Constantino, Duke of Bragança, had in 1558 offered the Jesuits in Daman an orchard and a few houses. They managed them well, and received other royal gifts and alms. João Dias Ribeiro, too, had given a certain amount towards the foundation of the College in the city, and came to be considered as its 'founder'.

The College of Thane functioned under the supervision of the College at Bassein. A grant from King Sebastian in 1569 helped in making it independent. It received 80 *pardaus* of gold each year from the rents of the village of Vellapa.[28]

King John III had been helpful to the College of Bassein in 1550. Later, King Sebastian in 1568 granted it various privileges, and also confirmed the donation of a widow, Dona Isabel de Aguiar.[29]

Crown Help

The Jesuits were among the various religious Orders that received help from the Crown. A report of Antonio Simões in 1623 mentioned the total for religious as 53,627 *xs.* and 4 *tgs.* (Dominicans 16,722-3-20; Franciscans 5,500-0-00; Augustinians 8,707-3-20 and Jesuits 22,697-2-20).[30] But payments were not always regular, and Fr. Antonio Freyre, complained that the travelling allowances for eighteen religious for a two-year period had not come in.[31]

Viceroy Antonio de Noronha had allotted the Jesuits and the Franciscans at Bassein a royal annual stipend of 2,070 gold *pardaus* to meet the expenses of the Christians there. The amount went in equal shares to the two. Governor Francisco Barreto gave an additional sum of 930 gold *pardaus* to round up the total to 3,000, on the advice of the King. Each thus received 1,500 gold *pardaus*.[32]

Governor Cabral was equally generous to the Jesuits in Bassein. He gifted them land and houses together with a cash of 1,500 *cruzados* of the 3,000 the King had set aside for the priests' expenses during the conversion work. The priests had till then lived on alms. The King had instructed his Governor to hand over to them 300 *cruzados* for their expenses there. Another 1,200 *cruzados* went towards the works of the Jesuits.

A widow in her esteem for the Society donated to the College some villages she had rented to the Crown. It fetched a revenue of 400 *cruzados*. She gifted before her death others totalling in all 1,100 *cruzados*. An income of 150 *cruzados* came in from other lands.[33]

The Crown had given a plot of land at Thane to the Society and four Jesuits lived on it. Viceroy Dom Constantino gave them a permanent residence at Daman along with a Crown subsidy, while Governor Cabral had given them a plot and houses for a permanent college and residence at Cochin. Later, the Bishop and the cathedral-chapter donated to the church, and private donations helped much towards the building of the college. The Crown gave an annual stipend of 300 *cruzados*, and there was another annual donation of 400 *cruzados*, left by a deceased person.

The College of Eleven Thousand Virgins at Daman started its activities from 1581. There had been a school since 1578 with two hundred children on its rolls. There was the College of the Mother of God at Thane in 1599, the College of the Holy Spirit at Diu in 1601 (also known as the College of St. Paul), and the College of Sts. Peter and Paul at Chaul in 1611. In 1580 there was a residence at Chaul, and a school for 300 children. In 1591 the Latin grammar class had 50 students.

Houses and Works Elsewhere

The other institutions which the Province had were the College of the Ascension of Mozambique (1613), the College of Our Lady of Birth at Agra (1630), and a school for elementary education and music at Bandra (1576). The College of St. Anne later changed into a University. The 1737-39 Maratha war destroyed the Colleges of Bassein and Thane, and the schools of Bandra and Chaul in 1740.[34]

Viceroy Francisco da Gama in his letter of 15 March 1624 had a word of praise for the work of the Jesuits on the fortifications of Daman and Chaul. Much against their Provincial's reluctance he succeeded in getting them to attend to the defence work of Bassein.[35] During the provincialate of Fr. Nuno Rodrigues, many sought their services for work in the hospitals too.[36]

The granaries were in the hands of the Jesuits since the days of the Count of Alvor, Francisco de Tavora (1682-86). They managed them well and bought more fields with the profits they made. They had intended to provide cheaper and more plentiful supplies of rice to the poor of the land.[37]

Surat

Fr. Deusse was Superior at the Surat residence where the French Jesuits working in Carnatic had a place to rest when they came from Europe by the overland routes. Though they worked under the Propaganda, the Capuchins opposed them at Surat, and wrote to Rome to ask the Sacred Congregation to close the residence. The first Carmelite Vicar Apostolic of the Great Mughal, Dom Peter Paul, came to Surat at the end of 1699 to convey the order to the Jesuits who left Surat soon afterwards.[38]

Other Jesuit Missions

The Raichur mission though the last to start its activities was next in importance to Mysore. The Kittur mission had among its parishioners those who had come from Goa for temporal reasons, and a few Portuguese who had come to escape from their crimes. The work there did not offer much consolation. Frs. Andres Stobl and Joseph Tiefenthaller served in the mission of the Grand Mughal, and at Agra and Delhi. They looked after the spiritual needs of the Asians and of the Europeans, many of whom were in the Emperor's service. Conversions from Islam were few. Yet, they secretly baptized many children when they were on the point of death.

There were about three missionaries in the Sunda mission to minister to the Christians who had come from Goa in search of better jobs. The war curtailed the number of priests. The annual expenses for all the missions were 20,000 *xs.* and the loss of the north Province affected much the missions and their regular income.[39]

The Royal Hospital

The Jesuits had managed the Royal Hospital at Goa since 1579. Their Superiors-General, Frs. Mercurian and Acquaviva had wished their men to surrender the task in 1583-84, but the King would not agree to the transfer. Excise dues from victuals, soap and opium met the medical expenses of 11,630 *pardaus*. The Comptroller of Revenues and the other officials could not use the income for any other purpose. The Hospital Treasurer, whom the Jesuits would approve, had to be present while registering the excise dues. The physicians had to maintain a standard rate for all medicines.[40]

In 1585, at the request of Governor Dom Duarte Menezes, the priests had taken over administrative charge of the Hospital. The Overseas

Council wanted the Administrator to quit since he was difficult to handle. Ten years later, they handed over charge to Viceroy Matias de Albuquerque over differences with him on financial control, but a word from King Philip saw them take up the task again two years later.[41]

On 15 December 1698, the Viceroy informed the King that the Jesuits wished to give up their duties at the Hospital since it was not proper to their ministry. Sickness and a lack of medicines had killed many at the Hospital. The Viceroy had asked the religious of St. John to come in, but the Overseas Council thought the Jesuits were best since they were skilled in medicine and excellent infirmarians (*sogeitos de grande sciencia medicina e singulhares boticarios*).[42]

One priest and two brothers stayed at the Hospital. There would be about seventy Portuguese patients in summer, and over a hundred in winter. The natives and the incurables had to seek the treatment of the House of Mercy. In 1748, the Jesuits sought royal confirmation of their usual practice to appoint officials of the Hospital. The Overseas Council opposed the move. They agreed to their appointing the Treasurer, but objected to their wanting to remove him without reference to the Court of Justice.[43] The Jesuits' administrative services were honorary all through their term. When Dom Cristovão Carcome Lobo took charge, his earnings were a hundred *xs.* a month.[44]

Jesuit Infirmaries

Many would flock to seek the healing touch of the brother-infirmarian at the Margão hospital.[45] It was in their infirmaries that the Jesuits received and practised their medical skills, and this training helped them during their stays in missions around India. It was there that they nurtured herbs and roots, and prepared remedies for use. Seven of the priests who took over Jesuit-missions in the South in 1759, made use of some of these when they took up their new posts.[46]

The Three Mughal Missions

The Province had three missions to the courts of Akbar, Jahangir, Shah Jahan and Aurangzeb. Akbar discussed religion with those who formed part of them, and his love and sensitivity to them, proved his sincerity. Yet events showed that his motives were not always honest in inviting the religious. He had long hoped to secure the military help of the Portuguese. In 1600 he turned to them to break the siege of Asirgahr. Prince Salim turned similarly to them in his drive against his father. And in the midst of it all, the invited Jesuits turned out to be a mixture of patriotic politicians and zealous missionaries.[47]

The Portuguese first came in contact with the Mughals during Akbar's annexation of Gujarat in 1573. He had wooed them for their friendship by praising them for their missionary zeal. He won his way, the missionaries came to him but it took long for all to see through his game. The Jesuits had much wished to return to their houses in Goa, but the hope of a future break-through prodded them on.[48]

Akbar had first invited a Christian priest learned in science and history (whom Abu Fazl called Padre Farabatun) to come from Goa. His task was to help some young translators in their work from Greek to Persian.[49]

The Jesuit missions may have failed in their primary task of converting the Emperors. But they won many converts from among the poor. The English traders, however, were quick to declare that the poor turned Christian primarily for money and help.[50] The Jesuits while not engaged in converting the Emperor were ever on the lookout to disgrace the English. One of them while reading aloud in court the letter of King James observed that it was discourteous since it had at its inception the word *Vestra* (Your) without *Maiestad* (Majesty).[51]

For the Jesuits, Akbar was a big disappointment. He turned out to be neither the visionary, or reformer or ecumenist he pretended to be, but a shrewd schemer using religion to further his political base.[52] Yet the Jesuit efforts were unique in the history of missionary enterprise as an attempt on the part of a large group to convert a single individual.[53]

College of Agra

The founder of the College was Mirza Zu-l-Quarnain. He was a powerful nobleman, who became *Fauzdar* of Sambhar and later Governor of Lahore. He owned a property at Parel in Bombay. Dona Juliana Dias da Costa had offered Rs. 20,000 towards this College under the provision that a priest should serve the Christians there. She gave another Rs. 10,000 for the poor of Agra and Delhi. She had obtained the money from the rents of the village of Manorim.[54] Zu-l-Quarnain gave another foundation too, for the College in Tibet.[55]

Jesuits as Diplomats

The Jesuits worked at times to defend Portuguese interests and to obtain the goodwill of the neighbouring powers. The ruler of Chandragiri warmly welcomed the missionary Fr. Simon de Sá who had arrived in his kingdom, and granted him leave to set up a church. He promised him the revenue of several villages to meet his expenses and costs, and when it proved insufficient, he added another 1,000 *pardaus* each year till 1606. The artist-Brothers Frey Alexander and Bartolomeo Fontabona did much to win favour for the Jesuits at the court.[56]

The Viceroy had called upon Fr. Pedro Mexia, Rector of the College of Mylapore to negotiate an alliance with the ruler of Vijayanagara on plans to oust the Dutch from the Coromandel coast. He did so twice and his hosts at court treated him well.[57]

Fr. Ignacio de Arcamone had come from Honavar with news that Shivappa Nayak would not hear of 200 *khandis* at the rate of 28 *pagodas*. To prevent him from attacking the fort, the priest suggested the State buy upto 350 *khandis*. The State Council then decided that 250 could be a good deal, and if necessary a further 20 or 30 at the price stated earlier.[58]

Two Jesuits were stationed in Surat at an annual allowance of 200 *xs*. The Surat captain Mirza Mulza had asked for them in the hope that they would prevent the Dutch from gaining a foothold in Sind.[59]

Nationalities

The Jesuits belonged to various countries and there were times when nationalist feelings and passions came to the fore. Their General had to remind them to keep united since he likened them to sons of a single mother. A traveller on a visit to one of their houses in Goa, noticed many Italians besides Portuguese and Spaniards among them. The Italians were usually bound either for Japan or China. They were learned and accomplished. Of the four he met two were linguists, the third was a mathematician, and the fourth a painter.[60]

There was some rivalry between the Portuguese and the Spanish Jesuits. It came across in frequent complaints to Rome from Jesuits writing their stipulated annual letters or reports. There were references to Fr. Jeronimo Xavier, a grand-nephew of St. Francis Xavier. Many, including some outside the Society, resented his appointment as Prepositor of the Professed House in Goa. He was said to be choleric by nature.[61] Fr. Cristovão de Castro had warned Fr. Acquaviva against appointing Fr. Xavier as the Provincial.[62] They mentioned his partiality to the members of his own country (*tanto apaixonado por sua nação*).[63] In an effort to get rid of him, he was literally "pushed up" to head the last Mughal mission.

They repeated that the Province would not lose much from his absence from Goa since he had an inordinate love for his own country.[64]

There was a lack of unity between those who joined the Society in Portugal and those who joined in India. The former maintained they were more learned than the ones of India and the Superiors tended to side with this view. This situation was especially noticeable at the College of St. Paul's.[65]

To check national rivalries among his men, the Superior General had sent Fr. Alessandro Valignano to the Indies in 1574. He had hoped to clip Portugal's excessive control of the Society of Jesus in Asia. Her inability to provide sufficient and qualified men, had forced him to rethink the question of Portuguese demands. He placed a non-Portuguese Procurator of the Goa Province in Lisbon, and picked up a band of Spanish and Italian Jesuits for the missions in Goa. Fr. Luis Gonçalves de Camara as Assistant in Portugal did much to contain the hurt nationalist feelings of the Portuguese. He was confessor to King Sebastian, while his brother was the royal secretary and the most powerful official in the land. It were these events that marked the first serious breach of the *Padroado* privileges as they understood them.[66]

Nationalist differences existed among the different religious Orders in Goa, too. They were more noticeable particularly in China. The Jesuit experiments there failed due to rivalries and to matters that had nothing to do with the Church, China or India.[67]

In Goa, the Governors complained that the religious scandals were a blot on the scene. The Jesuits and the Dominicans were relative moderates. The others were incorrigible for hardly would the Augustinians cool off after their quarrels, than the Capuchins would begin. The Franciscans and the Carmelites would also behave likewise. Their quarrels had turned their cloisters more into quarters for soldiers than habitats for monks.[68]

The national differences among the Jesuits did not help to weave their Order into an international whole. Little was the sympathy or contact between the Spanish and the Scottish, or the French and the English Jesuits. As a result, it was a lot easier for their enemies to destroy them at a later stage so thoroughly and so convincingly.[69]

Jesuits as depicted in Travel Accounts

A Jesuit in Goa usually dressed in a long black gown, with a collar and ring round his neck, a high round cap flat at the top, and shoes without stockings on the feet. They did not wear hats or three-corned caps as in Europe but a kind of cap which resembled in form a hat from which the brim had been removed. When they died they were similarly arrayed, and laid without a coffin.[70]

A few travellers have left interesting details on their visits to Jesuit houses in Goa. A description of a visit on a certain 16 January to the Professed House, mentioned curious items. One walked first through a spacious arched-hall which had a pillar with a spout of water at its entrance. The hall had covered tables along its walls, and right in the centre stood a table for those who had penances to perform. The adjoining hall, too, had a table in its centre, and it lay full of fruit, bread and china plates. The Viceroy who was present, had the pride of place at the meal. The Jesuits would hover around and attend to the needs of all. They brought in the meat in little dishes of porcelain, and also the fish, all neatly done. The meal then ended with a musical show of florentines and of tarts.[71]

Pyrard de Laval mentioned that the clerics that he came across were very rich. They were each of them busy gathering much for himself. But the Jesuits, he believed, were different. On their travels they carried nothing on themselves but their breviaries (*não levam mais que o seu breviario*).[72]

A Case of Disedification

A Jesuit Brother at Chorão had the duty of guarding the church and teaching Christian doctrine. On a certain occasion he came out armed with a rifle and a lighted rope against the Muslims who had tried to set fire to the church. From Rome, Fr. Juan Polanco wrote a reminder to the Provincial, Fr. Antonio de Quadros of the unlawfulness of having recourse to arms. He mentioned that the others would expect them to use purely spiritual means in dealing with such situations.[73]

Mission Work

The Archbishop disliked the grandeur with which the Jesuits went through their ceremonies of general baptisms. He considered it a loss of the spirit of humility in the Society. They had baptized in the islands of Goa, Chorão and Divar 13,092 persons in 1560. But the following year, the number surprisingly fell to a mere 3,437.[74]

Viceroy Dom Pedro Mascarenhas had divided Goa into separate

regions for the Dominicans, the Franciscans and the Jesuits to work in without annoyance from each other. The plan worked well and disputes were few. Besides, each of the Orders had their own 'Father of Christians' whose job was to help those who wished to be part of the faith. He had to protect the catechumens and the freshly-baptized from the harassment of their pagan relatives and officials.[75]

Fr. Valignano had left instructions in 1595 for the 'Father of Christians' on his duties of instruction and assistance. In Salcete of Goa and in Cochin, he was a Jesuit; in Bardez of Goa and Salcete of the North, a Franciscan; he was an Augustinian in Nagapattanam; and a Dominican at Diu, Chaul, and Macao.[76]

Many had a word of high praise for the Jesuits' missionary labours. They thought they struggled for souls as fiercely as others did for gold. Their standards and goals were higher than those of the others who had been around much earlier. Their missions grew remarkably and impressively and even the otherwise hostile Protestants admired them.

In Japan and China the priests tried a different tactical approach. They did not demand a total withdrawal of a neophyte from his former ways. They accepted the social situation the way they saw it, though they tried to cleanse it of its caste inequalities and ritual procedures.[77]

Brothers

Brothers though they formed an important part of the Society, did not enjoy the same privileges or acceptance as did the priests in the Order. They were usually given subordinate roles in the set-up and were to be of assistance to the Fathers whenever the occasion demanded them to do so. Bro. Antonio Pereira while stationed at the Professed House had the regular duty of accompanying the priests whenever they went out on their errands. Fr. Valignano believed that a brother with a desire to study would lead a restless life alongside other students, and would be unable to cope with his work. He deserved to be sent to a distant house and given charge of the native servants instead, thus making himself very useful.[78]

Vernaculars and Jesuits

The Jesuits paid much attention to the study of the vernaculars. The rules of the Society maintained that in order to foster greater union among all Jesuits, and for the greater assistance of those among whom they worked, all had to study the languages of the regions wherein they resided.[79] There were many who took these words seriously to heart. Among those who excelled far above the rest were Frs. Henrique Henriques and Constanzo Beschi in Tamil, Jeronimo Xavier in Persian, and Thomas Stephens in Konkani.

Jesuits on Voyages

Jesuits had served on naval voyages as chaplains, six of them (four priests and two brothers) on three *armadas* in 1593 at the request of Viceroy Matias de Albuquerque (1591-97). Of the six who went to Japan and China, four were Frs. Lazaro Caetano, Manuel Dias, Antonio Rodrigues and Francisco Toscano. Along with the Bishop of Japan Pedro Martins went Frs. Antonio Rodrigues, Bartolomeu Gomes and Bro. Antonio da Costa. To Malacca went Fr. Manuel Gonçalves and Bro. Antonio da Costa. Fr. Nuno Tavares and Bro. Francisco Lopes went to Malabar, and a priest and a brother went to Aventureiros, while Frs. Jeronimo Rebelo and Manuel Pinheiro voyaged to Mombaça. Each night all would recite the litanies of the Saints to intercede for safety at sea, and on Saturdays would petition Our Lady. The religious also spent time instructing the servants and slaves in the tenets of the faith.[80]

The Italian Jesuit, Fr. Tranquillo Grassetti wrote in remarkable detail and with much keenness of emotion on his voyage on board the *Bom Despacho*, one of the vessels of the Portuguese Indian fleet of 1629. He was one of the thirty Jesuits who journeyed on it. He described the various groups on it, the cramped quarters, the sicknesses and tensions that grew as the voyage progressed. The priests would say daily masses whenever possible, in temporary chapels, hear confessions, attack the prevalence of swearing, solve disputes, cool tempers and calm and encourage the fearful during periods of stress and danger. At times, they distributed extra food to the needy, and oversaw the medical supplies on board and attended to the needs of the sick.[81]

Jesuit Help during the Famine

The famine of 1649 had been severe, with many deaths occurring during the months of June to August. The Jesuits did their bit and would serve cooked rice to the hungry and distribute alms to the penniless. These usually numbered a few hundreds, and would leave after they had had their fill and some instruction in the faith. There were similar scenes and activity at the parish church of Navelim.[82]

Other Activities: Jesuits and Plants

The Jesuits introduced many new plants from South America, of which the cashew was the most valuable. Others were the pineapple, the potato, the guava and the custard-apple. About the year 1575, they also took to mango-grafting which worked wonders and brought in much income.[83] They were the first to draw attention to the species of herb called *caamini*, of Paraguay, which possessed valuable medicinal properties. In Peru they had discovered the medicinal value of quinine, known as the Jesuits' bark in England, and had cured Charles II of a dangerous fever. In America they pointed out the properties of india-rubber and vanilla, carried to Europe from Tartary the rhubarb plant, and from China the turkey.[84]

Plans for a New Vice-Province

There were plans to reorganize the structure of the Goa Province for a better utilization of the resources.[85] The Jesuits thought of a new Vice-Province comprising the Mughal kingdom with its centre at Srinagar. It would include Tibet, Persia and Armenia, and would be subject to the Visitor of the Goa Province, in the same way as the Vice-Province of China was subject to the Visitor of Japan. They reasoned that the Goa Province had too many colleges and residences (St. Paul's, Seminary of the Holy Faith, Professed House, Probation House, Royal Hospital, College of Rachol, twenty five parishes, the mission of Kanara with a residence at Honavar, residences at Chaul, Daman, Bassein, Thane, Bandra, ten parishes, and residences at Tete and Sena in East Africa).

The Vice-Province would include parts of interior India and qualified Jesuits would work in those areas. The Provincial of Goa was usually unable to visit the lands of the Mughal kingdom, Tibet, Srinagar and Monomotapa on account of their vast distances. The new plan would help revive abandoned missions, and thus Ethiopia, Madagascar and several of the islands at which the Portuguese navies called, could have some religious presence.

The practice then had been for the Provincial to send once in three years, a Visitor to the Agra mission at much expense to the Province. Fr. General could henceforth send an ordinary Vice-Provincial from among the older members of the mission who could supervise the developments of the Agra college and the vast regions of Hindustan and Persia.

He could allot the money from the gift of Mirza Zu-l-Quarnain and which belonged to the Agra and Lahore missions for other works. The other Hindustan missions could receive the 50 *scudi* left for the Ethiopia mission by the College of Rachol, besides the munificent amount it had received from the Crown. They could also receive the interests on endowments that Naples gave the Eastern missions. Merchants coming from Syria and Alleppo could bring the money from there.

The plan arranged for eight men to come from Europe for this purpose and for five to join them in India. One of them would need to reside at the Colleges of Daman and Surat to gather funds. The place would remain available for the sick of the mission and for those of the Goa Province. The Japan and China Provinces had similarly used Macao for the convalescence of the sick Jesuits. Yet this Province would have to avoid having too many missions, since times were difficult, and it was difficult to enter the kingdom.

Annual Letter of 1755

An annual letter of the Goa Province and typical of many others sent to Rome, described its mission of Mysore as a glorious one.[86] Its main activities were the conducting of Spiritual Exercises and the administration of the sacraments. The mission had thirteen priests and over eighty catechists working in it. Some of them worked solely with the higher castes. The churches were small and of mud and had hay-thatched roofs. The priests visited each church once or twice a year depending on the enemy movements, the distances or the rains. They had often to sleep under trees, and suffered as a result from fevers and illnesses. They lacked food, and ate only rice, cereals and vegetables, which were seldom available. Caste rules prevented them from eating meat or fish. The chieftains and petty lords used to make many troublesome demands on them for gifts from abroad.

The people would attend the services from afar, and when they could not do so, would gather in a house for reciting litanies and rosaries, and for morning and night prayers. The catechists would prepare them for confession by helping them examine their consciences.

Material Means

Though the Jesuit annual letters said much about the successes and difficulties of the mission, they did not offer sufficient information about the material means they used to run the same. Yet other literary writings of the time commented on their wealth and the means they employed to gather it. There were some Jesuits at least who busied themselves in pursuits such as these and who contributed their bit to the economic success of the Society of Jesus in the East.

REFERENCES

1. *Documenta Indica (DI)*, XVII (1595-97), ed. Josef Wicki, p. i. Over 2,100 came to India from Europe and Brazil. There were 15,000 requests for the India mission.
2. Guerreiro, Fernão, *Relação Anual das coisas que fizeram os Padres da Companhia de Jesus nas suas missões*, I (1600-03), pp. 3-4; Cardim, Antonio F., *Bathalhas da Companhia de Jesus na sua gloriosa Provincia do Japão*, p. 290.
   Appendices nos. 2-5 describe the working of the government of the Society of Jesus, the colleges, houses and churches it had in the Goa Province, and lists the men who served either as Visitors or Provincials of India and Goa.
3. Rodrigues, Francisco, *A Companhia de Jesus em Portugal e nas missões*, pp. 60-1.
4. AHU: India, *maço* 90, 29 November 1755.
5. *DI*, XIV (1585-88), p. 653.
6. *Ibid.*, pp. 85-86, 663-664, 888.
7. *DI*, I (1540-49), p. 108. Charter of King John III in favour of the College of St. Paul, signed at Almeirino, 8 March 1546.
8. DAAM: *Monções* 3A, fls. 255-62, 332-4. A Royal letter of 6 February 1589 wanted the gifts to be given to the Jesuits. The Public Exchequer did not have to pay them 2,000 *pardaus* in cash if they refused to accept it in kind.
9. *DI*, VII (1566-68), pp. 582-583.
10. *DI*, II, pp. 575-576.
11. *Ibid.*, p. 371.
12. Wicki, Josef, "Dois Compendios das Ordens dos Padres Gerais e Congregações Provinciais da Provincia dos Jesuitas da Goa, feitos em 1664," (Henceforth Dois Compendios), *Studia*, nos. 43-44, 1980, pp. 440-441.
13. Saldanha, Mariano, "A Primeira Imprensa em Goa", *BIVG*, no. 73, 1956, pp. 102-3.
14. *DI*, II, pp. 150-3. Goa, 16 January 1556.
15. *Ibid.*, pp. 13-20. February 1556.
16. *Ibid.*, pp. 463-464.
17. *Ibid.*, pp. 573-4. Goa, 19 November 1556.
18. *DI*, VIII (1569-73), pp. 252-267, 379-393, 397-401.
19. Humbert, John, "Some Answers of the Generals of the Society of Jesus to the Province of Goa. Acquaviva-Vitelleschi 1581-1645," *AHSI*, XXXV, 1966, p. 324.
20. *Ibid.*, p. 329.
21. *Ibid.*, pp. 323-324, 326-327.
22. Wicki, J., "Der Bericht des Jesuiten Provinzials von Goa an die Königleche Akademie der Portugiesischen Geschichte," (Henceforth "Der Bericht") *AHSI*, XXXIX, 1970, p. 162.
23. Wicki, "Dois Compendios," pp. 377-378; Melo, Afonso J. de, "A Basilica do Bom Jesus," *BEAG*, XI, nos. 5-6, 1952, pp. 237-238, gives details of the church and house. Appendices nos. 17-20 have lists of the income and expenditure of the Professed House for some years of the eighteenth century.
24. *DI*, XVII (1595-97), pp. iv-vi, 367-381. The Professed House was also in charge of the Mughal and Ethiopia missions.

25. Costa, Francisco X. (ed.), *Legados Pios que oneram os bens situados nos concelhos das Ilhas, Bardes, Salcette e Mormugão do distrito de Goa pelo Chantre Francisco Xavier Vaz*, pp. 163-164.
26. Wicki, "Der Bericht," pp. 162-163; *DI*, XVI (1592-94), pp. ix-xi.
27. *DI*, II, pp. 577-578; Almeida Calado, Adelino de, "A Companhia de Jesus na India em meados do século XVII," *Studia*, no. 40, 1978, p. 355.
28. *DI*, XVI (1592-94), pp. 164-165.
29. *Ibid.*, p. 164.
30. AHU, India, *maço* 35, fl. 20v, 1623.
31. *Ibid.*, *maço* 13, doc. 37, 3 March 1638.
32. *DI*, VI (1563-66), pp. 452-453, Goa, 4 April 1565.
33. *Ibid.*, VII (1566-68), p. 583.
34. Rodrigues, *op. cit.*, pp. 58-59.
35. DAAM: *Cartas e Ordens*, codex 2595. fl. 7v.
36. *Ibid.*, *MR* codex 8, fl. 81v, 22 January 1601.
37. *Ibid.*, codex 58, fl. 342. Letter of the Viceroy to the King, 23 November 1694. The factory was a receiving and delivering house where the Factor stored goods and transacted business.
38. Humbert, J.," The Goa Archives in 1693", *Indica*, vol. 1, no. 1, 1964, p. 55.
39. AHU: India, *maço* 8, doc. 99, 9 December 1718.
40. *DI*, XVII (1595-97), pp. 606-608.
41. *Ibid.*, pp. v-vi; XI (1577-80), pp. 664-665; XIII (1583-85), p. 568; XVII (1595-97), pp. 45-52, 338-350, 845, 877; AHU: India, *maço 65, 17 December 1745.*
42. AHU: India, *maço* 41, doc. 85, 6 February 1700.
43. *Ibid.*, *maço* 58, 1748. The Jesuits had expelled Geraldo Correia de Azevedo Baceiar and had appointed Pascual Mendes Thomaz in his place, but the former had requested for a stay-order. The Jesuit Administrator of the Hospital at the time was Fr. Manoel de Figueiredo.
44. *Ibid.*, *maço* 102, 28 September 1760.
45. *DI*, XVI (1592-94), p. 321. All esteemed and loved Bro. Peter Afonso who died at St. Paul's. He attended to both Christians and Hindus. Many converted to the Christian faith as a result of his care. They called him the 'father of the poor.'
46. Meersman, Achilles, "Notes on the charitable institutions the Portuguese established in India", *ICHR*, V, no. 2, 1971, p. 104.
47. Smith, Vincent A., *The Oxford History of India*, p. 362. For a study of the Jesuit diplomacy at the various northern and southern courts, see Charles J. Borges, "State Diplomacy and the Society of Jesus in the *Estado da India, 5th International Seminar on Indo-Portuguese History*, Cochin, 1989, pp. 1-17 (mimeographed papers).
48. De Souza, Teotonio R., *Medieval Goa*, pp. 27-28.
49. Elphinstone, Mountstuart, *The History of India*, II, p. 282.
50. Camps, Arnulf, *Jerome Xavier SJ and the Muslims of the Moghul Empire*, p. 89.
51. Prasad, Ram C., *Early English Travellers in India*, p. 91; *DUP*, II, p. 311. The Royal Advisory Council at Madrid (23 November 1622) wanted the Jesuits to set the Mughuls against the English at Surat.
52. Hoyland, J.S. (trans.), *The Commentary of Father Monserrate SJ on his journey to the Court of Akbar*, p. ii. The Commentary found its way to Calcutta in the beginning of the last century and was discovered in 1906 by Rev. W.K. Firminger; Correia-Afonso, John, "The Second Jesuit Mission to Akbar (1591)," *Indica*, Vol. 28, no. 2, Sep 1991, p. 93.
53. Fr. Felix, "Mughal Farmans, Parwanahs and Sanads issued in favour of the Jesuit

missionaries", *JPHS*, V, no. 1, Calcutta, 1916, pp. 1-53.

54. Wicki, "Der Bericht," p. 166; Hosten, Henry, "Mirza Zu-l-Qarnain, a Christian Grandee of three Moghuls, with notes on Akbar's Christian wife and the Indian Bourbons," *MASB*, V, no. 4, Calcutta, 1916, pp. 115-194.
55. Wicki, "Der Bericht," p. 166.
56. Heras, Henry, *The Aravidu Dynasty of Vijayanagara*, I, pp. 464-493.
57. Meersman, A., "The First Attempts to Introduce the Church in Vellore", *ICHR*, XII, no. 1, 1978, pp. 71-78.
58. DAAM: *ACF*, IV (1631-37), fl. 23.
59. *Ibid.*, VI (1643-47), codex 1164, fl. 194v, 14 August 1652; VIII, fl. 46v. The Council used the services of Fr. Antonio Correa of the Canara mission to buy 200 *khandis* of pepper from Shivappa Nayak at the rate of 25 *pagodas* a *khandi*.
60. *DI*, XVII (1595-97), pp. 30-31; Wheeller, J. T., *European Travellers in India*, p. 13.
61. *DI*, XVI (1592-94), pp. 36-37.
62. *Ibid.*, pp. 205-206.
63. *Ibid.*, pp. 216, 259-262. It was usual for the Prepositor (the priest in charge) of the Professed House to stand next in line for the post of Provincial. Many of the Portuguese feared that it would hold true in this case too.
64. *Ibid.*, p. 890.
65. *Ibid.*, p. 827.
66. De Souza, T. R., "The Portuguese in Asia and their Church patronage," *Western Colonialism in Asia and Christianity*, ed. M. D. David, p. 16; Schütte, Josef F., *Valignano's Mission Principles for Japan*, I, Part I, pp. 82-88.
67. Hay, Malcolm, *Failure in the Far East*, p. 6.
68. DAAM: *MR*, 56, fl. 267, 22 December 1691.
69. Hay, *op. cit.*, pp. 16-17.
70. Fryer, John, *A New Account of East India and Persia*, p. 12; Ball, V, *Travels in India by Jean-Baptiste Tavernier Baron of Aubonne*, ed. William Crooke, I, p. 159.
71. Cunha Rivara, Joaquim H. da (ed.), *Viagem de Francisco Pyrard de Laval*, II, p. 75.
72. *The Voyages and Travels of the Ambassadors: whereto are added the Travels of John Albert Mandelslo from Persia into the East Indies*, p. 78.
73. *DI*, IV (1557-60), pp. 131-132. Rome, 13 December 1558.
74. Souza, Francisco de, *Oriente Conquistado a Jesu Christo pelos Padres da Companhia de Jesus da Provincia de Goa*, I, p. 102.
75. *DI*, II (1550-53), pp. 350-351; XVI (1592-94), p. iii. The entire island was divided between the Dominicans and the Jesuits.
76. Pissurlencar, Panduronga S.S. *Regimentos das Fortalezas da India*, pp. 56-57.
77. Scammell, Geoffrey V., *The World Encompassed: The First European Maritime Empires c. 800-1650*, pp. 285-286.
78. *DI*, XIV (1585-88), p. 789. It was a rule of the Society to venture out of the house always with a companion. Schutte, F. X. *Valignano's Mission Principles for Japan*, Vol. 1, Part 1, p. 168.
79. Correia-Afonso, John, *Jesuit Letters and Indian History: 1542-1773*, quoted on p. 58.
80. *DI*, XVI (1592-94), pp. 296, 302.
81. Disney, Anthony R., "The World of long-distance voyaging in the seventeenth century: The Lisbon-Goa Fleet of 1629 as a case study," *Studies in Maritime History*, ed. K.S. Mathew, pp. 143-158.
82. ARSI: *Goa* 34, II, fls. 409v-411 (*Relação annual de Provincia de Goa deste anno de 1649* - Annual Report of the Goa Province from 1649).
83. Kosambi, Damodar D., *An Introduction to the Study of Indian History*, pp. 333-334.

84. B. N. (sic), *The Jesuits*, II (*Their foundation and history*), p. 27.
85. ARSI: *FG*, 1443/9, file 24, Goa 1650. A suggestion which Fr. Joannes Maraccius, Procurator, signed and added to the document described the necessity of attempting the formation of a new Vice-Province in order to reach the missions of China and Japan.
86. AHU: India, *maço* 90, 29 November 1755.

2

MORE MONEY FOR MORE SOULS

The Jesuits worked at gathering funds since the promised Crown subsidies were often either not forthcoming or inadequate. They thus bought lands, received donations and endowments from pious lay folk, got a flourishing palm-grove business going, sub-let lands, accepted pawned goods and mortgages, and helped the State with funds whenever the need arose. In the process, they became powerful landlords and financiers.

Financial Viewpoint

Most of the religious Orders of the time dealt in trade since they believed that it benefitted not so much the individual as much as the Order as a whole. The profits went a long way to defray their expenses in managing old missions or in starting new ones.

Yet accusations against them were many. The traveller Linschoten described the Jesuits of Goa as cunning in trade. In business, he believed, they surpassed the dealings of all the secular merchants. It was not before long that the other Orders and the ordinary people had started to murmur greatly against them. "There is", he believed, "not any commoditie to be had or reaped throughout all India, but they have their part therein, so that the other orders and Religious persons, as also the common people, doe much murmur thereat, and seeme to dislike of their convetous humors."[1] And they dealt in everything from bullion and silk in the East to sugar and slaves in the West.[2]

The various religious groups engaged in trade, initially to finance their work. But before long the trade turned to personal gain. The scale of their transactions provoked the anger of the people. There were heated quarrels between the groups themselves, and also between the missions and the Church.[3]

The fancy profits in the spice trade inspired many missionaries to take part in the trade, and to claim immunity before the secular law. The Crown objected to its own loss of revenue as a result. It obtained from the Pope the authority for the Bishop to punish such erring clerics.[4]

Jesuit Trade

The well-known Jesuit preacher, Fr. Antonio Vieira maintained that the missionaries carried the Gospel to various parts of the world, while the merchants in turn took the missionaries. Yet the distinction was not all that clearcut and did overlap. The Province of Japan, the vice-province of China and Simão de Souza de Tavora, a *fidalgo* and ex-captain of Salcete, had equal ownership shares on the *pataxo* (pinnace) which took a party of eleven Jesuits and four Capuchins on a roundabout voyage from Goa via Larantuca and Macassar to Macao in 1658.

The trade of the Japan Province from their base at Macao was the one which provoked the most criticism. The Papacy and the Crown had both authorized it for the support of the missions. When the Dutch shipwrecked four richly-laden Portuguese ships at Macassar in June 1660, both the Spanish Catholics and the Dutch Calvinists termed the event as a judgement of God. The Jesuits had large shares in the business.[5]

The Jesuits in Brazil did have their own boats, though of a smaller nature. In 1592 they had two such boats. It was a necessity since the Fr. Provincial had to visit much of his Province by sea. The royal subsidies had been wanting and they found maintaining a sea-vessel within their financial means.[6]

The Visitor Fr. Francisco Barreto had warned against the hiring of a *pataxo* for carrying of goods to another Province. He considered it a matter that would appear scandalous to others. He granted them permission, however, to hire a part of the cargo on any of the boats for their purpose.[7]

Gifts and Donations to the Province of Goa

The Crown and people too, gifted either lands or money to the Society of Jesus for its various works. King Sebastian had gifted spices to the Provinces of Germany and Flanders, and to the Jesuit colleges and houses in Rome. Fr. General Claudio Acquaviva had appointed Fr. Jeronimo Cardozo as Procurator to obtain and distribute the spices.[8]

D. Jeronimo Mascarenhas, captain of Hormuz, had left a legacy of 40,000 *ducados* to the Society. Isabel de Aguiar was declared the foundress of the College of Bassein after she gifted three villages and some houses in Bassein with an annual yield of 300 *cruzados*.[9]

Francisco de Melo e Castro who had come to Goa in 1601, and served as *Vedor da Fazenda* (Revenue Officer) and State Councillor, died in 1664 leaving behind an amount to the Society. It consisted of perpetual masses at two *tgs*. each. He also offered the Provincial, Fr. Antonio de Almeida, 5,000 *xs*. Antonio Paes de Sande offered the Church of Bom Jesus 300 *xs*. for expenses in maintaining the oil-lamp at the chapel of St. Xavier, while Balthazar da Veiga bequeathed properties in Bambolim worth 10,500 *xs*. and with annual income of 840 *xs*.[10]

D. Frei Sebastião Pinto Pimenta, the King of Tsaparang gave the priests in 1626 Rs. 8,000 towards the foundation of a mission in his kingdom. But the Jesuits in all likelihood had invested it in buying properties in Bombay.[11]

Other Donors

Mirza Zu-l-Qarnain gave the Society Rs. 20,000 at the behest of the priests. Fr. Joseph de Castro took it to Goa and the Province used the money to buy two villages in the North Province for Rs. 27,000. He gave them a further sum of Rs. 4,000. The revenues of the Parel house belonged to the College of Agra. The Jesuits at Bandra had large plots at Parel, Naigaon, Wadala, Mahim, and Dharavi. They held the property in trust as a source of revenue for the support of various missions, such as Goa, Cochin, Agra, Japan and China. But in 1719 the British Government confiscated their property.[12]

Zu-l-Qarnain gave the Society money to buy Parel and another village in Salcete of the North. The former netted 8,000 *xs*. while the latter about 5,000. When the English took over Parel, Juliana Dias da Costa, gave the Jesuits a sum of 50,000 *xs*. The cost of the Jesuits travelling to and fro and the expense of sending provisions alone amounted to about 10,000 *xs*. a year.[13]

Complaints against the Jesuit Holdings

The Jesuits as a result of the various donations they received, had their detractors. Antonio de Melo e Castro and Manuel Corte-Real de Sampaio, both of whom succeeded as Governors-General after the term of the Count of St. Vincent, reminded the Crown in 1670 that there were long-standing complaints about the amount of landed property the Jesuits owned in India and their refusal to give details of their holdings to the Crown or to any government authorities.[14]

Jesuit Procurators

The Procurator of the Indian Province resident at the College of St. Antão in Lisbon had the duty of sending to India provisions such as books, religious and liturgical articles, cloth and foodstuffs (olive oil, meat, plums, cereals). In turn he received from his counterparts in Goa pepper, *bazar* stone, diamonds, ivory and aloeswood.[15]

Procurator at Goa

Fr. Gonçalo Martins was a consummate financier for the Portuguese Jesuits. In 1653, the King of Portugal wrote to the Viceroy recommending Fr. Martins for all help and favour since he had served as Procurator and had helped in the dispatch of cinnamon for the Duchy of Bragança. He had also been on different occasions ambassador of the Viceroy to Shivaji and to Mohammed Adil Shah. The Viceroy had dispatched him to the court of Shivaji to secure the ratification of the Maratha-Portuguese treaty of 1667.[16]

The Office of Procurator

The creation of the post of a Jesuit Procurator was an important idea of Jesuit management. The intention of the General, Fr. Mercurian was similar to that of his predecessor who set up the office. The incumbent had to facilitate the exchange of correspondence between the Jesuits of Europe and of the Indies, and had to establish contacts for their mutual information.[17]

The Italian Bro. Bernardino dos Reis was in charge of such matters for India and Brazil. In 1554, Fr. Manuel Godinho was Procurator of the Portuguese Province, and his successor was Fr. Francisco Henriques. The Crown stipend to each departing missionary was 100 *cruzados*. The Procurator had to obtain for them material including books, retables, and mass-wine. He had to petition the King for the confirmation of the foundations of the Jesuit colleges. In 1573, Fr. General Mercurian had appointed the Italian Fr. Alexandre Valla Procurator for the Portuguese missions. He functioned independently of the Portuguese Province and was succeeded by a fellow-Italian Fr. Sebastian Sabino (1576-1580).[18]

The duties of the Procurator were manifold. He had to be diligent in office and he functioned under the supervision of the Superior of the house he stayed in. He was expected to close his room and desk when away, and had to keep one set of keys with himself and another with his companion after having locked away the account-books inside them. He had to keep the yearly accounts ready before the departure of the ships with copies of them for Rome. He had to seal the letters and documents meant for the other Procurators and for Fr. General, and had to dispatch them without delay through the royal court.

His other duties included being aware of the arrivals and departures of the various fleets and availing of every fleet to send the mail. He had to keep the Superior-General at Rome regularly informed on all matters concerning the Indies. He maintained a record containing information of the foundations of the colleges and houses with their income, and sent a summary of these to Rome.

In a second book he had to enter all information from Rome pertaining to his office, of things sent and received, of the lists of those going to the Indies, of the time for the fleets, and of Provinces with details of the country of origin, age, years in the Society, state, studies and talent of each Jesuit. The account-book also included details of Crown dealings, the amounts spent for books and clothes, the minutes of the meetings, the articles for the Indies (wine, olives, and ornaments for masses), together with the amount of stipends for the departing missionaries who usually housed themselves at the College of Seville.

The Procurator had to write a list of the missionaries with their times of arrival and departure. He stacked the necessities for the voyage in a suitable storehouse, and had the money of the Province in his safe-keeping. His other duties included filing information of good sailings, arranging books for the missionaries, having an intelligent and able assistant, paying Rome for the expense of letters and other things for the Indies, discussing relevant issues with the Crown, and writing to Rome and to the Provincial of Andalusia.[19]

An instruction of 11 September 1574 instructed the Procurator to ready the necessaries for dispatch to Peru and to Mexico, to collect and to send letters for Rome in the same condition they had arrived, and to fill in the registers with the respective incomes and expenditures. He had to send the annual accounts to Peru and to Mexico, and had to be prepared with the various receipts and dispatches, and with the history of the foundations of the colleges and houses of the Province with the income peculiar to each of them.

He had also to see to the matter he had received from Rome pertaining to his office, and the minutes of the meeting in the Andalusian Province. He needed to discuss with the Provincial matters of importance whenever it was difficult to secure the information from Rome.[20]

Jesuit Procurators for the Queen

The Jesuits were procurators for the House of Braganças in Lisbon. In 1751, Fr. Estrada de Rodrigo as Procurator sent the Queen 300 quintals of spices free of charge. Some in Goa objected to this practice but he explained his position to them satisfactorily.[21] He was a hard-working man, but had an irascible temper. He had antagonized others when he once tried illegaliy to appoint his own collector to handle the taxes of the villages of Panulem and Corjuem in Goa.[22]

The office of the Procurator helped in a sound financial management of the Jesuit revenues and their properties. The Marquis of Pombal could not but admire their methodology, and he had instructed his Board of Administration to follow the system when he took over the Jesuit properties in 1759.[23]

Jesuits as Loan-Givers

The Jesuits had made an offer of one-eighth of their income to the State in 1664. It was in response to the Viceroy Antonio de Melo e Castro's call to the religious Orders in Goa to pay one-eighth of their income for expenses the State incurred in its defence. The Jesuits had also given a loan for the war in Colaba and the money was invested with interest.[24]

They had offered the Public Exchequer in 1727 a loan of 1,25,000 *xs.* and another of 14,000 the following year, at eight per cent interest. In return they had the administration of the villages of Corjuem and Ponulem till 1741 though the State Council wanted to take it back earlier. The State had appointed a revenue collector for the islands who was paid 100 *xs.* by the Crown. The loan of 14,000 had helped in funding a fleet to Mombaça and Patte in East Africa. The yearly income was usually 10,000 to 12,000 *xs.*[25] But the Crown had not approved the deal of the villages and had suggested that the State think of some other way of paying back for the loan.[26]

The Jesuits had a rice granary at Bassein which helped the fleets to have a quick supply of rice for dispatch. They sold the rice at a higher price than the people could pay. They bought villages in order to stock their granaries keeping always 600 to 800 *mudas* of rice which would be sufficient in case of an enemy attack. They earned 7,73,572 *xs.* as land-tax from nine villages.

Fr. Julião Pereira gave 12,000 as help for Mombaça, Fr. Antonio Pereira 10,000 for the same in the form of cloth pieces ordered from Daman, Inacio de Almeida gave 6,000 for the construction of the royal vessel *Our Lady of Loretto*, and Fr. Nuno bought a smaller ship, *Santa Catarina* for 3,019 *xs.*, 1 *larim* and two quarters. The Administrator, Fr. Antonio Guerreiro had given the Factor of the city the loan of 14,000 for the fleets, and Fr. Alexandre Souza loaned another 20,000 *xs.* for a fleet to the Straits. He also gave two ships, one for the factory of the city and the other for the shipyard of the Crown, and Fr. Joseph de Veiga handed over 4,000 towards half the expenses of a fleet on the high seas. All the above amounts totalled 2,58,180 *xs.*[27] Cosme Damião Pereira Pinto with the permission of the Crown on 23 April 1736 mortgaged his estate at Curca to the Jesuits for 40,000 *xs.* for a eight-year duration. He borrowed a further 30,000 *xs.* from the Jesuit Procurator of Japan, since he could find no one who could lend so much.[28]

The Jesuits had helped the State financially on the occasion of the Maratha war. A meeting of the 29 August 1737 had asked for contributions towards a special tax (*finta geral*). The Viceroy, Count of Sandomil had asked the Provincial in his letter of 20 August 1737 for an inventory of the silver in the houses of the Province. He had to mention what pertained either to each house or to the confraternities in the churches of these houses, together with the likely donation for this cause.

In his reply of 3 September 1737 from Chorão, Fr. João Marques mentioned his own illness and his regret in paying more. He could offer only 30,000 *xs.* When the Viceroy protested, the Provincial recalled how the Jesuits (the Rector of the Diu college and the Superior of the Bandra house) had in an earlier event come to the rescue of the State. He reminded the Viceroy that the Society had its own expenses not only for its houses and colleges, but also for the missions of the other provinces. There the missionaries were without any sustenance for themselves and for the Christians. As a final gesture, he offered 40,000 *xs.* to the Viceroy which he would pay in ten days although he was unable to get the word of the other Fathers for it.[29]

Jesuits as Slave-Employers

The Jesuits besides being loan-givers were slave-employers too. They enlisted the help of subordinates for work on their farms, in their palm-groves and in their gardens. The situation was similar to that in the Zambezi missions in Africa where the efficient management of the *prazos* (large farm-lands) would have been impossible had the Jesuits there not been able to rely on helpers who were devoted, honest and capable. They themselves were so few that they could have done little besides supervising the work in a very general way. The climate took its toll, and some of those serving there had often to return to Goa for treatment and rest.[30]

Both free and bonded helpers were members of the domestic staff of the Jesuits in the Japan Province. The majority of the former were native Japanese, while the slaves were either Negroes, Indians, Malays or Asiatic. The Regulation of 1612 laid down that the Jesuits had to treat charitably the fugitive slaves in their custody, and had to refrain from handing them over to their masters. It believed it was more prudent to get rid of the unwanted refugee and to ask a local Christian to arrange a solution between the master and the man.

The Jesuit attitude toward the oppressed classes in Japan was more in support of those who had than those who did not. That was in contrast to its more liberal policy in Brazil. The Society denounced the Portuguese for holding Japanese and Chinese slaves since Japan and China disliked the practice.[31]

A few Christian thinkers of the time did not condemn all forms of slavery. The Church Provincial Council of 1567, after complaining that there was much unjust slavery, laid down certain rules for maintaining a slave. One who qualified to be a slave had to be born of a slave-woman, had to be a captive in a just war, had to have sold himself voluntarily or been a child sold in extreme poverty, and had to be a convict for his crimes. St. Francis Xavier, too, accepted the then prevalent idea of just slavery. During the early years of their stay at Goa, the Jesuits employed slaves, whom they believed they had acquired justly. But with the exception of Sicily and the Portuguese dominions, nowhere did the Jesuits keep slaves. In 1569 the Superior-General decreed that the Society ought to set free the slaves it maintained in its houses.[32]

Attitudes towards Slaves

Of the many non-Goans living in Goa, slaves made up the largest single group. In the early seventeenth century many believed that most of the Goa population consisted of slaves. The Portuguese *casados* (married settlers) usually had about ten slaves each. Local Goans in the city also had a few slaves. Most of these were Negroes from Mozambique and parts of East Africa, and the rest were Asiatics. They served as caretakers, personal helpers or even concubines, and worked on some handicraft or at some profitable trade. Lists of carracks seem to suggest that some of them went to Portugal as either export or re-export items.[33] But the Jesuits knew that they could neither sell nor act as middlemen during the sale of any slaves.[34]

Jesuit Properties in Bombay

The Jesuit College at Bandra had much land and many rights on the island of Bombay. But the English Governor, Sir Gervase Lucas had refused to admit them. The Jesuits had recourse to force which the Governor considered an act of treason against His Majesty's Government. He confiscated their lands and deprived them of their rights, and the Jesuits lost the annual revenue from their orchards.[35]

The Portuguese envoy, Viconte de Monte Arcada, had sent a memorial to the King of England in 1695. It stated that the inhabitants of the island of Bombay after securing peace with the Grand Mughul were reluctant to restore to the Portuguese Jesuits the lands which they claimed they had lost during the war. They believed that the new peace treaty with the Mughal gave them ownership over these. The treaty signed a long time ago with Portugal was no longer binding on them. It had stated that the island could be in the name of the English but with the Portuguese as owners of the lands. The petition wanted the King to give back the Portuguese their ownership over the lands.[36]

Jesuit Houses in Goa

In 1589 the College of St. Paul's had 70 Jesuits and 100 students, 30 Portuguese and the rest native. There were 40 servants to help in the various duties. The College received 7,807 *ducados* from the rents of Bandra, Kurla, Sargui and Mori, and from other gifts. While 3,600 *ducados* was spent on the Seminary, on the churches in Chorão and Bandra, and on the sick, 4,207 went towards the expenses of the priests and servants of the College. The income of the College for 1724 was 1,700 *xs.*, 1 *tga.*, and 40 *rs.*[37]

The College also received 2,000 *cruzados* and it owned besides, the villages of Bandra and Corlem given by Izabel Pereira before her death. In addition, it also owned other lands, salt-pans, plain and unbroken lands.[38]

The Confraternity of the Holy Faith enjoyed a sound financial basis with the assets of the temples of Ilhas. Of the 768 *pardaus* from temple rents, 300 were meant for the College of St. Paul's and the Confraternity. The remaining amount went towards the salaries of the chaplains of the churches of Banastarim, Divar, Panjim, and Batim.[39]

The new College of St. Paul's had properties in Bombay. In the Mahim *caçabé* it had palm-groves with coconut trees, 10,656 of which yielded coconuts, and 516 did not. The rice fields in Mahim and the suburbs yielded 96 *mudas*, 8 *paras* and 6.50 *adolins* of white rice, and 11 *mudas*, 11 *paras* and 1.50 *adolins* of black rice. It allotted 287 wild coconut-trees for toddy-tapping. The salt-pan in Sewri yielded 17 *ticates* of salt. Besides the above, the College had shops, taverns and coconut-trees at Dharavi. The Mughal mission had 2,290 coconut-bearing trees at Mahim and Parel, and 520 non coconut-bearing. There were also 15 wild palm-trees. Two villages at Parel and Wadala had rice fields of white and black varieties, and salt-pans. Daman and Diu had 354 and 492 fruit-bearing palms-trees, and 3 and 237 non-bearing palms-trees, respectively.[40]

The College of Rachol had received a royal endowment. It was customary for the villages of greater Morombim to guard the College fields at harvest-time in order to ensure the payment of revenue due to the village community. The *ganvkars* had stopped the practice, and had fixed a charge for keeping the watch. They next approached the Viceroy for exemption from the job. They believed that the College ought to have done the watch at no extra charge.[41]

As regards, the island of Kumbarjua, in 1665 the Jesuit Procurator, Fr. Gonçalo Martins bought it entirely on behalf of the Goa Province from a Government agent, André Salema for 20,000 *xs*. There was revenue from a tax on prostitution, from the issue of licences to Hindus to celebrate their weddings on the island, and from the illicit transaction of trade commodities at a much lower duty than that collected by the State at the official customs check-post. The Governor Antonio de Melo e Castro, however, opposed the activities of the Jesuits who managed an annual revenue of 7,000 *xs.* in the early eighteenth century. They had besides, kilns for baking lime and preparing tiles.[42]

Fr. Domingos Alvares while the Superior of St. Paul's was also the Administrator of Kumbarjua. A few poor *curumbi* families lived on the island but had no property of their own. The tobacco tax-farmers sold the tobacco which was cheap at the rate of 3 *baz.* an *oitava* to swell their profits. They were unable to levy any fines on the inhabitants when necessary since they were too poor to own anything. The families were better off during the time of the Jesuit administration. The tobacco tax-farmer, José de Miranda had raised the price by one *baz.* but the people opposed this. Finally, Fr. Teotonio Ribeiro, the next Administrator helped in reaching some agreement.

The farmers then sold the tobacco at four *bazarucos* but could take only half the proceeds leaving the rest to the inhabitants. The latter donated their share to the Jesuit Administrator on the condition that he would build them houses to secure their goods in case of wars and disturbances on the mainland. He built in addition a chapel for them on the island.

The tax-farmer at the time, Macana Sinai, requested Fr. Manoel Soares, another of the Administrators, to build him a house with two partitions. He intended to stay along with his factor in one of the sections and to keep the tobacco and its proceeds in the other. He wanted three smaller tobacco shops in public places. These cost him 10 *xs.* a month. He agreed to pay the priest a monthly sum of 12 *baz.* The Administrator had to set up a watch to guard against smuggling on the river. He paid three men at the rate of 3 *xs.* a month besides other perks. But some of them indulged in smuggling themselves and he had to replace them. He earned in all 24 *xs.*, 10 from house-rents, and 14 from the tobacco sale. The river passage belonged to the Society which used to then farm it out to others.[43]

Some Jesuit Houses in the Province of the North

The Viceroy had allotted one per cent of the town revenue of Chaul to the Jesuits.[44] The College of Diu received from the Royal Treasury each year 648 *xs.* for the expenses of the priests studying Arabic, 1,000 *pardaus* for the Christians of Ethiopia, 200 *xs.* for the Seminary, and 500 *pardaus* for the five Jesuits in Ethiopia. Diu was felt to be the best link between the Red Sea and Ethiopia.[45]

The total loss in Salcete of Goa due the Maratha war was 4,00,000 *xs.* It was due chiefly to the loss of silver and sacred ornaments of the churches. The Marathas had also attacked the Jesuit house at Bandra, but the Jesuits resisted the attack with the aid of some British soldiers who were on their pay-roll. The total loss in the two-year war was 34,40,000 *xs.*[46]

Gill Vaz Lobo had owed the College of Agra 26,067 *xs.*, 3 *tgs.* and 59 *rs.* On his death, the Procurator for the Dead, allotted the amount to the State as a loan. The Jesuits refuted the claim, and requested the Crown for its return. They claimed that the amount was the only support the mission in Agra could claim as its own.[47]

Jesuits as Economic Agents for the State

The Jesuits often joined other government officials on their visits to the neighbouring kingdoms to discuss matters of the State. Fr. Gonçalo Martins went to Honavar to discuss a peace settlement with Vittal Malya. The Viceroy and his Councillors discussed the amount of pepper which was to be sent along, and whether Ramoji Sinai Kothari was to accompany them as interpreter or participant in the discussions. They considered also the necessity of a permanent representative at Honavar to study the state of war, and picked on Fr. João Rodrigues Viegas for the job for his experience and merit. They decided on a compromise with Kanara with milder conditions and at some expense to the Treasury.

Fr. Martins went to Honavar with 500 *khandis* of pepper at a cost of 28 *pagodas* a *khandi*. Ramoji joined him because of his reliableness and his knowledge of the land. They returned to Shivappa Nayak the boat the Portuguese had captured at Cochin.[48] The Council had also discussed whether Fr. Martins ought to return and leave Fr. Viegas behind.[49]

Jesuits also functioned in the capacity of administrators of the Northern forts. Fr. Alexandre de Souza was Administrator of Bassein in 1715. The State praised the religious for their work and for the gift of 20,000 *pardaus* towards the *armada* of the North. Yet, the Jesuits often had difficulties in dealing with the construction and repairs of the forts mainly due to a depleted State Treasury.[50]

The Malabar Province

The Malabar Province though juridically distinct from the Province of Goa had its properties in Goa and its resident Jesuit officials to administer them. It sought a confirmation of the *alvará* of Dom Rodrigo da Costa and Vasco Rodrigues Caesar de Menezes, to enable it to buy property of about 20,000 *xs*. It needed money to maintain its priests and its catechists. The Jesuits had serious financial problems ever since they had lent money to some Hindus who had later absconded.

The Crown wanted the Viceroy to inquire into the property of the Fathers, to find out what each of the Provinces had, and how much money the Hindus had received due to the negligence of the Procurator. He wished all religious Orders to submit the lists of their properties and revenues. They did so. It was clear to the Crown that the Jesuits were in need of money for their growing missions. It could not grant the petition in the form presented, but suggested an alternative. In the North Province, people had deserted their villages. The Jesuits could take some of these, help in rehabilitating them, and retain the revenues of the same.[51]

It had given loans totalling 4,45,121 *xs.* and received 35,598 *xs.* in interest. Yet the money was not always sure. It spent much on its Procurator and staff at Goa, for the journeys of its members, for the poor, for cases of litigation and for repairs. In 1733, it spent 9,098 *xs.* for vestments, wine and church furniture. Its Procurators often received gold and precious stones which at times proved false. It had loaned the Portuguese Province 12,227 *xs.* at five percent interest. In India the limit was ten percent. Catechist fees and gift-giving was a drain on the income and the gross income of the Province was 60,000 *xs.* per year.[52]

The income and expenses for the year 1734 for the Province were 23,404 and 27,631 *xs.* respectively. The Assolná estate yielded 8,000. An annual report of 1740 mentioned that the Marathas had taken the estates of Assolná, Betim, Quirol, Sorrotor, and Gauto Comprem, and that the loss for the Province was 18,300 *xs.* The Royal Exchequer had not paid them 11,854 *xs.*, and 15,860 on a loan of 2,30,000 *xs.* had been lost. The Jesuits were rich landlords but some maintained that difficulties and litigations prevented them from getting their dues.[53]

A few made attempts to relieve the plight of the poor they served. The Archbishop of Cranganore Francis Garcia, for instance, had established a *montepio* (a charitable bank) for the people of Cranganore. The poor could draw from it on the condition that they could borrow no more if they failed to make their regular repayments.[54]

The Japan Province

The Visitor Fr. Valignano spoke of the warm generosity of the Viceroy Duarte de Menezes who in 1587 paid the Province 2,000 *cruzados*. He had promised each month another 200 and also four Arab horses.[55]

The Visitor had written to General Fr. Claudio Acquaviva about the difficulties of the Province to make payments towards the common expenses. He wanted care to be taken to collect the revenue of the Province (in Bassein) and to dispatch the things necessary for it. The contribution of his Province to the common fund would come only from the income it received either in India or in Europe. The Province had 12,000 *pardaus* in silk and 2,000 *pardaus* in anchorage in the port of Nagasaki.[56]

Other Religious

Though the Jesuits had their financial difficulties, the State did not quite believe their gravity. She was, for instance, better disposed towards the Oratorians. These had asked for permission to retain 10,000 *xs.* in landed property either through endowments or through purchase, and had approached the Crown with their request.

The Overseas Council affirmed the praiseworthy work they were doing and offered them a sum of 6,000 *xs*. But some among the members suggested a lower sum of 4,000 since the group usually had Brahmin recruits who entered their Order with large endowments. They recalled how the religious Orders always had enough money to float loans to the municipalities.[57]

The Jesuits, too, had been financial beneficiaries to the village communities and private parties. Their properties in Goa and in the North prove the extent of their hold on the finances of the time. They received and sent money to their offices in Rome and in Lisbon. The money they gained they used for building their churches and for their travels on missionary errands. And they lived generally well as their monthly accounts attest.

Besides, their Procurators did their jobs of gathering more funds for more souls with religious zeal seeing their endeavours as important as preaching the Gospel. These brought them into greater dealings with the State and the other foreign and local powers in India. While their own Superiors warned them of caution, the others viewed them with suspicion and antagonism.

REFERENCES

1. Linschoten, John Huyghen van, *The Voyage of John Huyghen Van Linschoten to the East Indies*. I, p. 164; Meilink-Roelofsz, M.A.P., *Asian Trade and European Influence*, pp. 130-131.
2. Scammell, Geoffrey V., *The World Encompassed: The First European Maritime Empires c. 800-1650*, p. 274.
3. *Ibid.*, p. 288.
4. Mathew, K. S., *Portuguese Trade with India in the Sixteenth Century*, pp. 31-32.
5. Boxer, Charles R., *Portuguese India in the Mid-Seventeenth Century*, pp. 48-49.
6. Leite, Serafim, *Historia da Companhia de Jesus no Brasil*, IV, pp. 169-171.
7. ARSI: *FG*, 1443/9, 74 B, Goa 27, clause 18. 1660.
8. *DI*, XIV (1585-88), p. 927. He had to see to the clearance of the goods and the tax-exemptions from port and customs authorities.
9. *Ibid.*, XVI (1592-94), pp. 170, 218. He had first come to India in 1574 and again in 1588 and his remains lie in the Basilica of Bom Jesus. de Aguiar was buried in the sanctuary of the church of the College of Bassein.
10. Carmo Nazareth, J. M. do, "Legados Pios a Egreja do Bom Jesus," *O Oriente Portugues*, IV, pp. 173-176; *BG*, no. 3, 1862. The founder of the College of Chaul gave 97, 000 *rs*.

11. Hosten, Henry (ed.), "Letters and Other Papers of Fr. Ippolito Desideri, SJ, A Missionary in Tibet (1713-21)", *JRASB*, IV, no. 24, 1938, p. 594.
12. Hosten, "Mirza Zu-l-Qarnain, a Christian Grandee of Three Great Moghuls, with Notes on Akbar's Christian Wife and the Indian Bourbons", *MASB*, V, no. 4, p. 137.
13. *Ibid.*, p. 137; DAAM: *MR*, no. 79, fl. 131.
14. DAAM: *MR*, no. 34 (1668-70), letter of Goa, Jan, 1670.
15. *Ibid.*, codex 2570. Book of register of articles sent and received by the Jesuits, 1664-1708.
16. *Ibid.*; *MR*, no. 23 (1653), fl. 263. Details supplied by Henry Heras in *JBHS*, 1928, pp. 6-7.
17. Zubillaga, Felix, "El Procurador de las Indias Occidentales", *AHSI*, XXII, 1953.
18. Wicki, J., "Die Anfange der Missionsprokur der Jesuiten in Lissabon bis 1580," *AHSI*, XXXIX, 1971, pp. 321-322.
19. Zubillaga, *art. cit.*, pp. 400-402.
20. *Ibid.*, pp. 398-399.
21. AHU: India *maço*, 99, 14 December 1758.
22. *Ibid.*, *maço*, 56, 1751. The Jesuits made use of these contacts to influence matters at Court.
23. Correia-Afonso, John (ed.), *Indo-Portuguese History: Sources and Problems*, pp. 76-77.
24. *MR*, no. 957, fl. 34, no. 960, fls. 46-48; AHU: *maço* 35, 8 Jan 1733.
25. AHU: India, *maço* 11, 1728. Fr. Provincial João de Mello was present at the meeting of the Revenue Council held on 23 October 1727.
26. *Ibid.*, *maço* 62, 1750.
27. *Ibid.*, *maço* 8.
28. *Ibid.*, *maço* 62.
    Appendix 22 gives an idea of the various loans the Jesuits gave to the municipalities, the village communities, and to individuals.
29. *ACE*, V, pp. 435-46.
30. Rea, William F., *The Economics of the Zambezi Missions: 1580-1759*, p. 111.
31. Boxer, Charles, *The Christian Century in Japan 1549-1650*, pp. 226-227.
32. D'Costa, Anthony, *The Christianisation of the Goa Islands*, p. 24.
33. Disney, Anthony, *The Twilight of the Pepper Empire: Portuguese trade in Southwest India in the early seventeenth century*, p. 18.
34. *DI*, XV (1588-92), p. 56.
35. Gense, James, "First confiscation of Jesuit properties in Bombay", *The Examiner*, Bombay, September 10 and 17, 1938.
36. IOL: *Home Miscellaneous Series*, 36. Shrewsbury Whitehall sent the memorial to the King on 27 August 1695.
37. *DI*, XV (1588-92), pp. 479-83. See Appendices 7 and 13 for lists containing income and expenses of St. Paul's for some years in the sixteenth and seventeenth centuries respectively.
38. IOL: *Pombal's Collection and letters from the Viceroy's Translations 1507-1806*: 1/3/147, vol. 525, fl. 101.
39. Rocha, Leopoldo da, *As Confrarias de Goa (séculos XVI-XX)*, 1973.
40. AHU: *maço* 10, doc. 77, 22 March 1720.
41. *Ibid.*, *maço* 48, 14 September 1731. See Appendix 15 for a list of income of the College of Rachol for the mid-seventeenth century.
42. De Souza, Teotonio R., "A Pious Hindu commemorates in Marble the Activities of the Paulistas in Kumbarjua," *Goa Today*, Panjim, February 1977, pp. 14, 22. Fr. Martins

was highly choleric, not academically-minded, but adept at administrative matters. He was in charge of the finances of Chaul and Goa, Mozambique and Japan at various times. He acted as peace-maker after the invasion of Goa by Adil Shah in 1654. He went to conclude a peace treaty with Shivaji after his invasion of Bardez in 1667.
See also De Souza, Teotonio. "Gonçalo Martins : A Jesuit Procurator, Businessman and Diplomat in the *Estado da India*". *Mare Liberum* (Lisbon). no. 5, July 1993, p. 119-128.

Appendix 14 gives figures of the income of the island for 1667-1731, while appendix 17 mentions the Jesuit properties there for 1726.

43. AHU: India, *maço* 27, 23 October 1714. Fr. Domingos Alvares wrote the letter on 19 December 1743 to pass on information to the Procurator of the Crown.
44. *ACE*, III (1644-58), pp. 230-1, 21 February 1653. The signatories at the consultation were Conde d'Obidos, Antonio Souza Coutinho, Francisco da Silva Sotto Maior, Martim Velho Barreto, Francisco de Melo e Castro, Antonio de Souza Coutinho and Mamty Ve.
Appendix 21 gives the income and expenses of the property at Betalbatim in Goa which the College of Chaul had for 1717-23.
45. Humbert, "Some Answers of the Generals of the Society of Jesus to the Province of Goa. Acquaviva - Vitelleschi 1581-1645," *AHSI*, XXXV, 1966, pp. 342-343.
46. Danvers, Frederick C., *Report to the Secretary of State for India in Council on the Portuguese Records relating to the East Indies contained in the Archivo da Torre do Tombo and the public libraries at Lisbon and Evora*, pp. 78, 89-90.
47. AHU: *maço* 62, 1750.
48. *ACE*, III, pp. 239-240, 7 April 1653. Fr. Martins mentions about the great change he noticed in Vittal Malya. King Shivappa Nayak was sick. Fr. Viegas was asked to spend the monsoon in Honavar with powers enough for its defence and the boats.
49. *Ibid.*, pp. 322-324, 5 March 1654.
50. Humbert, "The Goa Archives in 1963," *Indica*, vol. 1, no. 1, March 1964, pp. 57, 60.
51. AHU: India, *maço* 20, 1723.
52. Ferroli, Domenico, *The Jesuits in Malabar*, II, pp. 346-347.
53. *Ibid.*, pp. 349, 350-351.
54. Thekedathu, Joseph, *The Troubled Days of Francis Garcia SJ Archbishop of Cranganore (1641-59)*, p. 161. The book describes the holiness and goodness of the man, and the immense good he achieved. But his stubborn views caused him much trouble.
55. *DI*, XIV (1585-88), p. 653. See Appendix no. 8 for a list of the income and expenditure of the Japan Province for 1585-88.
56. *Ibid.*, XVI (1592-94), pp. 13-14, 249.
57. AHU: *maço* 9, 20 May 1719.

3

ROME-RULE

Money was a much needed item for the Jesuits of the Goa Province. They made use of various means to get more. At times the means were canonically wrong. Their Frs. Superior General would either write directly to the Frs. Provincial cautioning against these practices or would send their special Frs. Visitor to study the matter firsthand. These came armed with extensive powers to probe spiritual and financial matters and to give instructions. They covered details of everyday living, inter-religious relationships, political and material transactions.

It was all partly necessary since Jesuits often ventured too far ahead and that was at times disastrous for the Order as a whole. It had both lost much and gained much as a result. Its constitutional writings and instructions showed the heights to which its men had to rise. Yet, there were many who by their devious ways incurred the unnecessary wrath of others.

The View of the Church

In the Middle Ages, the Church regarded buying and selling, lending and borrowing as a case of charity. She had a prejudice against acquiring riches, and considered it avarice. Merchants and money-lenders were not business strategists, but monsters of iniquity. Invariably, the parish priests would deliver a sermon on the seventh commandment, choosing as their text the words of the Book of Proverbs, "Give me neither riches nor poverty, but enough for my sustenance."[1]

Early Church Councils had forbidden the clergy and laity the practice of usury, and laid down rules for dealing with offenders. The clerics who lent money to persons in need, or who took their possessions in pawn and received profits beyond the capital sum lent, lost their offices. They could not avail of Communion or be given a Christian burial. They could make no offerings, and ecclesiastics who failed to punish them were themselves to be suspended until they made satisfaction to their bishop. The most notable ecclesiastical attack on usury came in the legislations of the Councils of Lyons (1274) and of Venice (1312).[2]

The View of the Jesuits in Japan

The case of the Japan Province of the Society of Jesus was special and the Visitor, Fr. Alessandro Valignano had to reconcile many differences with regard to trade in order to run the Mission. Pope Gregory XIII granted that the trade the Province conducted, was a matter of charity rather than of commerce. His successor, however, curtailed many of the concessions. He had promised increased aid, but it was most often slow in coming.

Fr. Valignano had secretly sent some gold to India as part of his trading operations. The Superior-General, Fr. Claudio Acquaviva had warned him against it as the Viceroy was in the know of the affair. Besides, the extent of the Province's trading activities had earned the Society a bad name. The Province bought a certain amount of silk from the Portuguese merchants and sold it at a profit for the mission. The General wanted the Visitor to both prevent the Procurators from making contracts in the name of seculars and to receive money on their behalf. The Japan Jesuits had permission to deal in silk alone, but some of them fancied other materials too. Fr. Vitelleschi had to inform the next Visitor, Fr. Francisco Vieira, of the details. Yet, the men in 1623 termed their operations *non erat mercatura sed opus charitatis* (not business but charity).[3]

Jesuits at times appeared guilty of transgressing the canonical requirements in the matter of trade. In Africa though they sold ivory they could do so only of elephants which had died on their property according to the Provincial order, thus observing canonical regulations.[4] Canon law defined trade as buying a commodity with the intention of selling it unimproved for a higher price. Pope Pius IV in the brief *Romanum* of 4 October 1563 had forbidden all ecclesiastics in the Portuguese Indies to trade, and Pope Urban VIII renewed that by the Constitution *Ex Debito* of 22 February 1633.

General Acquaviva had heard from the reports of Frs. Francisco Cabral and Pero Martins of the extent of trade, of the buying and exchanging of *reales* (Spanish silver coins) which were highly prized in India at that time. He forbade individuals from engaging in trade, yet allowed the Japan Province its silk trade.[5]

Various Roman Instructions

Alms

The instructions that came from the offices in Rome did not cover merely matters of trade, but could often cover various matters of everyday living. Jesuits while preparing to take their final vows begged from door to door for a period of three days. In Goa, most often they received large sums of money. The Superior-General writing towards the end of the sixteenth century, objected to the acceptance of the sums. The practice of begging, he reminded all, was to instill a spirit of humility in the members and not to gather money for its own sake. In case of a legitimate need for money, they had to inform the donor of the motive of their practice and request. If money was eventually received, the Professed House alone could have the ownership it.[6]

Manual Work

Fr. General had objected to the behaviour of a Brother who had refused to do any manual work himself and who had made use of *hamals* (porters) instead. He warned the Superiors of religious houses that using the services of prabhus (private secretaries) for one's desk-work went against their practice of the vow of poverty.[7]

Fr. General, Tirso Gonzalez condemned the practice of having personal servants in one's employ. It was common- place at the Santa Monica convent. He maintained that the servants in the houses though attached to the property could leave their jobs if they wished to do so. Many of them used to go to Bandra since Bombay offered them better salaries.[8]

Fr. Francisco Barreto, Visitor to the Goa Province in 1660 left instructions on the manner and number of slaves in Jesuit houses. On many occasions, the large number of blacks in Jesuit houses had caused discomfort. They would be insolent and fight in groups. He suggested having a few to cut down on costs. The College could have not more than twelve and the house not more than six. The houses, he felt, would function better under that new arrangement.[9]

There were rules for servants (*moços*) too. At Rachol, they could do the reading at table when the Jesuits were few. They did not have to serve at table or engage in other works when the brothers were at hand. They had to be simply dressed, not luxuriously and favourably (*regalados e favorecidos*) in order not to scandalize others or appear as servants of the rich. They could be on temporary service and would be paid as time went by. They had to be at least twenty years of age, and the Superiors would need to choose and approve them.[10]

Financial Accounts

Fr. General Gonzalez wanted parish-priests and missionaries to furnish returns of all their income and expenditure. He prohibited the use of a palanquin and restrained servants in Jesuit houses from trading or from receiving money to invest.[11]

Issues on Poverty

Fr. Vitelleschi instructed his Visitor, Fr. João Baptista to check on various infringements against the vow of poverty. No one could carry away his *escritorio* (writing-desk) when on a transfer. It was wrong to retain in one's keeping money of 30 *pardaus* or more in value. Revenues from tobacco in the Northern Province were on the increase and brought in 50,000 *xs*. annually. But Jesuits were warned against sharing tobacco with their friends.[12] There was much movement of Jesuits from Goa to the Northern Province. The house to which a Jesuit was destined had to meet his travelling expenses and not the house at which he rested in transit.[13] In Goa and in the Zambezi missions, the Jesuits made use of either river-craft or palanquins to travel to various places.[14]

Jesuits had to refrain from keeping the money of a third party without the permission of the Superior. The case of Bro. Villas was fresh in the minds of many. As Administrator of the College of San Hermenegildo (Seville), he had traded in a big way with the funds of the Society, and had caused it much financial harm.[15] Pope Alexander VII had in his brief *Sacrosancti Apostolatus Officii* condemned the abuses committed by the European clergy, in Goa. The General reiterated the warning in his letters to the Procurators and Administrators.[16]

Warnings for Superiors

Rome pointed out that some Superiors acted as if they were accountable to no one in financial matters. Fr. Paulo Oliva as Vicar-General had asked the Provincial, Fr. Stanislaus Malpica in 1662 to inquire whether Rectors and Superiors parted with anything of value by either selling it or by gifting it away without leave of the Provincial. He wished them to be more sparing in giving general permissions, especially to scholastics.

Often Rectors were at fault in rushing to the aid of the State without proper reference to their higher Superiors or communities. The Rector of the Rachol College had given Jesuit funds when the Royal Treasury was bankrupt during the Dutch blockade of the harbour in Goa in 1659. He died in 1661 before the General's indictment could reach him.[17] In 1664, the Jesuits had offered the State an eighth part of their income.[18] That was in response to a State proposal that the Religious pay an amount towards the common need.[19]

Fr. Oliva reminded the Provincial that the General alone had the power to sell or grant property on lease. He wanted all the lease contracts ratified on condition that on the death of the holder of the property, it would return to the Society. No Superior had the authority to dispose of property without the permission of the General. The maladministration of the College of Bassein property had resulted in a a debt of 3,000 *pardaus* although it had a revenue of about 4,000. The College also had an income of 15,000 *pardaus*, and the Church of the College 5,000 *xs.* from the village of Purim.[20]

Superiors of houses often did more than charity called for. The Vicar-General Fr. Carlo de Sangro in his order of 2 January 1645 suggested that alms-giving though commendable had to be the amount sanctioned by the Provincial after due consultation. He fixed the amount at 20 *pardaus* in order to stop abuses which took place in times of economic crisis. Though Superiors were ready to help others, they overlooked that they had first to pay off the loans their own religious houses had incurred.[21]

Annual letters from the Provincials gave details of the material and spiritual state of the Goa Province. Letters from the Consultors kept Rome informed of the activities the Jesuits engaged in. Some of them were unhappy that they could not receive deposits from the common people. This would have, they believed, prevented the people from losing at the hands of the traders and bankers. The Rector of the Daman College, however, had permission to accept royal deposits and to act as Royal Treasurer.[22]

Fr. Oliva wanted his men to combine charity with sanity. The Professed House had taken a deposit to offer loans to outsiders (non-Jesuits). There was a danger of these turning into bad debts and thus becoming a burden for the House.[23]

The Frs. Provincial could not dispose of any property without consulting either the Province or the College concerned. The Consultors would then have to sign the minutes and send them to Rome with their own respective comments.[24]

The Provincial could accept goods of sufficient worth with their accompanying obligations, a mass each year for instance, yet he had to judge what was best, and without any grave obligation. He could agree to sell off estates to pay off debts. Jesuits could trade in property only with benefactors of the Society.[25]

The Provincial had the authority to transfer real estate worth 200 *pardaus* thus changing the will of the donor. He could do so if the need was urgent and if he could not wait for a reply from Rome. Yet he had to inform Rome of his decision as soon as it was possible. Those going to Japan could not take the money of seculars along although they were good friends of the Society. The Procurator could exchange money even though it would entail some loss. The Provincial had the duty of sending 600 *xs.* each year to the Procurator in Lisbon.[26]

Superiors could help each other to pay off their respective debts and the Provincial would have to determine where doubts would present themselves. Debts had led to fears that missionaries could not come to India from Europe at least for some years. The Procurators of India and Brazil could use the funds of each other in case of grave necessity.[27]

The rules for the Provincial included being familiar with the rules of the Institute, having a capable secretary, a Procurator and a Father of Christians, and visiting Bassein each year for four months from December. He had to visit Malabar once during his tenure between April and November. His duties were to post men for the right jobs, to have them in readiness during the monsoon, and to promote native seminaries and language schools.[28]

The Mission Procurator had to attend to the dispatch of correspondence between India and Rome. The former privilege of the Portuguese Provincial to open the mission letters was to cease. By appointing a non-Portuguese Visitor and Procurator the link between the mission field with Rome rather than Portugal was closer.[29]

The General had allowed Jesuits to purchase property in Portugal in the name of any local college or house in order to pay the expenses for the Province of India in Portugal. Fr. Jeronimo Cardoso, the Procurator at Lisbon had complained that those in Goa did not honour his letters of credit. Hence he could not buy and send things for the colleges in the ships. He suggested that there be separate Procurators for India and Brazil. It was not right to ask the Crown to buy landed property for Japan, or to meet the expenses of those going to India from other Provinces.[30]

The Professed House

The General had accepted the gift of Canon Sebastião da Costa towards the foundation of the Professed House. The money would come in instalments as alms and not as annual revenue. The Professed House could not have a regular income according to the instructions of the Society of Jesus. Hence, it could not accept masses until everything had been done towards its foundation.[31]

No one could make silver vessels without specific alms being allotted for their manufacture. The Jesuits had used money from the Mirza Zu-l-Quarnain fund to construct the new silver casket for the body of Francis Xavier. In 1641, the Professed House had received several important bequests towards the completion of the casket. The donors included the Queen of Spain and Antonio Teles da Silva.[32]

Fr. General Gonzalez had accepted the donation of João Dias Ribeiro and his son Domingos for the Professed House. He concurred with his predecessor that it was not against the poverty of the Professed House to run a farm at Bambolim in order to pay for the religious feasts in the church of Bom Jesus, provided the surplus went for the church maintenance. The administration of the property had to remain under the *Provedor dos Defuntos* (Caretaker of the Deceased), who in his capacity as legal administrator appointed the Jesuit whom the Provincial would suggest.[33]

Cautions for Brothers

Brothers were helpers to the priests and had to rest content with three vows and subordinate positions. It was not necessary for them to waste time fruitlessly in studying humanities. The younger among them had to deal with persons outside their communities. Superiors could not make it easier for them to pick up knowledge. They could not give them permission to offer curios to students outside. When posted to the properties they could not live by themselves but had priests for companions. They could neither be full-fledged Procurators nor have money without the proper authority.[34]

Money and Gifts sent to Portugal

Jesuits sent money to Lisbon for things they had purchased there and which came yearly in ships from Portugal. Yet much depended on the way the General dealt with these matters in his replies to the Provincials. One could retain some money for one's need but not for business. Superiors could grant their subjects leave to give money to their parents in case of extreme need.

No one could send precious parcels, scents, containers of *aguila (aromatic boxes), curios, medicines, pedras, escritorios*, or tobacco of 20 *xs*. an *arratel*. One could, however, send things like reliquaries, Agnus Dei, rosaries, old books (*cartapacios*), *pedra bazar*, and medicines. Superiors could not give or accept money or objects as presents in gratitude to persons close to ministers of the King. The Provincial often had to negotiate with these on matters concerning the Society and this could be embarrassing to both sides.[35]

Japan-bound Jesuits could not carry money on behalf of others in China. The Superiors could not give anyone permission to do so for others who might have been good friends of the Society. The Procurator could exchange money for some expenses and had to send 600 *xs*. each year to Lisbon. The rule restrained anyone from carrying or sending money to Portugal for one 's parents or friends. It applied to Superiors and Rectors, too. They often were indebted to persons who wanted it carried there.[36]

Real Estate

The Superior of a house could transact the sale of houses of any value, but not before seeking the advice of his Consultors. He could lease out coconut-groves for a period of thirty years and three lives *vidas a ganhos* or in *emphiteusis*. Yet he had no permission to accept any colleges, houses or property under heavy obligations.[37]

Jesuits could accept land only if it was possible to sell it later. They could not avail of its profits if it had been given for churches and pious works. But if they had received it without any mention of the recipients in the houses, they had to send it to a college nearby. If the donor had gifted it as a perpetuity for members of the houses, they had to inform Rome on its possible conversion into a college. If they were unable to do so, the property had to go to the Bishop or the inheritors of the debt.[38]

Colleges could not seek alms, though they could receive them if they were freely given. They needed the prior permission of the Provincial stating the reasons and the amount since there was no general permission in this regard. They could sell the fruits of their property in return for purchases, but could not buy anything for sale elsewhere. They could purchase property in one place and sell in another. They had, however, to fulfill three conditions: not holding on to more than was necessary, doing nothing against the law, and retaining the remainder without its sale.

They could avail of the revenues of the churches provided they had sufficient funds. They could give the *mezinha de esmola* to the Professed House but without any obligation.[39] Those colleges that had a sufficient number of immoveable properties had to desist from buying more than they could handle, and the Provincial could not legislate to the contrary.[40]

Political Activity

The Fifth General Congregation had insisted that no Jesuit could engage in political dealings. Nor could he give counsel to wage war, or be an envoy of those who wished to wage it. Those guilty of doing so would lose all office and honour, and forfeit the right of active and passive voice in matters of voting in the Society. They cited the case of Fr. Francis Xavier who always refrained from offering advice on the discovery of islands, the entry into any kingdom, and the raising of rents for the Royal Treasury. If he did do so, it was solely with reference to the spread of the Christian faith. All he worked at was to liberate the Christians from the humiliations they sometimes suffered at the hands of the officials of the King.[41]

Other Issues

Objections from Rome covered many other issues too. It is interesting to notice how varied the legislation of Rome was. Jesuits could not use skirts (*saias*), nor sandals (*alparcas*) while on the farm, but could make use of *chinelas*. The members of any house could not go armed when on business. They were asked not to avail of the service of a barber to clean their ears or to cut their nails. They had to celebrate baptisms and the feast of St. Paul with moderation. They were refrained if they were not parish-priests, from maintaining private small safes (*caixinhas*) in their churches and oratories. The Superiors could detain any member of their religious communities in his own cubicle for a period of penance. But they had to be careful that the detained did not appear as convicts.[42]

The Jesuits had farms at Bandra, Mahim, Marol, Ghatkopar, Thane and Bassein. A priest or a brother was in-charge and bought or sold for the benefit of St. Paul's (Goa), and the houses of Agra, Malabar, China or Japan. They handled a lot of money and the General expected them to deposit the money each day with the Procurator of the house.[43]

Fr. General Vitelleschi ordered in 1618 that the Jesuits could not dismiss the *canarin* students and seminarians from their studies. He wanted them to admit all of them. He wanted the dismissed ones to return.

It was a practice in 1580 to exclude the local students from higher studies like philosophy.[44]

No one could sell the things belonging to the Japan or China Provinces without the permission of their Superior. In 1571, Dom Sebastian had given the Jesuits permission to buy in Bandra villages which gave an income to the Japan mission. They later asked for permission to import copper from China. Philip I wrote to Viceroy Duarte de Menezes to refuse it. Dom Henrique had first given the permission in 1579 to bring 100 quintals of copper from China. It was to help wipe off the debts of the College of St. Paul's.[45]

Jesuits could not involve themselves in buying pearls on behalf of seculars. A priest once came from the Fishery Coast with about 12,000 *pardaus* to buy pearls which he claimed he did with the knowledge of his Superiors. The risks and scandals involved in such trade on behalf of others called for his removal. Buying and selling went on in the Province in the name of necessity. It polluted the poverty and purity of the religious houses.[46]

Fr. Vitelleschi wanted a ban on all new buildings till the debts were paid. Between 1585 and 1635, the Province had built the Professed House, the College of Bom Jesus, the new College of St. Paul's, the College of Rachol, the church and residence of St. Anne in Bandra, and the churches in Salcete. Besides, the arrival of the Dutch and the English had caused a financial strain in Goa.[47]

Some wanted Fr. Joseph Gomes transferred from the Professed House, since he had an excessive greed for money. He had lent money on interest deposited with him by the Secretary of State. The House had become a rendezvous of the principal new-Christian merchants of the city with the priest playing a major part in the affair. He meddled in the lawsuits of the externs with the hope of making some gain for the Professed House. He had also lent some money on interest through one of his New-Christian friends.[48]

Visitor Fr. Barreto's Instructions

Fr. Francisco Barreto, Visitor, had instructions for the Goa Province in 1660.[49] He instructed all to dispense with the custom of covering their heads with mantles and surplices on the occasion of the Good Friday processions. He suggested that lights lit on the towers on the feast-days need not remain burning all night. He hoped to cut down oil costs and to prevent the boys in charge of them from committing thefts. He wanted uniformity with regard to the playing of music at table in all the colleges and houses. He fixed supper for six-thirty after which they could rest and recite the litanies. He prevented the priests from doffing their *birettas* (hats) to each other. It was usual for the Superiors to do so to the ones who served them.

The Procurators of other Provinces residing here in Goa did not have to pay for all their expenses at the start of the year, but could pay half the amount in advance. If they had differences among themselves they had to seek the help of an experienced priest to sort them out. The Superior had no authority to interfere or to deal with the materials of another Province. If a Jesuit of another Province had died in Goa, his Procurator had to collect his all, including his salary and other benefits if he was a priest. The priest-companion and *socius* (assistant to the Provincial) were given no special designations like secretary, nor could they hang any such names but their proper names, on their doors.

Procurators could have the use of a clerk to conduct their affairs, and of a boy to carry their umbrellas. The Fr. Visitor did not want Jesuits to go to Surat to conduct business, since it was a big market-centre, and the people tended to view their presence there as of traders doing business.

Superiors had to have the prior permission of the Fr. Provincial and Fr. Visitor to undertake constructions, but without incurring debts for the college. They could sell off properties in order to buy others, but were restricted from handing over cultivated land on lease since it would lead to the alienation of property of the Society.

About new entrants to the Order, Consultors did not have to give reasons for their decisions in writing, nor accept anyone without studying their purity of blood. No Procurator of any Province could hire a *patacho* (ship) for provisions. If they did hire a place on board one of them, they had to do so without any cause for scandal. Parish-priests had to separate the maintenance of large properties from their pastoral concerns the better to do their work, handing its charge to another.

It had been the practice for the Jesuits to go on Good Friday to various churches at night and to return later than nine. Henceforth, the Visitor wanted them to visit the main churches in the day, and the ones closer home at night. Only a big group could get permission to return later than nine. The Province had been accepting too many masses with the burden of saying them. It used the interest from such income to buy property, leading the people to gather that the Society had too much money. It harmed the interests of the residences and colleges. Jesuits could from then on accept the obligations of only a founder of a college or of very important benefactors. They could not borrow money on loan from out of the amount they had received for masses of the dead.

The houses spent a lot of money on silk material for churches. These had large paintings which damaged the walls. All this had to be undertaken only in better financial times. Procurators were prevented from lending money to anyone except to each other. Jesuit guests to Goa from other Provinces and from Rachol and Salcete had to stay at St. Paul's, while the students from the North just fresh from studies, had to move to the Professed House.[50]

Rules for Assolná

The Visitor laid down rules for the property and church of Assolná, too.[51] The parish-priest could not permit the celebration of weddings of non-Christians close to the church, or the playing of the *tabla* (musical instrument). He received a stipend of 60 *xs.* for his clothes and for the hearing of confessions. The *fabrica* was in charge of the various pits, and the poor received the income from two palm-groves. The Bro. Procurator on the property could not go to the Rachol College as often as the parish-priest went.

He was allowed, however, visits on feast and vows-days, and during Holy Week. He had to make two equal divisions of the income for the Novitiate of Chorão and the College of Cochin as Rome had decreed. He could not send the entire money to either of the houses for the division.[52]

The expenses of houses were divided according to the *pro rata* system (the income of various parties) following the orders of Fr. Antonio Alemão, the Provincial and Visitor. The same rules were current when the Provincial and the Rector of the Novitiate distributed alms to the poor of the village. The Provincial could give not more than 20 xs. drawn half on the account of the College of Cochin and the other on the Novitiate. But Fr. Barreto had wondered why the Provincial had accepted 50 *xs.* as allowance on his visit to the village church, since the College of Rachol had provided suitably for him. He suggested that if for some reason, the Provincial had spent the amount, the Novitiate over which he had temporal jurisdiction, had to account for it.

All had to pay equally towards the expenses of the guests. If there were some unexpected guests who had come either to recover their health or to prepare themselves for preaching or for a rest, the expenses would pass on to the Novitiate.

The Procurators used to give away many of the coconut groves and cultivated fields on a permanent lease (*cottubana*) resulting in a loss of income. The Visitor considered this illegal and prohibited such perpetual alienation of cultivated land. No one could renew such contracts on their expiry or on the occasion of the death of the owners. They would then revert to Jesuit property.

He mentioned that the priests celebrated far too many feasts in Salcete which kept them more than busy with preaching and travelling. He did not want them to introduce any more feasts. They had to cut down on the preaching and he wished that many more had trained themselves for the job rather than the same few.

They could combine the patronal and confraternity feasts, maintain the same number of confraternities in the churches, and entrust new devotions to the existing ones. There were to be no fireworks since they caused a nuisance with people not knowing how to handle them. The priests had to take care to avoid the indecencies which took place in Loutolim and Chinchinim during Lent and Holy Week. They tied 'Jesus' to a pillar and rotated him around, and did the same after they had crowned him. In lower Rachol, they used to pierce him without specific permission to do so, and handled him artificially on the Cross. But the Visitor wanted all to celebrate the feasts solemnly as was the case at the Professed House or at Margão.[53]

Instructions of Visitor Fr. Miguel de Amaral

He expected the Procurators of all Provinces at the Professed House at Goa to help during the feast days of Christmas, Easter, Holy Spirit, and the Renewal of vows. They had to hear confessions, and help at the altar, but could exempt themselves if their work took them elsewhere. The Visitor also reminded them to be careful about the guests they brought to the Professed House.[54]

A Reflection

One notices the wide legislation that came from Rome to oversee the lives of the Jesuits of the Goa Province. It touched usually matters of poverty and property. At times it referred to incidentals while the religious were involved in deeper matters. But then, even the Frs. Superior-General and other officials could do very little to put a halt to many of the practices. Besides, too much supervision from Rome and from Superiors prevented the Goa Province from evolving along more local lines. Rivalry, misunderstanding and some injustice among the members themselves, and their disdain for local opposition were to get the Order deeply immersed in antagonism from the local population, at least in some of the villages of Salcete.

REFERENCES

1. Tawney, R. H., *Religion and the Rise of Capitalism*, pp. 66-67.
2. *Ibid.*, p. 58.
3. Boxer, Charles, *The Christian Century in Japan 1549-1650*, pp. 119-120, 425-427.
4. ARSI: Goa, no. 35, fl. 102v. Quoted in Rea, William F., *The Economics of the Zambezi Missions: 1580-1759*. Refers to the order of the Goa Provincial writing in 1674.
5. *DI*, XV (1588-92), pp. 324-325, 821.
6. Humbert, John, "Some Answers of the Generals of the Society of Jesus to the Province of Goa. Acquaviva - Vitelleschi 1581-1645," *AHSI*, XXXV, 1966, pp. 328-329.
7. Humbert, "Some Answers of the Generals of the Society of Jesus to the Province of Goa from Carrafa to Tamburini 1647-1726," *AHSI*, XXXVI, 1967, p. 91.
8. *Ibid.*, p. 99.
9. ARSI: *FG*, 74-B/9/1443, no. 27, fl. 5v; *DI*, XV (1588-92), p. 56.
10. Wicki, Josef, "Dois Compendios das Ordens dos Padres Gerais e Congregações Provinciais da Provincia dos Jesuitas de Goa, feitos em 1664," *Studia*, nos. 43-44, 1980, pp. 448-449. The stipulations were by Fr. General Acquaviva in 1601, 1603, 1604.
11. Humbert, *art. cit.*, XXXVI, p. 96.
12. Humbert, XXXV, pp. 336-337.
13. Humbert, XXXVI, p. 84.
14. Rea, *op. cit.*, p. 60.
15. Humbert, *art. cit.*, XXXVI, p. 73.
16. *Ibid.*, pp. 78-79; De Melo, Carlos M., *The Recruitment and Formation of the Native Clergy in India (sixteenth-nineteenth centuries)*, p. 171.
17. Humbert, *art. cit.*, XXXVI, p. 81; *ACE*, IV (1659-95), pp. 2-3.
18. DAAM: *MR*, codex 31, fls. 32, 34, 48, 111.
19. *Ibid.*, fls. 46-48.
20. Humbert, *art. cit.*, XXXVI, p. 83; DAAM: *MR* codex 79, fl. 330r.
21. Humbert, *art. cit.*, XXXV, p. 344; ARSI: Goa no. 5, 37; n. 10, fl. 180.
22. Humbert, *art. cit.*, XXXVI, pp. 83-84.
23. *Ibid.*, pp. 84-85.
24. *Ibid.*, p. 85.
25. Wicki, *art. cit.*, n. 43-44, pp. 362-366.
26. *Ibid.*, pp. 362, 409.
27. *DI*, VIII (1569-73), pp. 409-410; XIV (1585-88), pp. 625-627; XV (1588-92), p. 54.
28. Schütte, Josef, *Valignano's Mission Principles for Japan*, I, Part I, pp. 178-179.
29. *Ibid.*, pp. 85-86.
30. Wicki, *art. cit.*, nos. 43-44, p. 482; *DI*, XIV (1585-88), pp. 604-608.
31. Humbert, *art. cit.*, XXXVI, p. 92.
32. *Ibid.*, pp. 85-86.
33. *Ibid.*, pp. 94-95.

34. Wicki, *art. cit.*, p. 434. These were Fr. General Acquaviva's stipulations in 1598 and 1601, and Fr. General Vitelleschi's in 1621 and 1623.
35. *Ibid.*, pp. 473.
36. *Ibid.*, pp. 343-532 *passim*.
37. *Ibid.*, p. 483.
38. *Ibid.*, pp. 366-367. Fr. General Everardo Mercurian gave the ruling in 1575.
39. *Ibid.*, pp. 382-383.
40. *Ibid.*, p. 384.
41. Wicki, J. (ed.), *Primeira Parte da Historia dos Religiosos da Companhia de Jesus da Provincia de Goa composta pello Pe. Sebastiam Gonçalves*, p. 270.
42. Wicki, *art. cit.*, no. 43-44, p. 369.
43. Humbert, *art. cit.*, XXXV, p. 337.
44. Wicki, *art. cit.*, nos. 43-44, p. 368; *DI*, XII (1580-83), pp. 450-451.
45. *DI*, XII (1580-83), p. 419; *DI*, VIII (1569-73), pp. 406-407.
46. *DI*, XVI (1592-94), pp. 21-22, 32-33.
47. Humbert, *art. cit.*, XXXV, p. 343.
48. *DI*, XVI (1592-94), pp. 359-360.
49. ARSI: *FG*, no. 1443/9, file 27. Subsequent files have orders for the other individual houses of the Province.
50. *Ibid.* The twenty-six stipulations covered matters of finance, community life and church affairs.
51. *Ibid.*, *FG*, file 30, 1661; *DI*, XII (1580-83), pp. 639-640; XV (1588-92), p. 41; Meilink-Roelofsz, *Asian Trade and European Influence*, p. 361.
52. D. Pedro de Castro had on 4 July 1581 given the property in favour of the College of Cochin. The Goa Provincial accepted it on behalf of the College. Despite all clarifications, the House of Probation had been enjoying this property ever since the donation was received.
53. *Ibid.* It was given at Assolná and signed on 10 February 1661.
54. AHNM: *Legajo* 271, no. 98. Goa, 30 November 1708. No. 98 refers to his instructions of not buying or accepting a captive slave in any of our houses. He had sought the opinion of four Jesuit theologians before giving this decision. The priests were Frs. Ignacio de Andrade, Francisco de Souza, Joseph da Veyga, and Pantomo de Guizenrode.

4

AVC (ASSOLNĀ, VELIM, CUNCOLIM): Native Resistance

The Society of Jesus gained much property in Salcete, particularly, in the villages of Assolná, Velim and Cuncolim. It came to it partly through donations and partly through various methods of acquisition. The lands were then sub-let, and the village communities felt strangulated and could do little in the face of Jesuit control.

The State, too, appeared helpless while it heard various representations against the foreign clerics. The rift widened between the religious and the people, and no meeting-point was possible given the divergence of the respective positions.

The Woes at the Customs-House

There were complaints at the customs-house at São Lourenço that the Jesuits were encouraging the local population to evade the payment of taxes on food provisions. They would transport coconuts and spices illegally and would cite government legislation in their favour when questioned. They would be rude to the staff on duty while using the customs-house to dispatch their many dutiable goods.

They would send various gifts to the department officials whom they wanted to please. They and the parish-priests of the twenty-five parishes in Salcete paid nothing to the State resulting in a financial loss to the Crown. Their servants were a haughty lot and would turn insolent when any questions about payments came up. They imitated their masters who would come decked out with their *birettas* (hats) and swinging their umbrellas swearing their way through (*soltando palavras*) with concern for none.

Their slaves, servants and *bois* (palanquin-bearers) would move about at the customs-house without obtaining the customs' seal, or without presenting their goods for inspection. The priests would cross the river at all hours of the day and night in boats (*manchuas* and *bargantis*), but lacked the courtesy to enter the customs-house and greet the officials.[1]

The High Court Members

The members of the Goa High Court, too, resented the behaviour of the Jesuits. In a signed memorandum to the King, they described the superior airs they put on, how meanly and despicably they treated the natives, and how they tried to control the ministers of justice, especially those who did not do their bidding. They would find ways to harass them and would resort to arms as in the case of Jorge do Amaral de Vasconcellos, *Ouvidor-Geral de Crime*. They used harsh words (*palavras descompostas*) against him after he had tried to pass a sentence against them in a particular case. They had sent armed slaves into his residence forcing him to defend himself. They managed, too, to capture some of his servants whom they marched off to their College of St. Roque.[2]

Complaints of the People

The people of Salcete had informed the King of the oppression they suffered at the hands of their enemies. These were the Viceroy, the ministers of the Revenue Department, and the Jesuits. They considered the last the very worst of the lot and even the Viceroy had found it difficult to contain them.[3] A letter of 23 March 1604 described their religious intolerance and their corrupt practices. The Hindus of the city were prevented from crossing the mainland to perform their religious services, but some of the religious granted them the permission in return for money. This knowledge had scandalized many.[4]

Complaints of the Viceroy

The Viceroy, Miguel de Noronha, the Count of Linhares (1629-35) had his own anti-Jesuit sentiments. While replying to the accusations of the Jesuit Provincial, Fr. Antonio de Andrade (1630-33), he mentioned that he had regard for the priest and had been courteous to him despite the pain that his men had caused him as Viceroy. He did not correct or punish them, and they repaid his kindness with evil. He was aware that the Provincial had sent many accusations against him on the *St. Gonçalo which had shipwrecked at the Cape. The Jesuits had made of the previous Gover-*

Aires de Saldanha and Dom Jeronimo de Azevedo, their stooges, and deprived the State of its revenue. He was prepared to submit many more details if the need arose, and was ready to accept death should he be found guilty on any count. He was convinced that these religious would never be satisfied till they had taken over entirely the revenue of the State and his own responsibilities too.[5] He added that he was hard-working and that it would be difficult to find another more honest than him in India.[6]

An Inquiry into Jesuit Properties

Viceroy, Dom Felipe Mascarenhas (1645-51) had ordered an investigation into all the land assets of the Jesuits and had found them guilty of misappropriation. The King in his reply had thanked the Viceroy for this information. Yet, curiously, he believed that the law against the religious acquiring more properties, need not apply to the Jesuits. They had done and continued doing excellent work for the conversion of the people.[7]

Such was the influence of the Jesuits that even the highest official in the State believed that with them for friends he lacked no favourable agent at the law courts. He feared the world were they to be his enemies. The Franciscans and the municipal councillors at Goa thought likewise, and a proverb summed it all: One need fear more the nib of a Jesuit's pen than the point of an Arab's sword.[8]

The King had, in his letter of 3 April 1632, informed the Governor that he had received complaints from the people of Salcete against Justice Isidoro de Lemos. He sought an inquiry. The Viceroy in his reply dated 28 January 1633, explained that the accusations related more to the Jesuits, the sole masters of the lands (*senhores daquelas terras*). His ministers who went there on their duties, usually found it very tough going indeed.[9]

For the Jesuits traded with the neighbouring kingdoms from Salcete, using their boats on the river Sal for their commercial activities. They did business along the Kanara coast, too, with the Adil Shah, and sold the goods in the many shops they had in Goa.[10]

Many feared their overbearing ways and their power. The Viceroy had indiscreetly given them the legality to term anyone dangerous (*prejudiciais*) or urchins (*vadios*), and to sentence them to the galleys. They thus managed to get rid of many of their opponents.[11]

Their Anti-Religious Activities

Viceroy Antonio de Melo e Castro (1662-66) had in his letter of 28 January

1666 to the King attacked the anti-religious activities of the Society. He believed that the economy of the State was in shambles and a misery since no one could buy goods first-hand. Every middleman worked out his profit before goods reached the common people. The Hindu merchants bought cloth from Balghat, while others purchased it wholesale on the mainland to sell it off in Goa by retail. The prices turned exorbitant by the time the Portuguese sought to purchase the materials.

He had tried to control the price of food-items. Yet the officials of the Crown and the Jesuits had opposed him in their attempts to preserve their own private interests over the needs of the common folk. The officials had indulged in smuggling and would add 1 *baz.* to every measure of rice, gaining a clear profit of 15,000 *xs*. The *bangaçaleiros* (licensed wholesale-stockists) had maintained their own secret arrangements with the officials whom they paid amounts between 500 and 2,000 *xs*. to raise the prices.

The officials and the noblemen used to meet the convoy (*cáfila*) en route and would offload the grain with the help of their men. They would then stack it away secretly and would sell it off privately at previously arranged prices. For in Assolná, the Jesuits had granaries bigger than those of Goa in which to store much of what the *cá fila* brought in. They would use them to put away the produce of Assolná, Cuncolim and other Salcete lands. It was from there that they disposed of the grain to places which offered them a higher price, which were usually the Muslim lands.

They functioned similarly in Bandra. The Viceroy had advised them to call off their scandalous transactions, but they used their pulpits to react and to term his objections as an outright interference in their affairs. They had also worked the people against the Viceroy when he had sought to make more grain available for all.[12]

The Viceroy had to face charges against himself from the Inquisition. The officials questioned a witness on whether he had heard the Viceroy say that the Fathers of Portugal and Spain were Fathers of the Society while the Fathers of the Company in India were those of the Company of Holland. The witness denied having heard the statement.[13]

The Inquisition took no action against the Viceroy. There were some who held the view that the Jesuits in the East were more a commercial than a spiritual group. For reports showed that during the truce negotiations at Goa in 1664, the Dutch East India Company's envoy, Johan Maetsuyker, and the Jesuits were involved in commercial transactions between Goa, Macao and Batavia.[14]

The Viceroy had in his letter of 28 January 1666 detailed the various abuses of the Jesuits in the North and in Salcete. They would use an *armada* belonging to them as an escort for the *cáfilas* to Cambay and Bandra. Though they owned the latter village they paid no dues to the Crown. He was thus forced to send a fleet to Bandra to stop their activities.

They would corner most of the foodstuff coming from Kanara for their Jesuit stores at Assolná. He had, however, managed to stop the practice by setting the *sanguiceis* at the mouth of the river as the convoys arrived.

Referring to Kumbarjua, de Melo e Castro mentioned that the Jesuits harmed the Custom revenues. The island was too close to the river-passages of St. Braz and St. Tiago and most of the gold, coral and other goods passed to the mainland through that route. Cloth items came along the same passage to escape duty-payments. So many were the abuses at the time of Fr. Gonçalo Martins that the villagers had called for his removal and had placed an infantry-company there instead.

The Viceroy pointed out that the Jesuits managed to take over large properties as *testamenteiros* of the dead, and acted as judges both civil and criminal in the village courts. He added that there were few properties in Salcete which the Jesuits had not given out on rent at ten per cent interest.[15]

The King in his letter of 4 April 1662 had ordered the same Viceroy to submit accounts of the properties of all the Religious in India. He did as he was told, but this led to bitter personal attacks on him by those examined. Even the Royal Justice found it impossible to handle them.

The Criminal Justice had once ordered the auction of the Assolná fields, but the Jesuits had stalled the move. The officials could not bear their insolent behaviour and had informed the Governor accordingly. They had submitted the report to the Secretariat, but it had mysteriously disappeared although the ministers were in service at the time. The document had described the exodus of the villagers of Assolná to Cuncolim to escape the harsh treatment of the Jesuits.[16]

The Ganvkars of Velim, Ambelim and Assolná

The *ganvkars* of Velim, Ambelim and Assolná had submitted to the Crown through the offices of the Overseas Council, a document dated 5 February 1745.[17] The Jesuits had received an endowment in the three villages which they had evaluated at 2,250 *xs.* King Sebastian had authorized them to buy immoveable property up to a maximum value of 6,000 *xs*. Their evaluation was incorrect since it cost over 40,000 *xs*. The rents the villagers paid amounted alone to 1,500 *xs.* which was usually five per cent of the total produce.

The priests had dispossessed them of their property and had further deprived them of their right to complain or file a suit. In frustration, they had approached the Crown with the copies of their earlier protests to the Municipality. In response, the Crown had decreed that but for those with rights in accordance with the *Foral*, none could have ownership rights of property in Salcete. It applied to the *ganvkars* too. The regulation stated that no one could admit himself to the village contrary to any of the clauses of the *Foral*.

The *ganvkars* returned to their former positions, the newcomers found themselves out, and the current provisions stood invalid. Yet, it all remained on paper alone. The *ganvkars* continued to be poor, while the Jesuits grew the more powerful (*mais apotentados*). The latter dealt with the people most harshly, and many believed they earned more than the State in India, for the islands brought them much wealth and revenues. A High Court ruling expressed the fear that the others would have no more property at the rate the priests were acquiring it.

The *ganvkars* feared the priests would further harass them because of their protests which the Crown had failed to listen to. Viceroy Pedro Mascarenhas, the Count of Sandomil, had on 5 April 1739 written to the Crown after listening to the opinions of the priests, of the Crown attorney and of the procurator.

Their problems did not stem from their relationships with the Jesuits alone. There was the Maratha attack on Salcete on 31 January 1739, and the attitude of the State itself. The former had occupied their lands and had taken many captive. They released them two years later as a result of the peace treaty signed between them and the Viceroy. The villagers were once again in the possession of the *ganvkari* and other village-properties in accordance with the statutes of the *Foral*.

The State had been dealing differentially with them and they recalled the case of João Jacob de Mendonça, *ganvkar* of Çamorlim in Bardez. In his position of assistant captain he had betrayed the entire province to the Bhonsle. He received a sentence and lost his properties. But the entire village he resided in, did not suffer as a result. Governor Dom Luis Caetano de Almeida had later freed de Mendonça, and his son did not forfeit his own rights or privileges. They questioned the treatment they had received in their case. They wanted a similar judgement with no harm to their descendants. The Viceroy had fined them the entire revenue of their villages, which totalled over 20,000 *xs*. at the time. The figure was higher before 1739, but their payments regular.

They next pleaded with the Crown to confirm their possession. The

Crown order of March 1743 asked the High Court to decide the case with help from the royal attorney, and later to inform the Crown. The Fr. Procurator of the Malabar Province had appealed against the move, but a Crown order of 19 April 1743 upheld the decision of the High Court as final. The *ganvkars* believed the priest while submitting his case in the High Court, had misinterpreted the Crown order, and had denied them the restitution they deserved.

They filed a counter-case before the *Juiz dos Feitos*, Ignacio de Figueiredo, who as friend of the Jesuits, stalled all the proceedings on the issue. He went that monsoon to Portugal to argue in favour of his patrons. The *ganvkars* were helpless, for the priests had used their influence to submit many documents, some of them erroneous. They had deprived the former of even a right to study them before they came up for hearing before the Court.

They wondered how the priests could become *ganvkars* and stake their claims to the privileges that came along with the honour. The rule was clear and no one could dispense another in this regard. The Fr. Procurator and his assistant, Fr. Thomaz de Fonseca, the parish priest of the same villages, had gathered the signatures of other priests and seculars. They sought to give the false impression that the *ganvkars* were a minority in their opinions and were moreover only moradores (temporary residents).

The Jesuits in the villages included an assistant parish priest, his Brother-assistant, a Brother store-keeper of the parish, and chaplains of the churches. But it was impossible for them to become *ganvkars*, reasoned the others. Neither could their servants and their helpers, or their Shudra salt-makers and fishermen. They were merely temporary residents, while the villagers over seven hundred in number, were the true *Chardos* and *ganvkars*.

The villages were theirs by right. They sought Crown help against the violence and tyranny of the Jesuits, and feared for the safety of their own attorney, Antonio Rebello de Almeida, whom the priests had intended to imprison and to destroy.

Ganvkars of Ambelim and Assolná

The *ganvkars* of Ambelim and Assolná had sent a petition to the Crown, which on the advice of the Overseas Council decided against handing over the villages to the Malabar Province Jesuits until the High Court decided the case. The Province had the property for over a hundred years. The

Marathas had occupied it temporarily, and the royal decree of 20 March 1744 decided that the Province ought to get it back intact.[18]

Another Crown injunction had prevented religious from acquiring more landed property, and had instructed them to file a fresh petition if they intended to do so.[19] The *ganvkars* of Ambelim, Velim and Assolná resented the Jesuits of the Malabar Province acquiring land though prohibited from doing so by the provisions of the *Foral*. Courts had pleaded helpless to come to their aid and only a direct royal action could be of use. Witnesses feared to depose in the courts. The priests had managed to collect certificates to suit their claims and with their money had the best advocates available. No sooner did they file their cases, than the courts passed judgements leaving the people no time to respond. But when the reverse was the case, the priests would enjoy a period of two months within which they could answer. They were always able to block any move of the others and to threaten their attorneys.

Fr. João Alexandre, the Procurator of the Malabar Province in Salcete, was the virtual overlord of the area. With the help of the tobacco contractors, he would search people and force them to leave their villages. The revenue income suffered as a result. The people were unable to pay the high prices of the tobacco farmers and found cheaper tobacco in Sunda.

Each year over 8,000 *corjas* of rice would arrive here from South India. Tobacco was a State item, which the Hindu farmers managed. They would confiscate some of the vessels from the South, claiming that they carried tobacco in them. This halted commerce and the people of Salcete were the sufferers.

The Jesuits themselves had twelve watchmen of their own to guard the river passage against tobacco coming into Salcete from Sunda, thus harming the royal revenue. They enforced their watch ruthlessly, and two-thirds of the villagers had fled Cuncolim to escape their tyranny and that of the revenue farmers.

The Malabar Jesuits had further imposed tithes in villages under their charge which covered items like rice, coconuts, salt and fruits. They totalled 2,106 *xs*. and 36 *rs*. The *ganvkars* feared an auction would create problems. The Marathas had auctioned everything for 20,271 *xs*., and the high bidding later led to an exodus of the villagers. They wanted the State not to leave the collection to the revenue farmers, but to trustworthy administrators instead.

Fr. Thomas da Fonseca, the parish priest of Assolná, had got his servants to sign his petition against the *ganvkars*. It was, however, illegal to do so since the servants were merely temporary residents. The Crown

Procurator, Verasimmo Antonio da Silva, had intended to invite all the signatories before him for verification. But his sudden death had only made the priests the beneficiaries. They managed, too, a quick clearance of their request to the Judge of Dispatch to buy land worth 5,000 *xs*. The action had been unlawful since the High Court alone could give a permission in such a case. But having mentioned all the details against the priests, the *ganvkars* feared for their lives.

The Jesuits took charge of their Assolná property for the second time in 1744. But they did not bother themselves about the tobacco and arrack taxes. The Fr. Procurator sought an exemption from the Revenue Council for these items. As a result, the Public Exchequer stood to lose 6,000 *xs*. annually. The Crown Judge had received the matter for reference. Finally, the Jesuits won their case. They had based their request on false information stating that their property lay on the border, and that the villages were deserted.

The auctioned tithes exceeded 3,000 *xs*. annually, but the Fr. Procurator paid a mere half claiming that the Count of Cuncolim paid as much due to special royal privileges afforded to him. The tobacco farmers did not inspect his area, there was no auction of the tithes, and his procurator would pay what he felt best. The Revenue Council had been most liberal towards him in fixing the last bid at 1,500 *xs*. though it was worth 3,000 *xs*..

The Farmers of Ambelim, Velim and Assolná

As the villages of Ambelim, Velim and Assolná belonged to the Jesuits, the farmers complained that they received insufficient income. Fr. Antonio Menezes, the Rector of the Novitiate was asked whether he would be ready to pay 250 *xs*. of the rent for the fields belonging to the temples of the three villages every year in quarterly installments in the following manner: he would have to pay 202 *xs*. and 40 *rs*. to the parish priest of Our Lady of Martyrs, Assolná, for the salary of the Vicar, beadle, and *fabrica*, and another 47 *xs*., 4 *tgs*. and 20 *rs*. for the collection of the temples. If he agreed he could continue to enjoy the rights of the land.[20]

Property Issues between Provinces of Goa and Malabar

The problem of property in Assolná was a thorny issue not only between the people and the Jesuits, but also between the Jesuits themselves. There were disagreements between the two Provinces of Goa and Malabar. The

Vicar-General, Fr. Goswin Nickel had informed the respective Frs. Provincial and their Frs. Procurator to accept under obedience the judgement of Fr. Francisco Piccolomini, the Superior-General (1649-51) as absolute, and to refrain from any further recourse to the secular courts.[21]

Though Dom Pedro de Castro had donated the properties of Assolná in 1587 juridically to the College of Cochin, he intended them for the Novitiate of Chorão at Goa. This led to much heat and enmity between the two Provinces and the civil government.[22]

Fr. Piccolomini had decided that when the government officials would need to inspect the title-deeds of the Assolná property, it was the Procurator of the College of Cochin who would have to furnish them as he had been doing till then.

The King had opposed the above donation and had referred to the secular court the dispute involving the Novitiate and the State over the three villages. The Goa Provincial had to depute Fr. Castro from Goa to Portugal in 1589 to defend the case.[23]

The first income from the properties was 1,200 *scudi*, while the expenses of the house were 7,500.[24] The Jesuits had the lands of Pedro de Castro and appeared to have more than the State on the islands.[25]

The Provinces and Assolná

The Novitiate of Chorão and the College of Cochin disputed long over the ownership of the Assolná property. The Novitiate won the rights eventually.[26] The income of the property was 81,760 *xs.*, 2 *tgs.* and 18 *rs.*, while the expenditure was 63,225 *xs.*, 2 *tgs.* and 23 *rs.*[27] Property, worth 2,000 *cruzados* had been given by Gaspar Viegas.[28]

Fr. A. Laerzio writing to Fr. General Acquaviva in November 1588, had mentioned that the first income of these properties was 1,200 *scudi*, of which 750 were for the expenses of the house and the rest for the conversion work. And the Crown made it clear that the Jesuits could not convert the revenues they obtained into land.[29]

Dom Sebastian had given permission to the College of Cochin to acquire landed property worth 6,000 *xs.* The Viceroy had confirmed the donation of Pedro de Castro, and the Comptroller of the Treasury had valued it at 2,250 *xs.* Castro had given the villages to the Society for the foundation of the Novitiate, but made the donation in the name of the College of Cochin since the Novitiate had no permission to possess them.[30]

Island of Rachol

It was a bone of contention between the Jesuits and the owner on one hand,

and the *ganvkars* and the government on the other.[31] Francisco Dias, a Portuguese, was the owner of the island, *Xashticho Juo*, and had received it on a perpetual lease of six and a half *pardaus* of gold as rent in 1559. He had cleared the dense forest and had engaged in some cultivation. That is till he was forced to flee to the neighbouring Muslim country to evade punishment for his crime of sodomy.

The *ganvkars* claimed that the island could not be the property of the State. It bordered on their property and the *Foral* gave them the right to it. Pedro Alvares Pereira, the judge of the Appellant Court, argued that the island was in a navigable river, and rightly belonged to the Crown.

The *ganvkars* had on 11 November 1587, given the island on lease at a public auction to the Jesuit Rector of Salcete, Fr. Miguel de Leitão. But the Crown disclaimed the contention. Governor Francis Barreto had initially given it to Francisco Dias, and it did not and could not belong to the *ganvkars*. The latter questioned the view in court which upheld their demands. The Rector of the College of Rachol, Fr. Estevão Velho, next produced a document from the archives of the Church of Our Lady of Snows to prove that the auction had in fact taken place on the occasion of the festival of *panchratri* (five nights). Fr. Leitão had to pay 300 *tgs. brancas* as rent for the first years, and from 1594, 75 *tgs. brancas*.

The *ganvkars* showed how involved they were in the maintenance of the island all through the years. They had paid for the bunds, for the poles and timber needed on the island. Francisco Dias, ought to have refunded them for the expenses involved, but had since died.

Farming Success

The success of the Jesuits in farming excited the jealousy of the lay Portuguese settlers. The former had more than doubled the output of their lands through their more rational approach to cultivation. The valuation of the three villages of Assolná, Velim and Ambelim was in 1578, a sum of 2,010 *xs*. By 1635 it was 5,500.[32] There were 92 land-contracts between 1705 and 1769 in these three villages between the Jesuits and the local people. The yearly interest they received was 1,27,980 *xs*., 2 *tgs*., and 23 *rs*.[33]

The consolidated plots and large palm-groves of the religious also gave rise to a type of bonded labour known as *mundkars* who had to bind themselves to the land as a result of the small loans which they could not repay. The religious were kind to them, yet their condition worsened when the religious were no more, and they found themselves under new secular landlords.

Five houses in Goa alone had given out loans worth over 3,50,000 *xs.*, mainly to the general assemblies of the village communities and some individual village communities. Though the Jesuits were maligned for being anti-Hindus, yet they had given 23,800 *xs.* in loans to several Hindus residing in Kumbarjua.[34]

Though their land-grab and monetary munificence did at times go hand-in-hand, they appear to have fostered some divisions among the lay natives. Besides, their racial superiority made them unbending before the native clerical expectations. Their growing riches brought them opposition from many different quarters.

REFERENCES

1. AHU: India, *maço* 21, doc. 118, 20 December 1651.
2. *Ibid.*, doc. 191, 22 December 1651.
3. *Ibid.*, *maço* 15, doc. 110, 29 December 1643.
4. DAAM: *MR*, 9, 10 and 11, codex 12, fl. 4, 4v.
5. ANTT: *DR*, n. 29, fls. 153-4, 17 December 1631. Fl. 35 mentions that the Viceroy worked many hours a day and slept a bare three hours at night.
6. *Ibid.*, fl. 35.
7. Abranches Garcia, *Archivo da Relação de Goa*, II, doc. 652, 14 April 1649.
8. Boxer, Charles, *The Portuguese Seaborne Empire: 1415-1825*, pp. 344-345.
9. DAAM: *Ordens Regias*, no. 2, codex 1492, fls. 49v-50.
10. *Ibid.*, no. 2, codex 1498, fls. 48v-49, Goa, 28 January 1633.
11. *Ibid.*, *Cartas e Ordens*, no. 1, codex 779, fls. 90v-93, c. 1618.
12. AHU: India, *maço* 27, doc. 28, 28 January 1666.
13. ANTT: *maço* 2, doc. 22.
14. Boxer, Charles, *Portuguese India in the Mid-Seventeenth Century*, p. 49.
15. AHU: India, *maço* 28, doc. 36, 1 March 1669.
16. *Ibid.*, *maço* 75, no. 60.
17. Wicki, Josef, "Dois Compendios das Ordens dos Padres Gerais e Congregações Provinciais da Provincia dos Jesuitas de Goa, feitos em 1664," *Studia*, nos. 43-44, 1980, p. 461.
18. AHU, *maço* 64, 7 February 1746.
19. *Ibid.*, *maço* 68, 29 January 1747.
20. DAAM: *ACF*, III, fl. 115. Fl. 109v deals with the plots of the Jesuits in Salcete belonging to the temples.
21. *Ibid.*, p. 364; ARSI: Goa 22, fl. 400-404.
22. *DI*, XV (1588-92), p. 115.
23. AHU: India, *maço* 75, 1745.
24. *DI*, XIV (1585-88), pp. 208, 641-642; XV (1588-92), pp. 389, 524, 735, 777; XVI (1592-94), pp. 368-369.
25. AHU: India, *maço* 68, 2 March 1744.
26. ARSI: Goa 22, I, fls. 203-275.
27. DAAM: no. 1203 (*Receita e despeza dos Jesuitas 1693-1756*– Receipts and Expenditure of the Jesuits, 1693-1756).

28. *DI*. XV (1588-92), pp. 652, 735. Pedro de Castro had given a donation to the Novitiate on 26 February 1592; *DI*. XIV (1585-88), pp. 630, 641.
29. *Ibid*., XV (1588-92), pp. 115, 439.
30. *Ibid*., XIV (1585-88), pp. 628-632, 641-642.
31. ANTT: *Cartorio dos Jesuitas, maço* 87, no. 18.
32. De Souza, Teotonio, "The Voiceless in Goan Historiography: A Case for the Source-Value of Church Records in Goa," *Indo-Portuguese History: Sources and Problems*, p. 123.
33. DAAM: Ms. 7600 *Tombo de Cutumbona de Assolná, Ambelim e Velim 1705-1769*, fls. 1-276 *passim*.
    Arte Palmarica was a tract written by a Jesuit and describes the methods of planting coconut trees and the care to be taken for their maintenance. It mirrored the success the Jesuits reaped from their palm-groves.
34. Souza, *art. cit*., p. 123.

5

JESUITS VERSUS THE REST

Many were the forces the Jesuits met in their various fields of activity. They worked alongside them and were often a step ahead or succeeded in flourishing better. The Viceroys, Governors, and other high-ranking officials in the administration did their best to check what they regarded as the high-handedness of the Jesuits and their interference in the administrative and financial matters of the State, or perhaps to be more precise, in their personal interests.

The clergy, the travellers and the people, too, had their own tale to tell after their dealings with the Jesuits. Their accounts, at times, make chilling reading, and raise doubts about whether it was all true. But then, the members of the Society of Jesus in Goa were virtual overlords of the place during the times they lived in and forced their ways and attitudes on many.

A View from the Travellers

Diamond Trade

The French traveller, Jean-Baptiste Tavernier, disclosed that the Jesuits of Goa did a brisk trade in rough diamonds. They would disguise themselves as fakirs or pilgrims to escape notice in their trade. They then carried these to Europe. He had once met one of them attired thus, travelling to San Tomé on business for the Viceroy of Goa.[1]

The chief of the factory at Vengurla had on a certain occasion received information about two Jesuits who were on their way to the mines to buy 4,00,000 *pardaus* worth of diamonds. He left instructions that they should inform the master of the customs at Bicholim about the purchase. The Jesuits believed that no one knew of their deal besides themselves, and sought to cross the river after their undertaking. But no sooner had they done so, than they were searched by the officials and relieved of their treasure.[2]

Jesuit Cruelty

The Jesuits, according to Niccolao Manucci, spared no effort to increase their income, as masters of the Goa islands, in their service for the greater glory of God. They would not hesitate to protect the abandoned women of the city. But sorry was the fate of those who dared to interfere with them for any reason. Their criminal justice, he felt was something both frightful and cruel. They would strip the ones they believed were criminals, bind them to a tree and flog them so thoroughly that they would later need treatment at the hospital.[3]

The Royal Hospital

The Royal Hospital which the Jesuits managed, received an annual sum of 14,000 *xs*. The expenses were limited as patients stayed only for a short time, yet the Jesuits maintained that there was hardly anything left over to pay even for the oil-lamps in their college. Manucci claimed that he mentioned all those facts not in a spirit of vendetta, having been a recipient of many a civility and favour from them for which he owed them gratitude. Yet he felt himself under an obligation to speak the truth rather than hide it in the name of obligation and friendship. The Jesuits neglected to care for the sick at their hospital. Those who entered with simple fevers soon found them turning serious. The Konkanis or *Topazes* (native or half-caste Christians) served in the hospital and would force patients to pay for even a drink of water. The sick would take themselves to the underground cells, and the dampness would kill them a few days later. The Fr. Administrator would then auction their belongings for a price much less than at a public sale. Or he would send them to the North to seek a better price.

Their Wealth and Power

Their wealth, he believed, was immense, surpassing that of the Crown in all of the Portuguese possessions in India. They had in Goa 3,60,000 *pardaus* a year compared to the 3,00,000 of the King. They were rich, traded much and wide in every kind of merchandise, and held various government and administrative posts.

The Governors and the lieutenants of the fortress at Bandra, would fear to fire off a single cannon without the permission of their Jesuit administrators. In 1666, Manucci had witnessed Fr. Fortunato Seraphino, the Jesuit Administrator, speaking harshly to the Governor of Bassein, Christovão de Souza Coutinho, for having fired off the cannon without his permission.

Another View

The description of Manucci of the Jesuit hospital is in total contrast to that of Pyrard de Laval, who did not believe that there was a better-run hospital in the world (*Hé pois este hospital o melhor que na minha opiniço há no mundo*). He described the way the Jesuits conducted their daily affairs, their hospitality, their attention, the meals they served and the religious duties they performed. They kept patients usually on the first floor, reserving the ground for the new arrivals if any, from Portugal. They put the Portuguese in charge and had *canarins de Goa* or *bramanes cristãos* working as servants.

The Hospital stood by the river-bank. It received a royal subsidy of 25,000 *pardaus*. The Jesuit novices from St. Paul's would go round the city begging for old clothes for the sick. Bread was delicious, small in size and they would give further helpings when asked for, along with meat, broth and the daily fare of rice. They cleaned the place twice a day. Two of the priests would spend their time consoling the sick and administering the sacraments. The usual illnesses were fevers and dysentery. The Father in charge of the place would give a new outfit of clothes and a *pardau* to each of the ones who left on recovery. Occasionally the Archbishop, the Viceroy and the rich *fidalgos* of the city, would visit the hospital and while departing leave financial gifts behind. The beauty of the place struck many who visited, as did the clean rooms and the corridors adorned with historical motifs.[4]

The Jesuit Bro. Infirmarian (*boticario*) at the Royal Hospital ran a well-supplied pharmacy. The Assistant Infirmarian of St. Paul's once complained that spurious *pedras cordiais* unlike the originals of Bro. Gaspar Antonio (the recipe was kept secret) were then in the markets (in Goa and in Portugal) for sale. He requested the State to renew an existing ban on such sale. A royal decree of 6 March 1691 ordered that the Casa da India (where all goods from India were delivered) could not release any such cordial stones unless accompanied with a certificate attesting to their having been made at the Jesuit infirmaries.[5]

The officials of the Municipality of Goa had informed the King of their wish to see Bro. Luis da Silva, the Infirmarian at the Royal Hospital, back at his work. He was well-known for his charity and his medicine, and had moved elsewhere on transfer. They considered his successor, Bro. Miguel Vieira unfit for the task. But the Viceroy in his reply to the King dated 2 January 1717, assured him that the new appointee, an Infirmarian by profession, was doing well, and that the soldiers were pleased. Besides, he trusted the Jesuit Provincial's reasons for the replacement.[6]

At Sea

The Jesuits had once dispatched a *pataxo* (boat) to China and another to Portugal with their merchandise. They did so at night and had already crossed the river-bar. The one for Portugal got through, but unfortunately for them, the Dutch, who were around for a strike on the city of Goa, intercepted the one bound for China and sank it. The Jesuits in their long black gowns had been manning the boat. One of them who tried to escape, found it difficult to do so and paid with his life after the violence he attempted on his captors.[7]

Passion Plays

The Jesuits did much to popularize the passion plays they conducted in their churches. Manucci mentions how a Fr. Mansilhas while preaching in a church in 1703 was so upset at seeing members of the cast fighting that he came rushing down the pulpit and struck the 'Christ' and the 'Hebrews' with a baton. The audience at the church was much amused. It later became customary for the preachers to mount their pulpits with batons to lash at those they found distracted during the sermons.[8]

Their Affected Airs

Some considered the Portuguese Jesuits as illiterate as the rest of the clergy of their time. Yet, they observed a more reserved and decent conduct than the other religious Orders. They did not miss their drive for legacy-hunting and donation-collecting from the lay people. They usually wore broad-brimmed hats always flapped round like umbrellas with dejected eyes to portray humility, and with that non-caring look to see the world in the face.[9]

Many both hated and courted them out of a fear of their power and vindictiveness, a fear bred by weakness, and which would disappear on their showing themselves in their true light. In times of famine, they would win over the people relieving them of their sufferings on condition of their conversion. But usually their converts were the proverbial *cristãos de arroz* (rice-Christians).[10]

Government Grievances against the Jesuits

The Royal Treasury had grievances against the Jesuits. The Count of Linhares dwelt on their behaviour in Assolná, on the matter of jurisdiction of the outpost (*passo*) in Chorão, on how they misled the Royal Treasury, on their attacks on the Portuguese navies in Bandra, and on their contraband pearl activities in Tuticorin and pepper dealing in Quilon.[11]

There were instances of conflict between the Jesuits and the inhabitants of Rachol. The priests wanted to take away to their College some silverware from the Church of the Fort. They refused the Viceroy's intervention and his plans to call witnesses. He persisted and called the Provincial in for a discussion. He later commented that the Jesuits would cling to anything they set their eyes on, with all their strength, and would refuse to call their faults wrong (*he couza forte que tudo estes homens querião levar a forssa e sempre he queixão fazendo elles o mal, e tendo a culpa*).[12]

The Jesuits were unwilling to give an account of the works at the forts in the North. The Crown had also asked for a list of the title-deeds, and Crown and State donations to the Seminaries and to the College of St. Paul's. But the Viceroy discovered that it was impossible to get the details since the Jesuits were much averse to furnishing them.[13]

The Viceroy had received many complaints against the Jesuits for they were absolute in matters of purchase and sale of the forts in India. The State could not build a fort at Sant' Ana since the beach there lay in their charge. They submitted false accounts and it was impossible to get the right figures. Though they had money to build a hospital in Mozambique, they had not completed it, and many had died as a result.[14]

The list of Jesuit properties during the time of the Count of Linhares in Goa, Bassein, Thane, Bandra, Japan and Ceylon amounted to 2,16,500 *pardaus*. Yet it appeared incorrect since the Jesuits did not co-operate with the revenue officer. In Ceylon they had over 100 villages, many with no valid title-deeds. Viceroy Dom Felipe Mascarenhas thought they put more effort into their fund-raising than into their soul-winning.[15]

The Count, however, was thankful to the Jesuit Provincials, Frs. Antonio de Andrade and Alvaro Tavares, for their collaboration in bringing about the Anglo-Portuguese Goa accord of 1635.[16] The Viceroy recognized the high quality of Jesuit service whicn he utilized for the State.

What he objected to was their interference in his administration. He found them more powerful than the Crown staff in Salcete. In Tuticorin they had refused to co-operate with the local officials and had set up a customs-post netting them 12,000 *xs.* a year.[17]

He had used the services of Fr. Paulo Reimão, as his intelligence agent (*seu inteligente*) at Surat. But the cordial relations between the two soon ended and the Count discarded him over the signing of the Goa Accord of 1635 between the English East India Company and Goa. The priest's rough draft was discussed and they felt he had revealed his true colours and was more in favour of the English and the Dutch than the Portuguese (*como este padre hé de nação Ingres, ou olandes fello com seteçentas parvoisses em favor e autoridade dos Ingreses, tive com elle a este respeito hua grande briga de que elle ficou pouco contente*).[18]

Their Political Meddling

The Jesuits had on a certain occasion, detained a *galeota* (a boat) without permission in the Bombay islands. On another, they had taken some jewels from Gan Naique, a dweller from Mahim who had nothing to do with any contentions and was solely engaged in his own affairs. The Viceroy warned the priests to desist from meddling in political matters.[19]

National Interests

The Portuguese merchant, Francisco Vieira de Figueiredo, had occasion to inform the State of the friendship between the Italian, Fr. Martino Martini, and the Dutch, stationed at Macassar. He believed the French and the Italian Jesuits were hostile to the Portuguese interests in Asia.[20]

Smuggling

The Crown had asked the Jesuit Provincial in Goa, Fr. André Pereyra to examine the case of Fr. Paulo Marques who had smuggled two boxes of *velorio* (raw silk) to Sena, and had defrauded the Public Exchequer.[21] The Provincial informed the Governor that his Jesuit predecessor had received similar complaints against the priest. But these were not true. Moreover, the accusation that the Jesuit residence in Sena was actually a factory, was sheer calumny. It was the work of the Factor who opposed the Superintendent of the Board of Commerce (*Junta do Comércio*), Nicolao Tolentino de Almeida. The latter had exposed his many tricks in the river Sena, about how he had hidden textiles in bundles of white cloths in large quantities in one of the ships of the Northern Province.

The Jesuits, said the Provincial, always placed at the port for inspection the goods that had arrived for their Jesuit houses from Mozambique. The Factor and the Superintendent were always present then. If the Board of Commerce had suffered in revenue, it was rather the work of those in charge, for the factory had false weights.

The Provincial explained to the Crown that he was making all this known in order to seek justice. Fr. Paulo Marques had already died the previous year. He suggested that it send a dispassionate minister to check all cases of smuggling. All those who had served in earlier years at Mozambique and at Sena could testify to the good behaviour of his men there.

The Province of the North

The best land in the Province belonged to the Jesuits, and yielded rich amounts of sugarcane, rice and fruit. There were several villages consisting of poor Hindus, Muslims and Christians living in wattle and daub houses covered with straw or palm leaves. Their condition was miserable. They had to till the land as much as they could to pay their landlords. They would often flee from village to village, only to be brought back by force. Those who held their land from large proprietors paid their rent in grain, often with the addition of personal service. Those who held it direct from the State paid the government factor a monthly imposition according to the value of the land.[22]

Jesuits in Bombay

The Portuguese had delayed handing over Bombay to the English, who suspected the hand of the Jesuits in the move. The very mention of the name 'Jesuit' would excite the hostility of the Protestant Englishmen. The Jesuits who were among the more eminent inhabitants and owners of the island, were absentee landlords. They had considerable landed property in Salcete, notably the famous Bandra College. Henry Gary, a Surat Council member and one who hated the Jesuits, accused them in a letter of 12 January 1663 of bribing the Viceroy to withhold Bombay with a gift of 40,000 *xs.*[23]

Sir Abraham Shipman wrote to Sir William Morice, Secretary of State on 10 January 1663, that the Jesuits as masters of Salcete feared to hand over the island of Bombay. They knew that Salcete along with the rest would fall into English hands since Bombay and the other islands were the most fruitful of all India.[24]

Administration in the North

The State did not see it fit for the Jesuits to continue with the administration of the North, since it was against their religious rules. But they pointed out that they had managed bigger profits than the administrators of the factories and the *mahajans* had done. They had looked after the granaries of Bassein, Chaul, Daman and Diu for forty years. Their enemies were those who could not make as much with them around. With an initial capital of 16,858 *xs.* for the granary of Bassein, they had made 1,18,821 *xs.* during the Viceroyalty of the Count of Ericeira. They had supplied rice at a modest rate to the people, and had helped the soldiers and their families. Certain settlements had started with an initial fund of 8,000 *xs.*, which had swelled to 30,000 *xs.* under them. In 1710, the Jesuits had helped add one more unit to the fleet at a cost of 22,000 *xs.* The Daman granary had begun with 25,119 *xs.* and climbed to 56,138 *xs.* The following year, revenues from taxes and the royal property netted another 14,000 *xs.* But their predecessors could barely meet their expenses when they were in charge.

The Jesuits did more besides. They helped in financing vessels of war, which protected the convoys and the merchant ships, met the payments for the twenty soldiers at the fort of St. Jerome, and paid for the ammunition of the Tarapur and Mahim forts respectively. There had been an extraordinary rise of 25,341 *xs.* but they saw the emergency through. Their dealings with their Superiors and their network of demand and supply from wherever cheap and possible, had made everything easy.

They started their stint at the granary of Diu with 200 *mudas* of husked rice and 100 *khandis* of *nachni*. The *mahajans* before them had nothing to show by way of improvement of the quantities they had. But the Jesuits returned to the State 8,000 *xs.* in profit. They achieved this although they had lost 76 *mudas* in a shipwreck between Bassein and Diu.

The Provincial, Fr. João Olivares had requested the Crown for permission to give up the administration of the granaries, but the request was turned down. He believed that one of the reasons why commerce in India had fallen, was because there were investments in landed property rather than in business. The Overseas Council had asked for further information on the whole issue in order to have a better picture. The Jesuits had asked for permission to acquire properties since they had had no income from the Royal Exchequer for ordinary and extraordinary expenses, and could not maintain their granaries and their settlements.[25]

The Provincial, Fr. Henrique Pereira, complained to the State that Manuel Ferreira de Lima, Administrator of the royal granaries, hindered his men in their work as administrators of Bassein. He had auctioned the village of Utan belonging to a certain Luis Gonçalves da Camara Coutinho for 1,55,100 *xs*. He did not give it to the Jesuits who were ready to overbid. Instead, he decreased the bid to 1,45,000 *xs*. to favour another friend, Antonio Coelho da Costa.

The Provincial recalled the honesty with which his men had administered the granaries for 39 years. They had started with 16,855 *xs*. and ended up with 3,75,200 *xs*. in cash and 855 *mudas* of rice in kind. The Council decided that the Jesuits were right and the village was up for auction again.[26]

The Crown had informed Viceroy Francisco da Gama of the interference of the Jesuits into the affairs of the customs-house at Chaul. It advised him to warn their Provincial and to inform him that his priests were fortunate that the Crown had not as yet informed their General in Rome about their unbecoming behaviour.[27] The Captain of Chaul, too, resented the working of the Jesuit Rector, Fr. Bartolomeu Freire. It had been a feature for a long time. The Jesuits were in charge of the administration of the forts and its works and kept its finances. But they refused to accept any suggestions and preferred to follow their own minds.[28] The Jesuits were later deprived of the administrative work in Daman, Diu, Chaul, and Bassein because they were unwilling to submit their accounts for inspection.[29]

Jesuits and the Other Religious

Fierce at times were the quarrels between the Jesuits and the other religious Orders over matters pertaining to territorial jurisdiction, residences and methods of work. Though all religious Orders toiled for the same cause, a lot of unholy rivalry prevailed among them. The Franciscans and the Jesuits did not see eye-to-eye in many areas of work, especially in the seventeenth-century Japan and Ceylon.

They worked separately in the northern and southern areas of Goa and cases of enmity and tension were fewer than elsewhere where they clashed. They clashed in Pondicherry, where the Franciscans reacted to the Bishop of Mylapore's decision in 1699 to entrust the apostolate among non-

Christians of the town and surrounding areas to the Jesuits.[30]

In Japan at least, the cause of the friction between the Jesuits and others was a difference in missionary outlook. The Franciscans wanted a clean sweep of the native customs and religion, while the Jesuits avoided direct attacks on native cultures. Mainly religious, but political and economic motives, too, all caused the gulf to widen between the Society and the others. While the former sought the higher-ups in society trusting the lower groups would soon follow, the latter concentrated on the ignorant and forgotten classes.[31] These disputes did much to tarnish Portuguese prestige in the East. Their activities and labours were beneficial in many respects, but their abuses intensified the open and latent antagonism of the native population towards them.[32]

Differences at Goa

Fr. Gaspar de Lisboa, a Franciscan, wrote to King Philip I in 1589 attacking the Jesuits for their many houses, including their sumptuous Professed House. He suggested that since Goa was in need of a convent for nuns, the Professed House could best serve the purpose. He thought the takeover would trim the Jesuit revenues. He pointed out that they had recently built a church in an area that was the pastoral domain of the Franciscans. They were owners of many villages there, and were very powerful and troublesome besides.[33]

The Augustinians and the Jesuits were at odds over the construction works at the College of St. Roque.[34] They reached an agreement, however after protracted discussions, on 16 August 1632, in the presence of the Viceroy, Count of Linhares, the Provincial of the Augustinians, Frei Luis Coutinho, the Prior of the convent where the meeting was held, Frei Bonifacio de Chagas, the Provincial of the Society of Jesus, Fr. Antonio Ataide, the Rector of the College of St. Roque, Fr. Alvaro Tavares, and the notary, Francisco Rodrigues.

To maintain peace and religious friendship and harmony, they had agreed that the construction would not extend beyond what was done. The Jesuits accepted not to preach except on the feasts of Sts. Peter and Paul, of Our Lady of Conception, and of those of the Society of Jesus. There would be no preaching too, in Lent, and during the Sundays of the year.

The issue of toilets (*secretas, necessarias*) caused much bad blood between both sides, and the Jesuits finally decided to shift them elsewhere from their earlier place that would have caused a bad stench to the Augustinians. They also agreed to reduce the height of the new staircase that they had intended to build at the end of the college dormitory. The Augustinians planned to move their Seminary of St. John the Evangelist to their convent at Old Goa. In return for the concessions by the Jesuits, they would not admit any students from Santa Fé into their Seminary, and would refrain from making any petition to the King against the transfer plans of the Jesuits.[35]

The Jesuits and the Dominicans had a long history of bitter rivalry. They differed in Spain on almost every issue, and elsewhere, this turned into hostility and hatred. The Dominicans had their own plans for America, while the Jesuits, on the other hand, considered China their turf and challenge.[36] The latter knew the practised art of propaganda for their mission, and successfully sent to Europe the first Japanese embassy.[37]

Conversion Methods

There were complaints that the Jesuits used force to effect their conversions. Brothers went around villages to round up Hindus and to cut off their *xendi* (tuft of hair on the head). They next served them meat, and carried off the children to their Colleges at Bassein or Thane. They did this in defiance of the decrees of the first Church Provincial Council of Goa forbidding any one from using force while converting.[38]

Jesuits and the Archbishop Brandão

Differences between Archbishop Antonio Brandão, former Abbot General of the Cistercians and the thirteenth Archbishop of Goa, and the Jesuits, had reached a high point. Relations had long been strained between the two. The proceedings of the Council of State on the application of the Jesuit Provincial, Fr. Fernão de Queiroz to quit the churches in Salcete, bear this out.[39] The Viceroy and his ministers at their meeting were not ready to accept the resignation of the Jesuits from their churches in Salcete since it was the King who had offered them the obligation, and the Viceroy had no authority to act otherwise. The Council, however, decided that should they leave suddenly as they had threatened to do, it would be the Archbishop's duty to provide the same churches with replacements.

For he had prevented the Jesuits from administering their churches, and had ordered them to hand over their books of accounts to the civil treasurers. He instructed them to hand over the property and moneys of the *fabricas* and *confrarias*, and to incur no further expense without his permission.

He had planned to inspect the title-deeds and books of their church at Majorda, which for long had been the property of the College of Rachol. He excommunicated Fr. Antonio Luis, the parish-priest, and advised Fr. Torcato Parisiani, Rector of the College, under pain of excommunication, to present the title-deeds of the church within twenty-four hours. The property had been a gift of the Crown to the College during the provincialate of Fr. Miguel de Almeida. The Jesuits had built the main part of the church on the then existing chapel of the Mother of God.

Some accused the Jesuits of being ignorant of the local language, of being unable to preach and to hear confessions. They, their detractors said, could not administer the Sacraments or celebrate masses on Saturdays and days of obligation. In order to gain more money, they had their own treasurers, and they would get many to sign their documents on false promises of reward.

The Provincial maintained that they had to expose themselves to the continual humiliations of some, though a few others held them in high respect. The people missed the devotions they had introduced. He wanted to forego charge of all their churches with the exception of those at Raia, Majorda and Assolná. It was not ill-will in the King's service that had forced them to withdraw. They had need of preserving their own pride and serenity, he added.[40]

The Archbishop had excommunicated Fr. Antonio de Betancourt, the parish priest of Navelim. But the latter had managed to imprison the twenty persons whom the Archbishop had used as witnesses against him. He had obtained the Viceroy's permission to have them put at the gunpowder-house. Among them was a young cleric with minor orders, Salvador Pacheco. He remained there in his habit and tonsure, and had finally under duress to enroll himself as a soldier.[41]

Jesuits and Archbishop Santa Teresa

The relations between Archbishop, Ignacio de Santa Teresa and the Jesuits, too, were far from cordial. The State Council had received a letter from the Jesuit Provincial complaining that his men were victims of calumny. The Archbishop had inquired into their personal lives, and had questioned women on their visits to the priests, some of whom testified falsely under threats. Rumours were always afloat, and it was impossible for them to continue. He sought permission from the Viceroy, Francisco Joseph de Sampaio e Castro, for his priests to return to the Rachol College from their parishes. The native clerics, he said, were capable enough to do a similar job. His men could then man missions, since parish work was alien to their Institute.

The Governor in his reply to the letter of 6 September 1722 of Fr. Provincial, João Olivares, urged him to continue. But the latter did not concur saying his men were not obliged to obey him, and that he ought to accept their decision. The various members of the State Council, including the Captain of the city, Dom Manoel Sottomayor, the Inquisitor, the Chancellor of the High Court, and the General of the Straits, agreed. They decided that the Jesuits ought to leave, and that their Fr. Procurator ought to submit before their departure an inventory of all their church property.[42]

The Governor had his own problems with the Archbishop and informed the Overseas Council that His Reverence was needlessly interfering in his secular administration, and was a difficult person to get along with. He did not maintain any proper accounts of the *fabrica* property, and refused to accept letters the State sent to him. The Governor endorsed the decision of the Jesuits to leave their posts since the work was alien to them. Besides, the parishes of Ilhas were doing well under the native priests.[43]

The Overseas Council suggested that it was no longer necessary for the Jesuits to continue in their twenty-five parish churches, but that they could devote themselves to new missions for the greater glory of God. It was incorrect for the Inquisitor to inspect their churches, and they believed their own Superior ought to continue doing so.[44]

The Jesuits tried to take over once again the Salcete parishes they had left in 1722. They won over several people in Margão and other parishes, and came to Old Goa by the end of October with the signatures of many, some of which they had obtained by force, to present to the Viceroy. They sought the help of the village police officials and guards to install the new parish-priest and to evict the present one on pretext of an enemy invasion. The inhabitants of Margão had once evicted the parish-priest of their church, and had replaced him with a person of their choice. They had feigned having come to help a sick lady receive the Sacrament of the Sick. On another occasion, Fr. Afonço Costa from Rachol carried in solemn procession the thurible on the feast of Our Lady of Conception at which service there were many present who had taken part in a revolt at Bardez.[45]

Jesuits and Native Resistance

Frequent were the clashes between the Jesuits and the local Brahmin clergy. In a nine-point memorandum to Rome, the Brahmins accused the religious of persecuting them, of being ignorant of the local language, of being unable to help the people to confess more often than once a year, of using interpreters in the confessionals, and of preventing the Brahmin priests from hearing confessions in their own parishes. They pointed out that the priests were powerful, had property and had obtained stay-orders on royal decrees by sending gifts to Portugal to evade action. They lacked the fear of God and spread false information against them and Bishop Dom Matheus de Castro who had to flee to Rome as a result. They prevented the general assemblies of the Salcete villages from meeting and had arrested their members and chief *ganvkars*. In many and devious ways they obtained certificates and writs for what they wished.[46]

In a spirited reply the Provincial maintained that the priests taught the Brahmins in their schools to count and sing, to read and write, to dance and play musical instruments. They also taught them Latin, philosophy, theology and morals till some of them could become priests and say mass. They maintained them at the cost of the Seminary of Santa Fé, and of the Colleges of Rachol and Bassein. They provided jobs with salaries in the colleges for those who could study no further.

His men knew the local language well enough to preach with courage and erudition. They had composed several books and for the present year had printed two booklets (*cartilhas*), two grammars, a *Flos Sanctorum*, four *Puranas* in which they dealt with the errors of paganism and the mysteries of the Christian faith. They had done so in very noble terms which very few of the Brahmins understood. They wanted Crown help to print the other books in manuscript form: *Flos Sanctorum* in verse, three vocabularies, a book of examples, a book on theology, another on the immortality of the soul, yet another on the mysteries of the faith, two *Puranas* in verse, a book on the Gospels for the year, the life of Peter, a book of examples for all feasts of the year, and a booklet of hymns. No native Brahmin priest had done as much. They preached on merely a few occasions, while the religious did so oftener and better.

The parishioners in the Jesuit parishes confessed frequently, and with better devotion than the Europeans. The Jesuit-established confraternities too recommended frequent confession. But the native Brahmin parishes had people who were slow in the faith. In Jua, for example, the Inquisition had to penalize them for worshipping their former idols, something unheard of in the parishes of Salcete.

The parishioners would come to the Jesuits for help in their quarrels, marriages or joblessness. They sought nothing from their Brahmin priests who were as dark-skinned as themselves and unworthy of any respect. The

Jesuits knew much of the language to dispense with interpreters in the confessional, and were never the cause of the native priests being unable to hear confessions.

The Brahmin women usually confessed to the white religious, and this hurt the Brahmin priests. The Jesuits did not have large properties to sustain their colleges and residences, and the power they had was one of good example and virtue. They had but little, but paid the Crown regularly for the debts they had incurred.

They did not persecute the natives. Rather, they had raised them to the state they were then in. If Bishop Castro had fled to Rome, he did so to avoid the Count of Aveiras, who had issued summons to arrest him and send him to Portugal for his seditious invitations to the Dutch to take over Goa and Salcete. The Jesuits let the village communities manage their own affairs and offered help only when the members sought it. It would be helpful, however, if one of them could be present at their meetings to report to the Crown on the discussions or to forestall sedition if any. The King himself could better explain the reasons why he had issued certificates in their favour.

The Brahmin priests believed that Bishop Castro had been always faithful in his zeal of souls, having gone to Bijapur and to the Court of the Adil Shah to preach the Gospel. He built a church at Bicholim and took care of the lapsed Christians through his priests. They had termed him anti-national after he obtained a brief from His Holiness instructing the Jesuits to vacate the parishes they were in. The native priests had their churches clean and well-equipped with silver and other ornamentation. They had schools where they taught reading and writing in the mother-tongue (*lingua materna*), and the playing of various musical instruments. The Inquisition had sought their help in detecting the errors of paganism. They spent much of their salary and property for the work they were doing.

The Jesuits accused the Bishop of being a traitor and a friend to the Dutch. The church he claimed to have at Bicholim was but a hut (*palhota*) in which he lived like a criminal evading punishment for his many crimes. He had a woman as his companion whom he called a relative, but a fellow native priest, Fr. Bernard Coutinho, the parish priest of Chorão, had warned him against it. He had also ordained some clerics illegally. There was no Christianity worth its name at Bicholim, and the Jesuits would go there to hear confessions and to offer help to the Portuguese slaves. The Provincial visited Karwar by road to see for himself the convent of the Bishop. It turned out to be a hut, twenty spans in length, and twelve in height, and with a bench for an altar. A non-believer usually looked after the place and would stack rice, cereals and fruits on it. Two clerics would visit the place twice a year for a period of eight days during which time the caretaker vacated his spot. In Goa they had described their church as sumptuous, though the English who had a factory nearby, found the whole arrangement scandalous.

The only wealth the Jesuits had was what they got from alms. Yet, their parishes had a regular income, and their churches were furnished with crosses, thuribles, cruets, candelabras, gilded retables and rich altar ornamentation. The native priests had no decoration for their altars, they had failed to pay salaries to the tune of 30,000 *xs.* and their churches lacked everything. They educated their students poorly and the parents of these, resented the punishments they meted out, but cared not at all if the religious did the same.

The faith suffered due to their faulty knowledge of Latin and Portuguese. The Jesuits boasted that two months were enough for them to pick up the local language and to preach satisfactorily in it. No native priest could match them in it. They lacked good preachers among themselves, and the few that did preach, repeated the sermons of the religious.

The native priests had nothing to show by way of conversions. But the priests and brothers from St. Paul's trudged all over Goa in search of orphans and catechumens. The native priests were always reluctant to help of their own accord, and looked avidly for reward and gifts like reliquaries, rosaries and crosses.

The Jesuits had informed the Inquisition of many an error in paganism. They had composed grammars to make the study of the language easier. The native priests prevented them from coming to their parishes lest they see through their seditious plots. It was not without cause that the Crown had warned the religious against leaving Salcete, convinced as it was that they were each akin to a captain of a fortress.[47]

Village Communities

Pedro Alvares Pereira, a judge of the High Court, and Crown Attorney that year, in a report of 12 February 1619, had detailed Jesuit abuses. The village books showed many *nem* entries concerning contributions sought for dances and flowers, for celebrations in honour of judges, *fidalgos*, and visitors to the Jesuits. They showed that the priests valued the paddy fields which they had taken on lease, at a mere fraction of their original price.

These they had sublet in turn at a higher rental. They had acquired the island of Raia claiming it was legal according to the *Foral* to do so. But, in fact it was in violation of clause ten of the Charter. They paid a mere 70 *tgs.* as rent, though the land was worth over 1,000 *xs.*

The Jesuits were harsh at times in their dealings with the people of Salcete. One of them had ordered the *canarins* of his village to provide him daily with fish. On a certain occasion when he brought in a lesser quantity than the usual, he received a merciless flogging in the presence of some distinguished visitors. The natives, as also the Portuguese and the State officials, feared to complain, lest they had the priests against them. They could write damning accusations against their enemies to the authorities in Portugal.

They had got the general assembly of Salcete to request the Crown to prevent any Portuguese from acquiring rights which were due only to the *ganvkars.* Yet their plan backfired since it was they who enjoyed the privileges they sought to curb in most cases. They had also requested the Crown to exempt them from paying tithes, since they were at the service of the people.[48] The *ganvkars* of Salcete had once brought to the notice of the Crown the behaviour of Fr. Afonso Dias, the *mestiço* Rector of the College of Rachol. He had at a Sunday mass sentenced one of them, a person old and much respected, to be lashed, and then to be exiled for a year. They considered the priest's behaviour scandalous and were much upset as a result.[49]

The King in his letter of 3 April 1632, informed the Governor that he had received complaints from Salcete against Isidoro de Lemos, the Justice, and wanted an inquiry. The Viceroy in his reply mentioned that the accusations were not those of the people, but were those of the Jesuits, in fact. They were lord of all and hated any minister of the State who sought to act against their interests.[50]

Jesuits in Margão

The villagers of Margão had complained about the oppression they suffered at the hands of the Jesuits. They had not suffered as much under the Marathas in 1739. The priests were rich, ambitious, vindictive, aggressive and restless. Only the present Viceroy, the Count of Ega could be the saviour of the people. They had wide powers to acquire more and had stout defenders in their superiors. The Archbishop was a friend of the Jesuits and believed the thoughts of even a lay brother in their group as gospel-truth. They had won over every ruler in India, and even a minor slight to one of the group was enough to set them all up-in-arms.

Their group included Fr. Bento Monteiro, whom they considered a religious only in name. He loved the adulation of all, and had gathered much during his stint as Procurator of the China Vice-Province. His guests at his home would include the Archbishop, the High Court ministers, the General of the Province, and the Inquisitor. Though the post of parish-priest of the church of Margão usually fell on an older Jesuit or one with authority, he was none of these. He had managed to install Manuel Marques de Azevedo as Deputy of the Holy Office, and had promised him even more.

He would entertain his friends at his home in the parish church for days on end, with women of easy virtue as dancing companions in the hall above the sacristy. But his Superiors and the Archbishop thought nothing of this. He extorted money from others, interfered in religious matters, was the cause of disharmony, and gave clerics a rough deal. He insulted people at the Confraternity and Board meetings, and often used the rod on officials who failed to give him money. He let corpses lie unburied for days on end if relatives did not make payments in time, and even exhumed them if he had not received all his charges. His fee was five and a half *xs.* for a sung mass without acolytes. He would arrest people and place them in his parish prison. He did not keep records of the wills and last wishes of the deceased in his parish, and mortgaged property by force.

On a certain occasion he struck those who sought an explanation for the delay in the burial of one of theirs, and bound them in a cell. They managed to escape, however, across the border and left their property and families behind. It was only the Count of Ega who finally came to their rescue and gave them a safe passage back home.

The parishioners had secretly approached his Provincial, Fr. Luis Lopes, for help against him but it turned out all in vain. They went next to the Archbishop but he could do little more. Finally, they turned to the Government with a complaint signed by one hundred and thirty-eight. This set the parish-priest all aflame and he managed to arrest three priests whom he suspected of involvement in this, including Fr. João Caetano Coutinho, who was very ill. The people usually believed that a dispute involving any two of the locals normally ended in justice for both, while if a Portuguese was in conflict with a native, it was the former who was the favoured one.

Fr. Monteiro had on 26 May 1758 come along with the State Judge, Alexandre Botelho Vasconcellos and armed soldiers to a spot in the village. They invited the people to work, but arrested six of those who came. They then led them away to the fort at Rachol, and promised them an early release should they withdraw their accusations.[51].

The Statue of Menino-Jesus

The *ganvkars* of Colva, Sernabatim, Vanelim and Gandaulim of the parish of Our Lady of Mercy, had informed the Crown of all they had done to popularize the devotion of the *Menino-Jesus* (Child-Jesus) while Fr. Bento Ferreira was their parish-priest. They had spent money for the installation and rich ornamentation of the statue, and had helped increase the contributions to 20,000 *xs*. until the time of the departure of the Jesuits from their Salcete parishes. But at a later date, the Rector and the parish-priest, Fr. Joseph Figueiredo accompanied by the Rector of the College of Rachol, arrived at their church and carried away the statue. They refused to return it, stating that it had always belonged to the Society.[52]

In his representation of 23 November 1729, the Archbishop, Dom Frei Ignacio de Santa Teresa had informed the Crown of the violent means that Manoel Ferreira de Lima, Civil Judge of the High Court of Goa, had used in helping the Jesuits capture the statue of the Child-Jesus of the Church of Our Lady of Mercy, Colva, along with its collection. The Judge in his letter of 5 January of the previous year, had discussed the case, then in the Civil Court. It involved the Jesuits and the parish-communities of Colva and Sernabatim regarding their respective rights to have the statue. The former won the case and the Court of Appeal confirmed it. The Viceroy had asked the Judge to attend to its execution himself, but the Archbishop objected to the move. He wanted the Crown to restrain the Archbishop and to study the case itself.[53]

The Archbishop had earlier narrated his own version. In his letter of 11 August 1729, he recalled that at six in the morning on St. Lawrence's day, the Judge of the Civil Court along with the Rector of the Rachol College, other officials and twenty-four soldiers, had entered the church while the parishioners were worshipping. Despite the protests of the parish-priest, Fr. Joseph Ferreira, while the Beadle stood by on the altar-stone, the others used a knife and a bayonet to weaken the hinges of the case holding the statue. It was a day of obligation and many resisted the intruders with loud tears, but the latter got into their palanquins with their deed done and catch in hand and left for Rachol.

The *ganvkars* petitioned the Crown for a return of the statue along with all of its income. They maintained that the earlier ruling did not have the permission of the King, who was patron of the church, and of the Archbishop. The Jesuits, however, claimed the statue had always been theirs and was never the property of the church.[54]

Jesuit View of Themselves

A document, *Lista das rendas e despezas da Provincia de Goa da Companhia de Jesus para o Senhor Conde Viso-Rei João Nunes da Cunha* (List of income and expenses of the Province of Goa of the Society of Jesus to His Excellency the Viceroy, João Nunes da Cunha) describes the pain and the difficulties, the Jesuits claimed they had suffered in their work from different quarters.[55]

They pointed out the attacks made on them because of their properties. They were confident that the document they had submitted would disprove the myth of their great wealth. The convents at Coimbra and at Alcobaça in Portugal, had more, they said. How could this Province, they asked, have more with its few colleges, residences and missions than other religious convents in Portugal? The *fidalgos* had the entire North and more but gave nothing away of it for divine service. In other hands, the properties the Jesuits possessed would not have yielded as much. Their yield was a little over *50,000 xs*. but others maintained that it was thrice that figure. The accusations and outbursts of others had become too much for them and they were ready to renounce their all to the Crown.

They admitted that the places they owned were theirs only on trust and for a good administration for the service of God and King. The College of St. Paul's still owed 25,000 *xs*. and had resorted to cutting down on expenses wherever possible. Happily, the higher price for coconuts and *bate* (husked rice) had been a windfall and helped them to make good the entire loss they had suffered as a result of a fire. They had asked for a loan of 25,000 *xs*. to meet a difficult financial crisis, and to save them from the bother of officials who would pick on their finances when unable to attack them on anything else. They presented their lists to the new Viceroy, the Count of St. Vincent, and informed him that such reactions they had received were meted out not even to the most despicable in the land.

In 1735, Fr. Provincial, João Marques had informed the Crown of the Viceroy's inimical attitude towards them. He had heard of the Viceroy's plans to invite two religious priests from Varatojo to open a mission in India, since he surmised that the Jesuits were not interested in mission work. That was untrue, and also unnecessary for Jesuit missionaries were in abundance here. He recalled the various works his men were busy with in Goa and its missions.

The Archbishop had stopped them from exercising their ministries and had prevented the common people from going to their churches. He had declared their masses invalid. They found it difficult to continue saying the masses for the dead. The Viceroy was aware of all, yet had called the two missionaries from Varatojo who did not know the local language (*lingua barbara*) which needed many years to master. The Provincial felt his men had the advantage of knowing the language, and the local customs.[56]

At the judicial inquiry against Bro. Antonio Fernandes, the Provincial claimed that the Dominicans and some other religious had assaulted the Jesuit. A group of black slaves under Frei San Simão, had surprised a group while they were moving in their palanquins, and had attacked them. The servants in fear left the sick and helpless Jesuit they were carrying, to defend himself, and rushed to find sticks for the attack. The sick man died five days later due to injuries and shock.

Self-Criticism

The Jesuits were usually wary of criticism from other quarters, but were not sparing of it with reference to each other. They would point out the faults of the other in their annual reports and accounts to Rome. Fr. João da Cunha wrote to the Superior-General, Fr. Acquaviva that the Rector of the College, Fr. Thomas Stephens, had used for the College of Bom Jesus what legally belonged to the church according to the will of the donor. These included a palm-grove and some rents. He had got the Christians to donate their properties to the church with the added clause that they would continue belonging to the Jesuits although they might not be in charge of them for any reason for a length of time.[57]

With all the power they wielded and the money they gained, the Jesuits did not do much to raise the social condition of the people they served. The converts were mostly from the lower economic or caste groups in Goa. Moreover, they were unable to compete with the Hindus in business or for jobs. Their restlessness in their new state of life and antagonism against the Jesuits grew. The religious with their land-grab policies had brought about an impoverished gentry. The religious confraternities they formed based on castes actually failed to promote social cohesion. The insolence some of them showed the religious and secular authorities drew them further apart from all. The picture was not very different in their missions in the other parts of the globe from that in Goa. Their various activities in a way gradually hastened the coming events of 1759.

REFERENCES

1. Crooke, William (ed.), *Travels in India by Jean-Baptiste Tavernier Baron of Aubonne*, II, pp. 238-239.
2. *Ibid.*, pp. 239-240.
3. Irvine, William (trans.), *Storia do Mogor or Moghul India 1653-1708 by Niccolao Manucci*, III, pp. 265 ff.
4. Cunha Rivara, José H. (ed.), *Viagem de Francisco Pyrard de Laval*, II, pp. 9-20.
5. Correia-Afonso, John (ed.), *Indo-Portuguese History: Sources and Problems*, pp. 77-78. Refers to the ANTT: *Cartorio dos Jesuitas* 83/68. 90/61-2 are petitions of the Apothecary of the Royal Hospital at Goa.
   Amaro, Ana Maria, "Goa's Famous Cordial Stone," *Review of Culture* (Macau), nos. 7-8, 1988/1989, pp. 82-103. Describes the secret recipe of the cordial stones. "It was said to be the most universal, useful antidote to all venoms, both for internal and external uses. The medicines were given a miraculous quality, and were prepared in a room which contained the relics of the stone's patron saint, holy water and whilst making the sign of the cross." (pp. 82-83).
6. AHU: India, *maço* 7, 27 January 1716. The King's letter to the Viceroy is dated 7 January 1716.
7. Irvine, *op. cit.*, p. 79.
8. *Ibid.*, pp. 200-201.
9. *A Voyage to the East Indies with observations on various parts there*, II, p. 273.
10. *Ibid.*, p. 293. He says, "always in those times, but often wherever they could discover objects with whose indigence they could work that they succeeded by their mercenary means".
11. *BFUP*, n. 12, *LM*, 19-C (1634-35), pp. 301-302, 7 January 1634.
12. *Diario do 3º (sic) Conde de Linhares, Vice-Rei da India*, (*Diario*) II, pp. 135-136.
13. *BFUP*, *LM* 19-B, doc. 57, Lisbon 7 March 1634, p. 473.
14. *Ibid.*, 15 (1631-32), pp. 30, 58-59, 89, 94.
15. Abeyasinghe, Tikiri, "History as polemics and propaganda: Some aspects of Fernão de Queiroz's *Conquista*," *II Seminario International de Historia Indo-Portuguesa*, pp. 792-793.
16. *Diario*, II, p. 268.
17. Disney, Anthony, "The Viceroy Count of Linhares at Goa, 1629-1635," *II Seminario Internacional de Historia Indo-Portuguesa*, p. 312.
18. *Diario*, II, pp. 186, 264-265.
   De Souza, Teotonio, "Embassies and Surrogates: Case-Study of a Malacca Embassy to Siam in 1595," *Indica*, Vol. XXVI, nos 1-2, 1989, p. 42. Paulo Reimão of English or Dutch descent, had been acting as an intermediary between the Viceroy and the President of the Surat-based English East India Company, William Methwold.
19. *IOL, Pombal Collection*, 1/3/147, vol. 525, pp. 97-98.
20. Boxer, Charles, *Francisco Vieira de Figueiredo, a Portuguese merchant-adventurer in South East Asia, 1624-1667*, p. 34.
   SASJ, *MR* no. 28, fl. 250. Governor D. Rodrigo da Costa had written to the King on 24 January 1690 mentioning that the non-Portuguese Jesuits in China were paid by the Portuguese Crown to harm its interests and to work in favour of other countries. He was referring to the French Jesuits (*MR* 5, fls. 105-111).
21. AHU: India, *maço* 27.
22. *Gazetteer of the Bombay Presidency: Thana*, ch. VII, p. 484.
23. Gense, James H., *How Bombay was ceded*, pp. 57, 60, 63-65.

24. Foster, William, *The English Factories in India: 1661-64*, p. 216.
25. AHU: India, *maço* 21, 20 July 1731.
26. *Ibid., maço* 46, doc. 17, 16 December 1731.
27. *BFUP, LM*, no. 4 (1595-98), p. 422. Lisbon, 28 February 1596; *MR* 4, fls. 27-634.
28. *Diario*, II, p. 186.
29. *ACF*, VI (43-47), codex 1164, fl. 196v. 6 June 1646; V, fls. 187r, v, 18 May 1641. In 1641, the Council had discussed a petition of the Superior of the Jesuits to free his men from the duty of looking after the forts in the North. They concluded, however, that the priests had shown much zeal in keeping the places well-provisioned and guarded and they should continue with their work.
30. De Souza, Teotonio, "Afro-Asian Church in Portuguese Estado da India", *ICHR*, XXI, n. 2, Dec 1987, p. 106.
31. Boxer, *The Christian Century in Japan 1549-1650*, pp. 231-236.
32. Meilink-Roelofsz, *Asian Trade and European Influence*, p. 131.
33. *DI*, XV (1588-92), pp. 455, 459-460.
34. ARSI: *Goa* 22, 16 August 1632; *DR*, Bk. 15, docs. 4, 99-102, 186-188, 268-273; Abranches Garcia, José I (ed.), *Archivo da Relação de Goa*, século XVII (1601-40), docs. 265, 324.
35. Souza, Francisco de, *Oriente Conquistado a Jesu Christo pelos Padres da Companhia de Jesus da Provincia de Goa*, II, p. 93. There was a residence for the sick on the Mount of Our Lady of Rosary. It went over to the Professed House from 1585. The latter got its permanent site at the *Terreiro dos Gallos* (The Cock's Field) at Old Goa.
36. Cummins, J. S., *Jesuit and Friar in the Spanish Expansion to the East*, p. viii.
37. *Ibid.*, p. 28.
38. *DI*, XVI (1592-94), pp. 158-159.
39. *ACE*, IV (1659-95), doc. 110, pp. 270-274. The see had been vacant for twenty-three years. For differences between him and the Jesuits: Nazareth, Casimiro C., *Mitras Lusitanas no Oriente*, I, pp. 176, 184.
40. Leopoldo da Rocha has well described the running battle between the Jesuits under Provincial Fernão de Queiroz and the Archbishop Antonio Brandão in his *As Confrarias de Goa (sèulos XVI-XX)*, pp. 176 ff. He calls it the controversy of *jus visitandi*.
41. AHU: *maço* 5, 23 December 1725.
42. *Ibid., maço* 11, 17 March 1727.
43. *Ibid.*, 5 January 1727.
44. *Ibid., maço* 37, doc. 7, 26 February 1693.
45. *Ibid., maço* 44, December 1731.
46. ARSI: *FG*, 1443/9, file 23; *Goa* 22, I, fls. 59-65 is a tract written by a Jesuit to disprove the accusations made against the priests of the College of St. Paul's.
    Borges, Charles, "Foreign Jesuits and Native Resistance in Goa 1542-1759," *Essays in Goan History*, pp. 69-80.
47. *Ibid.* The Provincial went on to describe the faults of the native Brahmin priests who were dark-skinned like the people they served. They gave no alms to the people, and were foreigners themselves since they descended from Brahman.
48. De Souza, Teotonio, *Medieval Goa*. Appendix A-4, pp. 225-229. Pedro Alvares Pereira is described as an intelligent, practical and expert official in Indian affairs based on a report by Viceroy Count of Linhares to Portugal on 6 January 1630 (DAAM: *MR*, 13A).
49. *DR*, Bk. 14, doc. 82, 87-90. There were also complaints against the Franciscans in Bardez and the Jesuits in Salcete. *DR*, Bk. 13, doc. 112, 27 March 1620.
50. DAAM: *Ordens Regias*, no. 2, codex 1492, fls. 49v-50. The Viceroy's letter is dated

28 January 1633.

51. AHU: India, *maço* 5, 10 January 1759.
52. *Ibid., maço* 6.
53. *Ibid., maço* 21, 20 July 1731.
54. *Ibid., maço* 9, 20 March 1726. The King had ordered the Viceroy to work out the restitution of the image and the Fathers had done so.
55. Almeida Calado, Adelino A. de, "A Companhia de Jesus na India em meados do século XVII," *Studia*, no. 40, 1978, pp. 351-366. The document is dated 13 December 1666.
56. AHU: *maço* 41, 17 January 1734.
57. *DI*, XVI (1592-94), pp. 276-278, 281-282.

6

JESUITS GLOBALLY

Many and varied were the activities of the Society of Jesus in their Provinces other than Goa and India. They worked hard and ingeniously to swell funds for their mission-needs. Their zeal saw them labouring in their colleges and residences and on their farms in Brazil and in Paraguay, in Asia and in Africa, in America and in Mexico. Their income came from the sale of sugar, of slaves and of livestock from their plantations and ranches.

They had their enemies in the process. They were traders generally who resented both their cornering of their profits and their efforts to uplift the people socially and economically. While their activities affected the economies of the places they worked in and for, they invited resentment against themselves. Some believed their transactions were at times greater in scope than those of other companies.[1] Yet, though their efforts were lessons in innovation, they also portrayed stubbornness to the signs of the then changing times.

Different Methodologies

The different Orders among themselves differed on methods of evangelization. The Franciscans wanted to cleanse all native cultures they came across and accused the Jesuits of not preaching Christ crucified. The Jesuits, on the other hand, made plans in Japan, to attract the ruling nobles believing the other groups would then follow.[2] Without demanding a convert's total rejection of his former ways, they tried to understand, accept and christianize the existing society. In India, they recognized the caste system with all its restrictions and inequalities, and allowed the continued practice of some of its rites.[3]

Economic Matters

Their methodological approaches did not prevent them from getting involved in economic matters. The Jesuit rule of prohibiting ownership of property could not keep off the members from devoting much of their labours and attention to their financial concerns. They considered it a realistic approach. Besides, their enviable administrative system won them much more success than for many others in the field. They started off as did the other religious Orders, receiving contributions from their friends and sympathizers. They invested much of it in land, and in the spirit of commercial capitalism, did not always observe the prohibition against interest.

As bankers and enterprisers, they were pioneering contributors. The central headquarters of the Order would come to the aid of any Jesuit Province that would find itself in economic trouble. These economic backings raised many a suspicion and exaggerated idea about the wealth of the Jesuits. The process became an important element in the anti-Jesuit feelings which undermined its position in the world.[4]

Activities in South America

The College of St. Peter and St. Paul traded in over five hundred Negro slaves in the course of the seventeenth century. It entered the slaves in its books of accounts as "items". Its other economic transactions were all a way of building and strengthening the Order's independence, and influence in the social and political fields.[5]

The missions in Brazil and Angola got part of their finances from the sale of sugar, slaves and livestock from their plantations, ranches and other properties. It was also the case of the Spanish missions of Mexico, Peru and the Philippines. Their large economic activities, it was said, surpassed in scope those of the first multinationals, the Dutch and the English East India Companies. The directors of both the Jan Compagnie and John Company were nationals of their respective nations, whereas the same was not the case of the Jesuit Frs. Superior-General at Rome, and the respective Provincials and Superiors in the Provinces. Some nationalities, however, would predominate in certain of the Spanish or Portuguese missions. Certain individual Jesuits occasionally objected to the Society's involvement in trade. Yet the great majority of them being aware of the constraints and hardships of managing their missions, saw no practical alternative to the practice.[6]

They relied on the powerful backing of their legal friends many of whom had once studied at their schools. With their help they came by title-deeds and did not allow questionable clauses to deter them from attaining ends that they felt justified the means. They needed all they could get their hands on in order to maintain their colleges and their missions, some of which were in the remotest parts of the kingdom.[7]

Often what they touched turned to gold. They were able to convert their *pesos* and their gifts, their purchases and their exchanges of land, into large estates and flourishing *haciendas*. They were able to do it by a fine blend of skill, force and calculation. They started with but a little, but it was not before long that they had the largest sheep-flocks, the finest sugar-plantations, and the best-managed estates.[8]

The Jesuit colleges often made use of their friends and other parties in certain negotiations in which they preferred not to figure directly. They were aware that they had no legal rights to acquire land. A certain person who had in 1594 two sheep-farms, made them over to the Society two years later. In 1607, acting as if he was still the owner, he asked for the Viceroy's permission to use them for cattle. He was in this case a dummy for the real owner, the College of St. Peter and St. Paul. Yet despite the opposition of the Indian municipality, the local Mayor approved the conversion of one of the farms. The missionaries did not consider it wrong to raise horses and mules on land which was strictly reserved for sheep.[9]

Brazil

It was in Brazil that the Jesuits developed their economic practice to its fullest. They realized from the start that a development of their lands could best secure the material resources that they needed. They did this so successfully that the royal subsidy came to be of little importance. The College of Bahia received the first grant of land in 1550. By the end of the century, it had grown with thirty more. In 1552 it had twelve heifers, by 1742 its farm of Santa Cruz had 7,658 along with oxen for work, 1,400 horses and 2,000 sheep. The College had developed manioc, and cotton which its inmates could use. It grew sugar and maize, coffee and cocoa, and a variety of fruit and vegetables. It set up also tile and pottery, soap and timber works.

Jesuit economic practice developed without much hindrance. The Portuguese had control of the country, the government was favourable and the manpower sufficient. The climate was favourable too. The extent and success of the farms gave rise to the rumours of abundant wealth, and yet the profits did not turn, as many believed, into silver or gold.[10]

By 1600 there were 172 Jesuits between Pernambuco in the North and São Paulo in the South, and 317 by the end of their stay. The missionaries had set up two hundred missions in two hundred years, besides a dozen colleges, seminaries, other training and recreational facilities. They got part of their resources from the Crown and private benefactors. They used their own initiative and skill to gather more and became reluctant yet active participants in the sugar business of Brazil.[11]

As maintenance subsidy, the Jesuits received iron bars from the Crown which they exchanged for other goods. Since the year 1564 they received annually for the College of Bahia 12,00,000 *rs*. Four years later the Crown promised the College of Rio de Janeiro 10,00,000 *rs*. In 1576, the College of Olinda was to receive 4,00,000 *rs*. but the figure was later doubled. The Colleges needed more, and the Crown allowed three of them in 1604 to collect their stipends in sugar after paying the tithes on the plantations of their choice. On the lands that the Jesuits received for the Colleges of Bahia and Rio de Janeiro in 1550 and 1565, respectively, they planted various crops and fruits like manioc, corn, beans, squashes, European vegetables, cucumbers, lentils, turnips, lettuce, figs, grapes, oranges and lemons.[12]

They had also pastured livestock, for in 1551, Fr. Nobrega had imported a dozen milk cows, horses and pigs. The Superior-General, Fr. Francis Borgia, and the first Provincial Congregation in Salvador in 1568 had objected to the Order's involvement in commerce and trade. Yet a few decades later the objections had almost disappeared.

In the last quarter of the sixteenth-century, the colleges acquired lands either by purchase, exchange, bequest or assignment. By 1598 the lands and buildings of the College of Bahia netted an annual income of 8,00,000 *rs*. with two-thirds coming from royal endowments.[13] The Superior-General, Fr. Claudio Acquaviva had given his men permission in 1590 to grow sugar. Thus, they had five sugar plantations in Bahia, three owned by the local College and two by the College of St. Antão in Lisbon. They had some misgivings too about supervising the plantations and handling the large number of black slaves on them.[14]

One comes across the superior attitude with which the missionaries came to labour in the Brazilian fields. Fr. José Azevedo, writing as Visitor of Brazil in 1556, described their work as necessary "to Christianize the cannibalistic natives and to moderate the rapacity and cruelty of the white colonists and half-breeds, who saw in the Indians only subhuman creatures to be slaughtered or enslaved." He had published a grammar and a dictionary of Tupi, the main language, and a book of sacred poems. From their arrival till their suppression, the Jesuits maintained that they defended the human rights of the Indians whether pagan or Christian and opposed their exploitation.[15]

Contribution in Brazil

They cultivated on a grand scale sugarcane, maize, sesame, beans, runnerbeans, watermelons, melons, many of the vegetables of Portugal, bananas, pineapples, oranges, jackfruit and cashew. They had big plantations of rice, maize, sugar and tea. They made use of new methods of growing rice and used animal and hydraulic power. Cinnamon and pepper were also grown and in 1690, two labourers from India came to Brazil to look after the cultivation.[16]

In 1677 after three years of planting cocoa in Maranhão, there were 2,000 plants worth more than 1,000 *cruzados*. The Jesuits had a monopoly to export wood, but there were reactions from the others to its scale. They had a saw-mill, and a yard for making canoes and small boats. In 1643, they sold 2,200 quintals of wood at 19 *vintens* a quintal. They also constructed frigates for their own maritime use in Brazil.[17]

The Society in its provinces of Maranhão and Grão Para had lime-kilns and pottery-works for products like bricks, tiles, and crockery. They manufactured vegetable soaps. Jesuit-houses had masonries, quarries and factories for iron products like axes, scythes and keys.

The Jesuit hospitals and infirmaries were famous in all the villages, and in 1757, the infirmary of the College of Para was said to have been the only one medical centre in the entire city. It had regular supplies of medicines from Portugal. These were given to the poor, but being free, the rich also availed of them. The priests in 1732 decided that the rich should pay towards the common good. The income that thus came in, helped in keeping a well-stocked infirmary for the benefit of all.

The infirmary of the College of Para occupied two halls with stores and stocks of crystal glasses with remedies, bags and utensils. There were balances, weights, measures, funnels, pounding bowls, ladles, copper containers, copper pots, flasks, grinding stones, cups and utensils. There was an image of Our Lady in each room. Jesuit brothers trained in medicine in Portugal came to serve in these hospitals and infirmaries. They helped not merely in giving medicines, but also in the eradication of small-pox in parts of Brazil. They rendered yeoman service during the epidemic of 1627-28.[18]

The Bishop of Bahia was suspicious of the dealings of the Jesuits. But they had no difficulty in convincing him that they were not involved in trade. They received goods and paid for all their expenses. They sent sugar to Lisbon for sale. With the proceeds they bought materials necessary for their mission in Brazil.[19]

The State in Goa had sent plants to Lisbon. The Crown had informed the Governor D. Rodrigo da Costa that they could be sent instead to Brazil to the Jesuits who were adept at using them to best advantage.[20]

The Province of New Spain

The houses and colleges of the Province of New Spain could avail of a fixed income, while its residences and Professed Houses had to be content with alms. But since the residences found it difficult, they converted themselves into colleges and had both sources of income. They could own farms and ranches, rent out houses and accept mortgages, but could not receive any salary or fees for their educational and pastoral ministries. They found themselves forced to look out for generous founders and benefactors, and to seek the help of civil and religious authorities. Their Superiors in Rome warned them against greed, speculation and personal profit. They gave over the direction of the finances of their colleges to others, and took it up only in cases of necessity. The Crown too was not of much help, and aided them only on their most necessary expenditures. They lived not in luxury but as persons in need.[21]

Africa: Zambezi

A study of William F. Rea (*The Economics of the Zambezi Missions 1580-1759*) discusses the economic contribution of the Jesuits during their one hundred and fifty years' stay in the Zambezi Missions of Africa. Fr. Gaspar Soares became the first Superior of the Mission from 29 November 1609. Jesuit letters and reports were pessimistic about evangelization in Africa, yet to give it up would be a blow to the Crown. The Mission carried on to keep the Crown favourable and to win valuable support for missionary work in other parts of the Portuguese dominions. The Mission had to build itself on a subsistence economy.[22]

The Jesuits had sought to influence the *prazo*-holders and the people of the region. They found the royal grants inadequate, and neither the College of Mozambique nor the Province of Goa could offer them much. Yet, the Jesuit mission on the Zambezi avoided all debt and succeeded in increasing its revenue.

The Dominicans, on the other hand, either ministered largely to the Portuguese or busied themselves in trade much like the other traders. The Jesuits got much of their income from their farms on the left bank of the River Zambezi, and from their share in the gold trade during the last three decades of their presence on the Rivers. The large loans they advanced proved the profits which they made. They were an index of the economic role their missions played during the period. They provided the means which enabled a considerable number of traders to carry on business. Yet, since a number of them defaulted it was doubtful whether the Jesuits made much of a profit. They could not have a widespread or lasting influence in agriculture since the other farmers interested themselves more in trade or in plunder. They managed during the years of their influence to show how better agriculture could gain anyone sufficient profit to provide credit for others.[23]

In East Africa, the Crown promised the Jesuits the stipend equivalent to the pay of two soldiers. But the promise was most often not fulfilled. Their Superiors had allowed them to buy or to accept property to help support their missions. In 1633, the Count of Linhares objected to these means and expected them to pay tithes on the land. The Goa Province had thus to spend 5,000 *xs*. annually on behalf of the College of Mozambique. There were complaints that while the lay people received the lands on the Rivers on a maximum lease of three lives, the religious Orders got the same in perpetuity. The Crown thus lost any claim to its ownership after that.

The Jesuits had instructions from their Superiors to keep ivory of their own lands. They could exchange it either for cloth or other commodities. But ivory from the lands of other people could not figure in their transactions.

The College of Sena could own a light rowing boat to help the Rector visit the houses he was in charge of. It would also be useful to transport the recent missionary arrivals from Quelimane. The College could also maintain a six-ton boat to conduct their dealings with Sena. Their men could draw profit from their own lands, but could not purchase goods for selling at a higher price.[24]

The use the Jesuits made of real property helped them towards a non-reliance on the fluctuating royal stipends and their own economic stability in their missions. Their College of Mozambique and the Zambezi missions received an annual of 250 *cruzados*. Francisco Soares donated nine *pastas* of gold which brought in 5,000 *xs*. a year, and they got another two each year out of the rent of two store-rooms within the fortress of Sena. These rents led some to terming them the greatest house-proprietors in Mozambique. The Rector of the College of Mozambique, Fr. Rodrigo da Estrada, who had had his earlier share of trouble in Goa, involved himself in a dispute with the widow of Gonçalves Guião, who had donated some land to the College. She retained it for herself and gave instead an interest-free loan of 6,000 *cruzados*. The amount was in the ill-fated *St. Tiago* and though she claimed she had made good her promise of giving the Jesuits the money, the claimants believed that she had deprived them of it.[25]

The Mozambique College had a large palm-grove yielding 500 *cruzados* annually. The College owed the Goa Province 2,500 *xs*. It had purchased the island of Kumbarjua in the hope of wiping out its debts, a matter that took thirty years to achieve.[26]

The economic and social influence of the Jesuits had been a check for the lay *prazo*-holders. After their exit, the Crown had to face the difficulties. The Jesuits had 18 *prazos*, around Tete and this formed some of the most valuable property in the whole of Portuguese East Africa. Initially, the *prazos* were difficult, but the Jesuits worked them, promoted agriculture and made them productive. They did not grow cotton since it was a Crown monopoly, nor sugarcane which was the most lucrative crop in Brazil.

The Jesuits had subordinates to help them who were friendly and devoted and when the former were arrested in 1759, the latter were ready to set their masters free, if they could. There were slaves, 710 in all. They worked on gold diggings. The gold industry formed an essential part of the economy. Gold was exported to India where it brought in exchange the cloth the Jesuits needed as currency to buy what they needed.

Ivory was another source of income, and every year three large Portuguese ships with cargoes of it left Mozambique for Goa. Jesuit economy was fairly prosperous to advance loans over a good period of time. The loans were an indication of the economic role they played in the missions. They provided the means for a good number of traders to carry on their business. The terms were easy and did not arouse bad feelings against them. They were the most stable economic element in Zambezia. The subsequent expulsion of the Jesuits was a serious blow to the economic interests of the place.

According to Rea, from an economic point of view the giving of credit was the most important function of the Missions. The Jesuits taught the people that better agriculture was possible, and believed that economic enterprise was an important segment of missionary life. They moved away from the earlier conventional method of gathering people into the mission and feeding them on the basis of a legacy or foundation. The new policy was a combination of body and soul to draw people to the Christian faith. Yet in spite of all their creditable efforts, the Jesuits never adopted an African way of life. Right up to the end of their stay on the Rivers they were Europeans and thought of themselves as such.[27]

Japan

Fr. Alessandro Valignano had considered Japan as the most fruitful field of missionary activity. For him the people were intelligent and cultivated unlike in India where they were base and uncultured. The Jesuits first dressed as Buddhist priests but soon changed them for the silk robes of the scholar. They adopted Chinese ways and gave expensive gifts to the influential. They traveled in sedan-chairs, and had to turn to being merchants and traders to maintain an expensive way of life. They prepared themselves to do everything possible to bring the Gospel to the unconverted.[28]

There were many, including the China Jesuits, who did not approve of the commerce of the Japan Province. Fr. Valignano was ready to give up the trade if 12,000 *ducats* at least came in some other form. He had suggested a landed income in Japan to help them become self-supporting. He needed money for the seminaries, hospitals and elementary schools. Trade was the only means of survival. They did not grow rich on the proceeds and they used the profits for the mission, which had suffered bad debts and other losses.[29]

The Jesuits were involved with the local country traders. One of them, Bartholomeu Vaz Landeiro was a major contributor to the Japan mission and had placed his resources and shipping interests at their disposal. He made sure he did not enter any port with his merchandise where Jesuit transactions were likely to be in danger. He had helped in their participation of the silk trade wherein they got 100 *piculs* of silk a year at an annual profit of about 6,000 *ducats*.[30]

To increase the income of the mission, Fr. Valignano reduced by half the annual contribution of Japan to the Goa Province fund which was then 2,000 *pardaus*. The Province made some money by investing in the silk and gold trade. 50 *picos* of silk yielded about 7,000 *pardaus*. and 6,000 gold *pardaus*. Its annual income was about 14,000 *pardaus*. In 1593, it invested 6,000 *taeis* of gold equivalent to 12,000 gold *pardaus*; 2,000 *taeis* in pearls which was 4,000 *pardaus*, along with another gold investment of more than 10,000 *pardaus*.[31]

Fr. Valignano laid down regulations for things meant for Japan from India. He appointed a Procurator in India for Japan. His duties included collecting and sending the subsidies and revenues, buying and dispatching the things necessary for Japan, and providing for the missionaries going from Goa to Japan. The Rector and Procurator of the College of Malacca had the duty of collecting and forwarding the money and things for Japan without detaining them in Malacca.[32]

The Fr. Procurator had also to collect the rents of the villages of Bassein (Marol, Ponvem, Kondoti, Mulgão, Borbata, Quirol, Moroci), and Taleigão in Goa, the 500 *pardaus* annually from the island of Caranja, and the Crown stipend. The College of Macao got rents from Arem, Mirem, Malvara and Thane (all in the North Province), while the Tonkin mission had income from the villages of Moroci, Sar and Maljaca. He had to buy wine, olives and other necessities. Under no condition could he lend the money of the Japan Province to others. He had to dispatch to Goa all of the disposable annual income from the properties. These came in the form of letters of exchange, currencies and merchandise. These were changed into silver or bullion and sent on to China. Between 1691 and 1735, a total of 1,202,039 *xs.* was remitted to Goa from the properties. Besides, he had to remind His Holiness, Pope Gregory XIV to send the papal subsidy of 4,000 *ducats which his predecessor had arranged for Japan.*[33]

King Sebastian had in 1574 sanctioned 1,000 *cruzados* annually for Japan and this amount was payable at the customs-house at Malacca. Yet the payments were irregular. Thirty per cent of the amount would be lost on exchange when the money was remitted via China. King Felipe of Spain later made an additional annual grant of 1,000 *ducats.* 12,000 *ducats* came from the revenue of Jesuit landed property in India, while the expenses were about 12,000 *cruzados* annually.

Fr. Valignano while under many constraints in 1578, entered into a mercantile contract with the merchants at Macao. Of the 1,500 *picos* annually shipped to Japan by Macao, 50 belonged to the Japan Province. Profits amounted to about 6,000 *ducats* annually. This together with amounts from Malacca, India and Europe totalled 12,000 *ducats.* Mercantile trade, some Crown payments and the capital transfers from the rental and agricultural properties in India together with the administration of donations and legacies from Macao were the main sources of income.[34]

Their expertise in managing donations and legacies won them many more. In 1636, Fr. Paulo dos Santos gifted them 12,000 *taeis* for the foundation of the seminary for the Japanese, Francisco de Figueiredo and his widow gave 11,728 *taeis* in 1680 for the foundation of a college, and 10,000 *taeis* came in from a contract between the Jesuits and Nicolão Fuimes and his widow.[35]

Fr. Valignano had asked for a papal authorization enabling the Province to lend money at 10 per cent interest. The local usurers charged as high as 70 to 80 per cent. The new rate would benefit the Christians and help to win more converts. They wanted the maximum loan to be six *cruzados*. The profits would help towards the construction of hospitals for the *samurai* and nobles, and the setting up of banks for poor Christians.[36]

The Visitor in his supplementary report of 1592 mentioned that numerous *daimyo* wanted the Jesuits to act as bullion-brokers in their business. Some of them started in a small way exchanging silver for gold in China. The Jesuits aware that the favours they would give would in turn bind the *daimyo* to them, played their part in the business between Canton, Macao and Nagasaki. Fr. Visitor allowed his men a maximum of 6,000 *ducats* a year. But the trouble involved and the gift-giving raised the cost of the Japan mission to 12,000 *cruzados annually.*[37]

The Jesuits were indispensable as linguists and had the right contacts in high places. They played an important part in the silk trade and sent cargoes to Nagasaki under other names after their expulsion in 1614. Their mission moved on the profits in the trade with Macao.[38]

The Chinese emperor in Peking gave the Japanese a tiny permanent base in Southern China and agreed to trade silks for silver. Japan had silver in abundance. The trade flourished, the middlemen grew rich, and the Jesuits became a vital link in the trade. They were the only ones who managed to speak Chinese and Japanese, and therefore could act as negotiators and interpreters. As trade increased they became more essential. The yearly trade was huge and touched the life of the *samurai*. They tolerated the Jesuits, and the spread of their religion lest they sailed away and the trade suffer.[39]

Ieyasu admired the commercial skill of the Jesuit-interpreters, and in 1602, appointed Fr. João Rodriguez as his agent at Nagasaki. He helped financially the Jesuits with 350 *cruzados* when they lost their annual silk investment in the Macao trade due to the Dutch capture of it in 1603. He wanted them to foster his foreign trade and to act as his intermediaries. They were the only capable linguists for the smooth running of the trade between the Japanese and the Portuguese.[40]

In 1608, the Vatican allowed the Dominican friars to work in Japan. Six months earlier, the Crown in Madrid had forbidden religious Orders to trade. The injunction was aimed at the Jesuits who made known their difficulties to manage the mission without the promised Crown help.[41]

The squabbles with the Spanish Dominicans had destroyed the Jesuit economic power. The Portuguese merchants entered into trade with Japan, the Japanese traded abroad in their own ships and the Dutch and the English came to Japan too. The English spread the fear that the missions were military posts for the conquest of Japan and this led to the end of Christianity in 1614.[42]

Macao, Manila and Nagasaki were each obscure in the mid- sixteenth century till they rose to positions of thriving commercial cities and Catholic missionary-centres fifty years later. Nagasaki for a few years was the sole domain of the Jesuit mission in Japan. But unlike the Spaniards, the Portuguese Jesuits concerned themselves equally with commercial and missionary interests.[43] There were strong pressures from Portuguese traders to prevent any danger to their commercial activities from the missionary activity. It worked as long as the respective interests did not clash. When they did, the traders usually scored.[44]

Some accused the Jesuit trade in Japan of being worth 2,00,000 *ducats* a year. But the Jesuits maintained that it was a twentieth of that figure. A Jesuit would usually help in the discussions at the College at Macao with Chinese merchants over the price of silk. The Superior-General, Fr. Vitelleschi had objected to the practice and asked that a more secluded spot for a warehouse be chosen. The Japanese and Portuguese used the Jesuits as their interpreters, and the latter traded on a large scale in secret.[45] The ship *Our Lady of Conception and St. Dominic Suriano*, belonged jointly to the merchant Francisco Vieira de Figueiredo and to the Jesuits, and carried Chinese gold and musk.[46]

The Jesuits in Macao had a substantial share in the trade of silk for silver with Nagasaki. They sent consignments to Japan even after their expulsion from the island in 1614. The loss of their revenues in the later 1730s in India, forced them to rely on finances from maritime-trading investments. This had affected the Macao country trading.

The Jesuits had all along involved themselves in trade and finance as partners and competitors with country traders. They were investors and stood at an advantage with their funds from their Indian sources. Their Procurators in their transactions used third parties, trustworthy laymen as their authorized agents. The rules expected the Procurators to have a natural talent for their post, to have few business associates, not to lend silver or other valuables, nor to employ anyone who offered to serve out of friendship or free of charge. They had to take care to assay the fineness of silver when buying bullion. Their superiors had to refrain from giving them unlimited latitude, yet neither had they to restrict their drive.[47]

China

When Fr. Trigault arrived in Europe from Asia in 1615 and published his account of China there were many offers from all over the continent. But the patrons of the China Mission feared that a large number of foreigners would enter their sphere of interest and jeopardize their working.[48] The Jesuits began their stay at China with their involvement at the Imperial Court. Their efforts were more successful and lasting than those of their colleagues in Japan. In China, they helped the various embassies of the Dutch, and Fr. Ferdinand Verbiest functioned as interpreter in Chinese and Manchu during these meetings. The 1679 trade concessions Macao received were largely his work.[49]

With their considerable influence at Court, the Jesuits had introduced the Emperor to many facets of European culture and science. Fr. Thomas Pereira made musical instruments teaching the elements of western music to members of the court and to the Emperor himself. He and his group worked on the court's love for clocks, fancy fountains and mechanical toys. They tried their best to comply with the Emperor's request for a western physician since a physician according to them would have a closer rapport with the Emperor than an astronomer would. A study of the atlas which they brought reveals their important contribution to China and to the cartographic knowledge of Europe.[50]

The Jesuits had their own reasons for helping the Dutch as they had earlier helped the Portuguese. They also tried to weaken the Dutch foothold in the China trade lest the competition damage Macao. They did their manoeuvring rather covertly since they were held to be reliable and impartial translators for the Dutch, the Portuguese and the Russians, and could not appear too obvious in their scheming.

The Jesuits best handled trade negotiations since they were often at Court and had their own developed connections and friendships. They had long realized that their presence in China would work only if based on a policy of accommodation and understanding with the members of the Ming Court. It led to the translating into Chinese of the Christian doctrine and western science. They became an integral part of the civilization they worked in, and could communicate with the people in their own language and in terms relevant to their culture.[51]

Result of Involvements

The activities of the Jesuits in some of the Portuguese dominions show their deep involvement in their cultures and economies. The involvement was varied and peculiar to each of the regions of work. In the process, the scope of their transactions gave rise to exaggerated fears of their wealth. The projects they worked on while benefiting some, drew many others against them. Their critics overlooked their innovations, and sought their eviction, an idea that became a reality in 1759.

REFERENCES

1. Boxer, Charles, *Portuguese India in the Mid-Seventeenth Century*, p. 50.
2. Boxer, *The Christian Century in Japan 1549-1650*, pp. 231-236.
3. Scammell, Geoffrey, *The World Encompassed: The first European maritime empires c. 800-1650*, pp. 285-286.
4. Morner, Magnus (ed.), *The Expulsion of the Jesuits from Latin America*, pp. 6-7.
5. *Ibid.*, pp. 102-103.
6. Boxer, *Portuguese India.*, *op. cit.*, p. 50.
7. Morner, *op. cit.*, p. 98.
8. *Ibid.*, p. 98.
9. *Ibid.*, p. 99.
10. Rea, William F., *The Economics of the Zambezi Missions 1580-1759*, pp. 53-54.
11. Alden, Dauril, "Sugar planters by necessity, not choice: The role of the Jesuits in the cane sugar industry of Colonial Brazil," *The Church and Society in Latin America*. pp. 139-170.
12. *Ibid.*, pp. 140-141.
13. *Ibid.*, p. 141.
14. *Ibid.*, pp. 143-144, 156.
15. Brodrick, James, *The Origin of the Jesuits*, pp. 227, 229.
    Francisco Davila (1573-1647). a Spanish priest, during a sermon preached to the Indians of Peru in 1646 said, "It is because of their prior faults that God has begun to chastize the Incas, making them die and the *runas* (Indians) along with them. And God has not done that simply by chance; he hs done it with his very great insurpassable knowlege. The whites have been the *alguazib* of God. They have come for that purpose." Comby, Jean and MacCulloch, Diarmaid, *How to read Church History*, vol. 2, London, 1989, p. 73.
16. Leite, Serafim, *Historia da Companhia de Jesus no Brasil*, IV, pp. 156-157.
    Antony, Philomena, "Missionary Expansion: Cultural and Agricultural Contacts between Colonial Goa and Brazil," *Discoveries, Missionary Expansion and Asian Cultures*, ed. Teotonio de Souza, 1994.
17. Leite, *op. cit.*, pp. 158-159, 162-163.
18. *Ibid.*, pp. 189-191.
19. Caeiro, José, *Jesuitas do Brasil e da India na persuguição do Marques de Pombal: século XVIII*, p. 41.
20. *BFUP, LM*, n. 53 (1687-89), doc. 104, p. 93.

21. Zubillaga, Felix, "La Provincia Jesuitica de Nueva Espana su Fundamento Economico: siglo XVI", *AHSI*, XXXVIII, pp. 3-167. *passim*.
22. Rea, *op. cit.*, p. 47.
23. *Ibid.*, pp. 171-174.
24. *Ibid.*, pp. 57-61.
25. *Ibid.*, pp. 61-66.
26. *Ibid.*, pp. 77-80.
27. *Ibid.*, p. 80; Zubillaga, *art. cit.*, pp. 3-167 *passim*.
28. Cummins, J. S., *Jesuit and Friar in the Spanish Expansion to the East*, pp. 42-43.
29. Boxer, *The Christian Century*, pp. 120-121.
    Souza, George B., *The Survival of Empire: Portuguese Trade and Society in China and the South China Sea, 1630-1754*, pp. 34-36. The Jesuits were ship-owners though they preferred to be part-owners of the shipping in which they invested with different country-traders.
    One of them, Francisco da Gama exported merchandise from India on his own account and freighted for others cotton and silk piece-goods and silver bullion on behalf of the Jesuits and the Portuguese.
30. Souza, *op. cit.*, p. 37. At Macao, the Crown administrators and country traders resented the Jesuit diplomatic and economic talents believing their funds were immense. In the late seventeenth and first half of the eighteenth centuries, however, their funds were relative in comparison to the capital resources of the Asian merchants (p. 189).
31. *DI*, XVI (1592-94), p. 520.
32. *Ibid.*, p. 95
33. *Ibid.*, pp. 96, 99-100, 106; Souza, pp. 191-192. According to Prof. Souza from 1684 to 1754 there was a shift of emphasis from revenues on maritime trading loans to proceeds from rents from villages owned by the Japan Province in the North Province of India.
34. Boxer, *op. cit.*, pp. 117-118; *DI*, XIV (1585-88), p. [illegible]; Souza, p. 190.
35. Souza, p. 191.
36. Boxer, *op. cit.*, pp. 203-204.
37. *Ibid.*, pp. 112-114.
38. Boxer, *The Great Ship from Amacon*, p. 12.
39. Clavell, James, *Shogun*, p. 59.
40. Boxer, *The Christian Century*, pp. 182-183.
41. Boxer, *The Great Ship from Amacon*, p. 71.
42. Scammell, *op. cit.*, pp. 286-287.
43. Boxer, "A note on the triangular trade between Macao, Manila and Nagasaki, 1580-1640," *Terrae Incognitae*, p. 51.
44. Noonan, Laurence A., *The First Jesuit Mission in Malacca: A Study of the use of the Portuguese trading centre as a base for Christian missionary expansion during the years 1545 to 1552*, p. 3.
45. Boxer, *The Christian Century*, pp. 243-246.
46. Boxer, *Francisco Vieira de Figueiredo, a Portuguese merchant-adventurer in South East Asia, 1624-1667*, p. 56.
47. Boxer, "Macao as a Religious and Commercial Entrepot in the 16th and 17th centuries," *Acta Asiatica*, pp. 71-72.
    Souza, pp. 192-193, 227. The Procurator was a man of commercial acumen who oversaw the collection of rents, the sale of agricultural goods, and the payment of taxes.
48. Cummins, *Jesuit and Friar*, p. 28.

49. Wills, John, E., *Embassies and Illusions: Dutch and Portuguese Envoys to K'ang-hsi, 1666-1687*, pp. 237-241.
50. *Ibid.*, pp. 1-61; Witek, John W., *Controversial Ideas in China and in Europe: A Biography of Jean-François Foucquet, S.J. (1665-1741)*, p. 5.
51. Wills, *op. cit.*, pp. 1-61, 122, 126, 164-166. The China Jesuits had entertained two very powerful officials by giving them presents in the Ambassador's name: a clock for Mingju and gifts which the Macao and Canton Jesuits had sent for Songgotu.

7

BACK HOME:
The Suppression of 1759

There was no one who could stop the Marquis of Pombal. He had worked to have the Society of Jesus supressed, and the Jesuits went home in disgrace having lost all they had struggled for and lived for. Many sighed in relief, for the unexpected did happen. The hope of the State was to earn much and thus to boost the sagging Portuguese economy and trade. It did get a sizable amount, but eager grabbing and lack of proper recycling of assets dashed hopes of a grand economic resurgence. More energy was spent in discrediting the Jesuits than in using the money and properties they had left behind.

The Jesuits had also themselves to blame. They had gained much yet had alienated themselves from the people they worked for. When the suppression took place, there were few who rallied to their cause and rescue. They returned home with none of the power and authority they had once wielded.

The Marquis of Pombal

Sebastião José de Carvalho e Mello (1699-1782), was a man of a remarkable physical physique and iron constitution. Portugal's Ambassador to London in 1738, he was much impressed by English commercial prosperity and maritime power. In 1745, he mediated a dispute between the Pope and the Queen of Hungary and Bohemia. Five years later, King José appointed him as Minister of War and Foreign Affairs. He won his fame for his handling of the Lisbon earthquake of November 1755, and found himself at centre stage of Portugal for the next 22 years.

He was largely responsible for the suppression of the Society of Jesus and for the confiscation of its assets in the Portuguese territories. Yet his previous behaviour towards the group appeared so very different from his later actions. He had always admired the Society and had paid special attention to it. He had thought himself a great Jesuit. He would dress his son in the garb of the Society and would parade him as a young apostle. When he fell out of favour with the King because of his coarse manners at court, he had begged the King's confessor, Fr. José Moreira, to plead on his behalf, which the priest did with great vehemence. He defended the Marquis as the minister beyond compare in all of Europe. The defence succeeded, but the meddling with things outside the sphere of one's duty had its most drastic consequences.[1]

The Marquis' hatred for the Jesuits grew stronger. He attacked them with motives which were difficult to fathom and to criticize. Frs. J. Carbone, José Moreira and José Ritler had all been close to him. Yet, in September 1757 he dismissed the Jesuit confessor of the King and prevented the others of the group from entering the court. He convinced Pope Benedict XIV of the need of suppressing the Society of Jesus. An attempt on the King's life on the night of 3 September 1758 was a pretext for him to do likewise in the Portuguese dominions. By January of the following year, he had confiscated all its goods.

His Reasons

He was convinced that the Jesuits were the primary opponents of his political plans. He believed that they were fomenting opposition among the Amerindians and halting some of the stipulations of the Treaty of Madrid of 1750. The Queen Mother had urged them in Brazil to report to her in confidence any instance of misgovernment. The Jesuits indiscreetly had denounced Governor Xavier de Mendonçào Furtado, the brother of the Marquis. When the latter discovered the informants, his hostility knew no bounds.[2]

The exit of the Jesuits, the Marquis felt, would help towards the much-needed reform in education. He next associated himself with the eminent people of his day, Ribeiro Sanches, D. Francisco de Lemos, and João Pereira Ramos e Cenaculo. He also invited from abroad men of learning and culture to the universities of Portugal.

He accused the Society of Jesus in Portugal of sedition and war against the government in America, of illicit trafficking, and of conspiracy on the King's life in September.[3] His three-volume *Deducção Chronologica e Analitica* (Chronological and Analytical Deductions) in 1767-68, was based on historical documents and State papers to prove that all of

Portugal's economic, political, social and religious ills were directly or indirectly the work of the Jesuits there. He forced the interpretations that one finds in the volumes, and went to absurd lengths to see that it was widely and truly read in the country.[4]

For many in Portugal and elsewhere, the Marquis was a combination of a depraved mind and a political genius bubbling with energy.[5] Some considered his reforms too hastily conceived and not sufficiently based on reality. Yet, his reforms were far-reaching for he had abolished slavery, had removed the colour-bar, reformed the teaching in the Universities, established monopolistic chartered companies, brought about changes in public finances and had tried to put a halt to the anti-Semitism of the day.

Goa: September 1759

The King's edict of 3 September 1759, asked for the disbanding of all the Jesuit forces in the East. The Viceroy, Count of Ega, Manuel Saldanha e Albuquerque, meanwhile had made plans for the imprisonment and shipment of the Jesuits from their Provinces of Goa, Malabar, Japan and the Vice-Province of China. He had come with a detailed briefing on the coming events, and his curt behaviour towards the Jesuits on his arrival in Goa, showed it. He informed them that he would not deal with them personally.

The Jesuits did have a wind of their imminent fall from grace, but chose to remain at their posts. The Viceroy took on himself the burden of the assault on and the detention of the priests, scholastics and brothers, 84 of whom were at the new College of St. Paul's. His assault on this college resembled a warfront. He had taken extra precautions for an counter-attack from the Jesuits and their servants. He need not, for those he sought succumbed meekly.

The daily regime during the Jesuits' year-long imprisonment consisted of being counted and searched each day, and having guards to oversee all their movements. They could not get into the garden and the continual damp air took its toll on the delicate healths of many. Some of the rigours were hard indeed, and the Viceroy bowed to the entreaties of the other Religious in Goa and distributed the prisoners in the convents of the Franciscans, the Dominicans, the Capuchins and the Augustinians. While the Augustinians added to their cup of woe, the Capuchins were all kindness and compassion.

The Viceroy had made plans to arrest the Jesuits who were in areas in India beyond Portuguese control. He sought the help of the rulers of

Kittur, Sunda and Raichur, each of whom refused to comply. Fr. Albert Zarth of the Kittur mission refused to give up his post. To his Provincial, Fr. Luis Lopes who asked him to do so, he replied that he would have willingly obeyed his dictates had they been given in freedom.[6]

As the octogenarian, Fr. Manuel Figueiredo handed over the receipts and payments of the house and the Province to his captors, he stated that he was the Procurator of a religious Province and not of a commercial society. It is debatable whether he was right in his distinction for the past had shown the Society well immersed in transactions and business.[7]

Expenses for the Deported

The hundred and twenty-seven Jesuits returned to Portugal on board the *Our Lady of Conception* and the *St. Vincent Ferreira* respectively. The State spent 9,144 *xs.* for their provisions and copper utensils. These included rice, biscuits, salt-fish, meat (beef and pork), cereals, salt, vinegar, oil, eggs, onions, ginger, chillies, mustard, cinnamon, tamarind, wine, cheese, saffron, potatoes, native wine, butter, 1,000 hosts and wine used for mass. The special diet cost 1,217 *xs.*, 1 *tga.*, and 40 *rs.* For their assistance there were seven black slaves and one named Paul from Kerala. The captain was Bernard Carneiro de Alcaçar and extra room on an already insufficient deck cost another 3,000 *xs.*[8]

They arrived in Portugal on the 20 May 1761 to be interned in the infamous jails of St. Julião and of Azeitão, not all of them, though, since 24 had died en route. 16 had left the Order, and but for the 45 who were exiled to Italy, the rest languished painfully and hopelessly till their day of release.

Directives of the Marquis

The Marquis of Pombal set about overhauling life after the exit of the Jesuits from the scene. In his directive to the Board of Administration he asked it to cut down on all the unnecessary expenses on the feasts in the Jesuit colleges. The Crown had decided to abolish the confraternities the Jesuits had established in their churches, and to discontinue the celebration of their feasts. The Archbishops would decide how best to celebrate the services in their former churches with decorum and without pomp. There would be a single chaplain and a sacristan in each of them to maintain a certain order and to oversee the respective properties which the King wished to retain in case of need.[9]

He had earlier discussed with the Board of Royal Revenue matters regarding the income and expenditure of the Jesuits, the former being 5,41,124 *xs.*, 3 *tgs.*, and 15 *rs.* on 31 December 1769, and the latter 3,20,800-0-00, with a balance of 2,20,324-3-15 and an error of 3,841-1-04.[10]

There were separate entries for the amounts spent for the feasts of Francis Xavier and Francis Borgia at the Jesuit churches. They discontinued the celebrations later. He allotted the Chapter at the Professed House 4,386 *xs*, 3 *tgs.*, and 14 *rs.*[11]

The Marquis had hoped to enrich Portugal with the property and money of the Jesuits. He instructed the Board to send to Portugal the gold, silver, and the pawned articles of the sacristies. He asked them to retain the crowns, chalices and patens necessary for the services. He wanted the impressive images safe in Portugal to avoid the greed of the plunderers in Goa.[12]

He wanted the Board to conduct an auction of all the items of the Jesuit houses and churches. The latter would be released of all obligations in keeping with his directive of 24 March 1772.[13] The auction netted 75,809 *xs*. which came in from pawned articles, from interests on loans, and from 15 *maticais* of gold from Mozambique.[14]

The Marquis cautioned the Board of Revenue to be careful in drawing up the accounts of the confiscated properties of the Jesuits. His carefulness in studying the returns showed in his observation that a sum of 439 *xs*. was 200 in excess, while a figure 522 *xs*. was 100 in arrears. The total for the debtors ought to have been 8,95,999 *xs.*, 1 *tga*. and 39 *rs*. and not 8,96,099-1-39.[15]

In Goa, the Count of Ega, carried out faithfully the dictates of the Marquis. It is coincidental that he too left Goa later in disgrace. His detractors imprisoned and blinded him on his return to Portugal, and he was forced to spend the last years of his life in ignominy. The charges against him were that he had misspent the money from the confiscation, had abused his authority and squandered public money, and had showed disrespect for the King by working against Crown interests.[16]

The Marquis of Angeja had informed the Board of Administration of the Revenue that the sale of Jesuit properties had not proceeded as his predecessor had hoped for, since the people did not have ready cash to pay for them. He hoped he would be able to execute the wishes of the Crown regarding their sale.[17]

He mentioned that thirteen cases containing gold and silver articles of the Jesuit churches along with a list dated 4 March 1777, had arrived on the *Santissimo Sacramento* and the *Our Lady of Paraizo* under the command of Captain Miguel Rodrigues Colaço. The articles, he believed, were not part of the articles which were earlier confiscated and taken to Portugal. He had decided to return the above cases to the Board on 28 March 1778 in the *Our Lady of Conception* under the captaincy of Joaquim dos Santos e Andrade.[18]

Cleansing Operations

In Goa, the Marquis was not merely interested in removing the physical presence of the Jesuits from the scene, but sought to remove all traces of their influence in religion, education and morals. He branded them as rebels, traitors, and enemies of the public peace in the kingdom, and of the common will of the faithful. They had created, he maintained, distinctions between the foreigners and the natives, and between the Brahmins and the Chardos. They had changed the original motives of the College of St. Paul's, and he hoped to revert the Seminary to its former state.[19]

He introduced fresh statutes for the natives and the clerics at St. Paul's. He fixed the number of admissions to one hundred. The students would receive their instruction in their native tongue, and would be under a Board consisting of the Archbishop, the Viceroy, the Captain General, the Inquisitor and the Inspector of the Treasury. They would censor all Jesuit teaching-material and would introduce the books the Oratorians had written and the grammars whose cost the Royal Exchequer had met. Latin would be one of the subjects. There would be a chair of rhetoric and another of Christian morals. The works of Sts. Thomas and Augustine would be on the syllabus with a total exclusion of all Jesuit-written books. They would invite some to teach who would stay, however, not at the College, but at their own respective convents. There would be classes in the history of the conquest of the East, and ecclesiastical studies, too, based on the text-books of Natal, Alexandre Fleury, and Bossuet.[20]

The King had in his letter of 4 April 1761, praised the Oratorians for their work and had trusted that they would fill the void after the exit of the Jesuits. He had informed the Count of Ega that all the goods of the Jesuits belonged to the Treasury and the Royal Chamber.

He grouped these into three categories. The first consisted of the immovable goods (not directly connected with the church services), items of commerce, houses and money lent to people without any terms. He wanted the officials to show consideration while recovering loans, and declared debts older than five years as written off. There would be an auction of the movable items of only the colleges and houses both in Goa and in Lisbon.[21]

The second group were the Crown and temple properties given to the Jesuits and consisting of fields, salt-pans, palm and areca groves. The instructions mentioned constant care and inspection of these. The villagers were to have them in proportionate plots on rent, and would have to pay the dues regularly. They had to replace the trees that were dead. The properties were many, and the College of Rachol alone had 311 of these.

The third group dealt with the lists of landed property connected with chapels for the saying of masses and performance of pious works. The Crown wanted a list of these together with details of the donors, the obligations and money involved, the annual income, and suggestions for the use of possible surpluses.

The Crown would inform the State of the manner of expenditure of the above money. The Board in Goa, meanwhile would have to pay the salaries of the guards and watchmen of the Jesuit college and church properties.

The Later Religious

The Crown reminded the other religious that their bad behaviour had lost them their place on the Bombay islands. No longer could they blame the Jesuits for their present ills since the field was solely theirs to labour in be it Propaganda or Padroado. They would need to rely on their own virtue rather than on any Crown compulsion. Religious superiors would have to train men with no temporal ambitions but a pure zeal for souls. Failing this, they would suffer the same fate as the Jesuits or the Franciscans, in Bombay. The former had their wealth, while the latter their many scandals.

It was for reasons such as these that the Crown considered re-establishing the College once begun by Miguel Vaz and Fr. Diogo de Borba, and starting a house for the Oratorians. They would have a building and a church, and would receive the property and income of the College of Rachol as maintenance. The new house would attend to the missions of Mysore, Kittur, Raichur, Sunda and the Bhonsle kingdom. The Board of Missions would supervise their working, withdraw permissions to it if necessary, and dispatch missionaries elsewhere. There would also be a new college for secular clerics at Rachol with Oratorians as teachers.[22]

Nicolao Francisco, the Prefect of Studies and Superior of the new College, informed the King about the usefulness of his own instructions to the students. He blamed the Jesuits for all the past disorders. The new studies rightly based themselves on the views of the Marquis. The Jesuits had harmed many by intrigues, fanaticism, superstition and slavery. They taught poorly, admired the banned *Bulla de Ceia* as if it was a pontifical law, and lectured on the suspect theories of fanaticism and probabilism. He on the other hand, taught doctrinally despite the opposition of all, Oratorians included, and had decided to leave. Yet, he hoped the Crown would maintain forever the greatness of the College.[23]

The Board of Administration

The Count of Ega had suggested that the State could put the wealth of the Jesuits to good use. Many could get jobs and the Board of Administration itself would need to consist of men of confidence who would work methodically and usefully. One of the articles of the Board described the functions of the ministers, the officials, the President, and the two deputies. The meeting had to be on the fixed day of the week. The duties of the President would be to promote the good administration of the Board, and to carry out the orders of the Crown. He would have to attend all the meetings, shoulder the duties not done by others, and act while the Board was not in session. A majority vote would decide issues, with his personal vote ranking higher than those of his Deputies.

The rules urged the Deputies to offer advice on any matter necessary for good administration and had to make their proposals known at the meetings. They had to appoint other officials, check their work, and clear the accounts. The secretary had to complete the register, the representations of the Board, write the resolutions, read the applications of private parties, keep the minutes of the sessions, check the accounts of expenditure and income of the Board, maintain a list of both the pawns and money given on interest to businessmen, issue letters of appointment to various officials, and make copies of instructions and regulations.

The Procurator had to be a capable person and well conversant with the law should he have to defend the interests of the Board. He had to collect the relevant information from the archives of the colleges. The Treasurer of the Board had to state the income, keep an account of the books, inventories, original intentions of the funds and their later change, maintain in a separate box the income of each college, keep separate boxes for the pawns of private persons, and preserve a box with the keys of all the above boxes, and the three keys of this box.

One or more ministers would oversee the public auctioning. The

Board would have to make a collection of all the capital and confiscated goods of the Jesuits in Goa, or in Daman and Diu. It had to appoint writers, beadles, and minor officials to help in the secretarial and collection work. It had also to appoint administrators for the various properties and residences. The Board had to do its utmost to fulfill the plans of the Crown. It had to provide for the missions and for the priests working there. It had to observe the details of the pious endowments, and take care of the colleges, houses and residences, especially during the rainy season. It would also have to pay a stipend of one *xe.* a day for each of the Jesuits then in the various convents till their deportation, for their food and medical expenses. It would pay the convents for expenses they incurred, and give salaries to the Negroes and servants at the Jesuits' service.

The Board had to provide for the Seminary and for the College of Rachol. It had to auction the properties of the College in public once each year, and the fruits to the highest bidders, especially when market prices were high. It had to return the articles which the people had entrusted to the college for safe-keeping, whenever they showed the receipts for them. The infirmaries of the Colleges of Rachol and of St. Roque had been very useful for all, and the Board would have to appoint suitable people to run them.[24]

The Windfall, but Unproductive

In South America, except for their well-built colleges, the Jesuits had none of the secret mines or hoards of silver and jewels that the royal investigators had hoped to discover. All that was found was the vast sugar estates, ranches and shops. But, by the early 1780s, all the Jesuit sugar plantations were sold in exchange and eventually lost.[25]

At Goa, the money which the State received from the Jesuits was soon to disappear as quickly as it had come in. 50,000 *xs.* went towards the manufacture of two frigates at Daman, 65,925 *xs.* for the purchase of 366 *khandis*, a loan of 40,584 *xs.* to the Royal Treasury for payments to the military garrison with a further 27,000 *xs.* for the same purpose. The other amounts which the Royal Treasury applied to itself from the Confiscation were 16,546 *xs*, 3 *tgs.* and 28 *rs.*, 18,453-1-32, and 12,088-4-35, the latter amount for the construction of a new boat at the Daman docks. But it turned inadequate and a further sum of 30,000 *xs.* helped towards its final completion.[26]

Jesuit Intolerance

Jesuit intolerance was one of the reasons for their downfall. The people in the sixteenth-century Goa reacted strongly to the violence and despotism of the Viceroys, to Jesuit intolerance, and to the horrors of the Inquisition. The Religious, when they could no longer draw large revenues from the State of India, reacted unfavourably to the government legislation under which they had accumulated wealth, and even opposed it.[27]

The Jesuits in Goa received a taste of the rough deal that they sometimes meted out to their subordinates. They found themselves summarily removed from their houses and colleges, places they had built and nurtured with much care and concern. They were the first to experience the venom of antagonism from their foes which affected in the course of the following decade their colleagues in other parts of the world.

Few were those who saw any good in them. The rest eagerly either grabbed their wealth, or sought to undo all their influence and impress in matters of faith and culture. The alienation which the Jesuits had gradually brought between themselves and the others, had eventually evoked hardly any sympathy for their cause.

REFERENCES

1. Weld, Alfred, *The Suppression of the Society of Jesus*, p. 10.
2. Sergio, Antonio, *Breve Interpretação da Historia de Portugal*, p. 123; Cummins, J.S., "The Suppression of the Jesuits 1773," *History Today*, 1973, pp. 839-848.
3. Sergio, *op. cit*, p. 268.
4. Boxer, Charles, *The Portuguese Seaborne Empire 1415-1825*, p. 191.
5. Sergio, *op. cit.*, p. 124.
6. Humbert, John, "Catalogus Patrum et Fratrum Societatis Iesu ex India anno 1760 expulsorum," *AHSI*, XXXI, pp. 324 ff.; Meersman, Achilles, "The Expulsion of the Jesuits from their Kittur mission in India," *NZFM*, pp. 221-224; Bacelar e Oliveira, José P, "Arrest, Spoliation and Exile of the Goa Jesuits according to Father Caeiro's *De Exilio*," *Indo-Portuguese History: Old Issues, New Questions*, pp. 123-132.
7. Caeiro, José, *Jesuitas do Brasil e da India na perseguição do Marques de Pombal: séulo XVIII*, p. 659. Pp. 628-941 deal with the ordeals the Jesuits faced in the Goa Province during the turbulent months following September 1759.
   Leite, S., *Historia da Companhia de Jesus no Brasil*, IV, p. 179, mentions that Governor Melo de Castro in his letter of 5 July 1760 valued the confiscated wealth of the Society of Jesus in Brazil at a mere 2,000 *cruzados*; Ferroli, D., *The Jesuits in Malabar*, II, pp. 490-521.
8. AHU: India, *maço* 99. See Appendix 25 (Jesuits Bound for Portugal: Expenses in 1760).
9. *DUP*, V, p. 96. Letter of 27 February 1776.

10. *Ibid.*, pp. 46-47. Letter of 8 April 1772.
11. *Ibid.*, pp. 146-147, 2 April 1778.
12. *Ibid.*, p. 94. Letter of 26 February 1776.
13. *Ibid.*, pp. 67-68.
14. *Ibid.*, pp. 75-76.
15. *Ibid.*, p. 104. Pombal fell from royal grace after the death of King D. José who died on 24 February 1777. The Marquis of Angeja replaced him as Inspector General of the Treasury.
16. *Ibid.*, pp. liii-liv.
17. *Ibid.*, p. 148.
18. *Ibid.*, pp. 164-165.
19. AHU: India, *maço* 93, 2 April 1761.
20. *ibid.*, *maço* 93.
    Martires Lopes, Maria Jesus dos, "Teaching Methods in Goa (1750-1800): Jesuits and Oratorians," *Discoveries, Missionary Expansion and Asian Cultures*, ed. Teotonio de Souza, 1994.
21. *Ibid*, *maço* 91, 16 March 1757.
22. *Ibid.*, 4 April 1761. Francisco Xavier de Mendonça Furtado signed the letter.
23. *Ibid.*, *maço* 91.
24. *Ibid.*
    Appendices 23, 26 and 27. They deal with the various Jesuit properties that came to the State as a result of the Suppression. While no. 23 mentions the income of each of the major Jesuit houses of the Goa Province in 1759, no. 26 tabulates some of the amounts that came in between 1759 to 1760 from rents and sale of produce of properties. In no. 27 one finds lists of the varied land-acquisitions the banished Society had.
25. Alden, Dauril "Sugar Planters by necessity, not choice: The role of the Jesuits in the cane sugar industry of colonial Brazil," *The Church and Society in Latin America*, p. 159.
    DAAM: codices 1727-28, 2041 deal with the confiscated properties of the Jesuits.
26. DAAM: codex 2549 (*Bens confiscados aos Jesuitas 1770-85* - Confiscated Properties of the Jesuits 1770-85), fls. 1-7.
27. Henry Heras, "The Decay of the Portuguese Power in India,", *The Journal of the Bombay Historical Society*, p. 3.

8

CONCLUSION

The other religious Orders too had their own histories to tell, but according to some, they have never been as interesting as that of the Jesuits. Or scandalous. The Jesuits came initially in a trickle to Goa but within the two hundred years of their stay, they had become a mighty force. Few could handle or control them. Their Generals and Provincials cautioned them through their various briefs, but a good number of them went their own way. For they believed the scene was different in India and warranted a special economic order.

Many a Viceroy and Governor pleaded helpless in dealing with them, while the local population accepted their lot hoping for better times. The numerous petitions sent to the Crown either by the Overseas Council, the clergy or the people, attest to the unhappy relations the Jesuits largely had with all. With a good liaison they would have been able to win over the men who mattered, to their side.

Finally, a bold and drastic stroke from the Marquis of Pombal got them away from harm's way back to the places from which they came. His move had a mix of personal vendetta and of a desire to improve the state of Portugal's economy. The Jesuits had heralds to wish them on their departures in Lisbon. But only an imprisonment in the infamous jails of their own land awaited them on their return.

A Look-Back

The Jesuits wrote at regular intervals on themselves and their activities to their Superiors in Rome. These were often a "pat-in-the-back" for themselves. There were treatises and compositions, too, which usually turned out to be their weapons of attack on the philosophies and religions of the day. They sang the glories of their triumphs, showed the pain of injustices they suffered at the hands of the State and the people, and believed in their unique role in converting the land to the Christian faith. Others wrote about them too. Strange, but their accounts most often described the Jesuits as cheats, incorrigible and a blot on the scene. Nowhere do we come across writings by Jesuits which showed them accepting such criticism for what it was truly worth. They pointed out defects in their descriptions of each other, but rallied to a man when the attack sprang from outside on them.

The Province of Goa maintained regular audits of its own accounts for each of its houses. Since these were an internal matter with no checks by outsiders, many believed the figures just did not match the wealth which they believed they had. The difference between their income and expenditure usually appeared very thin. Yet the Province had enough and more to lend amounts at interest rates of between five and ten percent. The State and village communities drew big sums, while individuals availed of small amounts, too. There was much money around. It was not without cause that the State believed that the eviction of the Jesuits from the scene would bring an economic relief to all around.

The scene had not been much different in Jesuit missions in other parts of the world. The reports that came into the Portuguese courts and offices for the good part of two centuries convinced the government that the Jesuits had to go. While it cited many causes, the economic stranglehold on everything was perhaps the major reason for the Jesuit downfall.

Jesuit Workings

The very nature of the Jesuit organisation made the group in Goa a powerful force. Intercontinental legislation and help brought the group closer together. Their national rivalries remained, but they did not prove a threat to their working and success.

Their men at the helm were trustworthy according to the dictates of the Order's Constitution. They occupied their seats after a lengthy period of testing and training, and one comes across no case of a Goa Superior bringing irreparable discredit to the intentions and cause of the Order.

The duties of gathering money and building the faith, went hand-in-hand, literally, and many were the Provincials who had served earlier as Procurators of their respective Provinces. The knowledge of the economic foundations had made them better aware of the needs and expectations of the mission they were heading to serve.

Result of the Suppression

The State and some of the people were the immediate beneficiaries of the suppression. The former offered loans or settled unpaid wages. It wrote off bad debts, and made it lighter for those who had been victims of Jesuit overlordship. It helped avert an economic dead-end. But what the Marquis had overlooked was that the State could never be a sufficient match for the organizational acumen of the Jesuit Order. The money that came in by way of public auctioning of properties, sale of pawned goods, return of loans and the interests, income on fruits and coconuts, soon disappeared into non-productive expenses. The windfall had come, but disappeared as quickly as it had come.

In the regions of South America and Africa, the eviction of the Jesuits saw a gradual degeneration of their properties and lands that had seen better and enormously more fruitful times. For the Jesuits had loved their lands and used them to full advantage.

When the State and other religious Orders failed to effect their hoped-for economic resurgence after the Jesuit exit, they stressed more on the supposedly harmful intellectual and moral teachings of the religious. But it was these very matters they had praised during better economic times for all.

The Jesuits had overlooked the writing on the wall. Their reluctance to accept any criticism had shielded them from coming to the rescue of those who suffered. They could have helped in reducing their own economic control, and thus offset the antagonism that built dangerously against them. When they had to go, there were few who wished dearly they had not.

9

BIBLIOGRAPHICAL AND ARCHIVAL ESSAY

The present essay is on the bibliographical and archival information on the history of the Society of Jesus with special reference to the Province of Goa. The Provinces of Malabar, Japan and the Vice-Province of China were for long part of the Goa Province. Its members had studied or worked in it and often returned to it for help or rest. Some of the studies that follow contain references to the other Provinces though primarily dealing with the Province of Goa.

Works by Jesuits on Jesuits

Fr. John Correia-Afonso has stated somewhere that the Jesuits have been "the best critics of their colleagues' work". Yet Jesuits have often been most apologetic about their own work as Prof. Charles R. Boxer has pointed out with reference to S.G. Perera and Ernest Burrus (Jesuit Historical Institute, Rome) in his reviews of their studies. In the case of the latter writer he warns the readers of his then recent work for its "200% Jesuit standpoint and his cavalier dismissal of all criticism of the Society, however justified" ("Macao as a Religious and Commercial Entrepot in the 16th and 17th Centuries").

Much is written about the Jesuits from various angles covering the different regions they worked in. One could usefully refer to Laszlo Polgar for a list of writings by Jesuits and on Jesuits. He has published the *Bibliography of the History of the Society of Jesus*, I, *Sources and Studies for the History of the Jesuits*, and *Bibliographie sur L'Histoire de la Compagnie de Jesus 1901-1980*, I, *Toute la Compagnie*.

For the purpose of the present study concentrating on the Jesuits in Goa, I have not taken up for mention in this essay general works which though good in themselves contain only a marginal treatment of the Society of Jesus in Goa.

A necessary reading for a Jesuit point of view of their activities during the sixteenth to the eighteenth centuries are Alessandro Valignano's *Historia del principio y progresso de la Compañia de Jesus en las Indias Orientales (1542-64)*, ed. Josef Wicki, Rome, 1944; Luis de Guzman's *Historia de las Missiones que han hecho los Religiosos de la Compañia de Jesus, para predicar el sancto Evangelio en la India Oriental y en los Reynos de la China y Japon*; and Sebastião Gonçalves' *Primeira Parte da Historia da Companhia de Jesus nos reynos e provincias da India Oriental*. Also indispensable are Francisco de Souza's *Oriente Conquistado a Jesu Christo pelos Padres da Companhia de Jesus da Provincia de Goa*, Vol. 1, and Fernão Guerreiro's, *Relação Anual das coisas que fizeram os Padres da Companhia de Jesus nas suas missões*, Vol. 1.

Anthony D'Costa's, *The Christianisation of the Goa Islands*, is a scholarly and interesting work and is useful for its information on the evangelical activities of the Goa Jesuits at the initial stages of its activities in India, and also for its impact on the society in Goa. Some like Prof. Boxer have criticized it as too apologetic ("apologia pro domo sua", *Bulletin of Oriental and African Studies*, n. 29, 1966, pp. 399-401).

John Correia-Afonso's *Jesuit Letters and Indian History: 1542-1773* proves quite extensively the value of Jesuit accounts and letters for the writing of Indian history. Several of his later writings also dwell on Jesuit history: "Indo-American contacts through Jesuit missionaries"; "Indo-Portuguese History in Jesuit Archives"; *Letters from the Mughal Court: The First Jesuit Mission to Akbar (1580-1583)*, and "Documents of the First Jesuit Mission from Goa to the Great Mughal." Fr. Joseph Velinkar has two well-documented articles ("Francisco Aranha, Builder of Salcete Churches;" and "Jesuit Educational Style in Sixteenth Century Goa.")

Pride of place for information on Jesuit history in India goes to the late Fr. Josef Wicki. The eighteen volumes of *Documenta Indica* he has edited since 1948 (some with the co-editorship of John Gomes) contain much valuable information from the Jesuit official correspondence in the sixteenth century for the Indian Provinces of the Society of Jesus. They are largely culled from the Jesuit Archives in Rome or from the Directorate of Archives, Archaeology and Museum at Goa.

I also found very useful for this study some of his many articles like "Der Bericht des Jesuiten Provinzials von Goa an die Königliche Akademie der Portugiesischen Geschichte" (The Information of the Jesuit Provincials of Goa to the Portuguese Royal Academy of History); "Die Anfange der Missionsprokur der Jesuiten in Lissabon bis 1580" (The Beginnings of the Jesuit Mission Office in Lisbon since 1580); and "Dois Compendios das Ordens dos Padres Gerais e Congregações Provinciais da Provincia dos Jesuitas da Goa, feitos em 1664" (Two volumes containing orders of the General Superiors and the Provincial Congregations of the Jesuit Province of Goa compiled in 1664).

Among other writings on and from a largely Jesuit angle have been those of Henry Heras, *The Aravidu Dynasty of Vijayanagara*; "The Decay of the Portuguese Power in India"; "Three Catholic Padres at the Court of the Ali Adil Shah I"; and *The Conversion Policy of the Jesuits in India.* Henry Hosten has many articles on the Jesuits, particularly in their missions in North India. Two of them are "Mirza Zu-l-Qarnain, a Christian Grandee of three Great Mughuls, with notes on Akbar's Christian wife and the Indian Bourbons"; and "List of Jesuit Missionaries in Mogor (1580-1803)".

I have drawn much from the very authentic accounts and lists of John Humbert, "Catologus Patrum et Fratrum Societatis Iesu ex India anno 1760 expulsorum," (Catalogue of the Fathers and Brothers of the Society of Jesus expelled from India in 1760); "The Goa Archives in 1963"; "Some Answers of the Generals of the Society of Jesus to the Province of Goa. Acquaviva - Vitelleschi 1581-1645"; and "Some Answers of the Generals of the Society of Jesus to the Province of Goa from Carrafa to Tamburini 1647-1726."

Domenico Ferroli's two volumes on *The Jesuits in Malabar*, and *The Jesuits in Mysore*, contain much varied yet useful information for the Malabar Province and the Mysore mission respectively. James Gense has concentrated on the Jesuit presence in Bombay in his *How Bombay was ceded* and in his two articles on their properties ("First Confiscation of Jesuit Properties in Bombay".

S. Noti writes interestingly on the indefatigable Jesuit missionary who survived the suppression, in *Joseph Tieffentaller SJ - a forgotten Geographer of India*. Cornelius Wessels describes the intrepid Jesuit adventurers in *Early Jesuit Travellers in Central Asia 1603-1721*. They were all part of the Goa Province and set off eventually to labour in its northern missions.

Teotonio de Souza has commented on several unsavoury aspects of Jesuit involvement in the rural life of the sixteenth and seventeenth centuries Goa, in "A Pious Hindu commemorates in marble the activities of the Paulistas in Kumbarjua"; and in his book, *Medieval Goa*. Correia-Afonso in a review (*Sunday Standard*, Bombay, 11 May 1980, p. 8) has commented on the writer's determination not to let the Jesuits off the hook too lightly, and refers to the author pointing out to some of the measures the Jesuits took in Goa such as helping the villagers against rural indebtedness.

De Souza has also discussed Jesuit involvement in the over-all context of the Portuguese *Estado da India* in some of his later contributions like "Spiritual Conquest of the East: A Critique of the Church History of Portuguese Asia (16th & 17th century)"; "Records in Portuguese on Shivaji's South Indian Campaign and its impact on the people"; "Afro-Asian Church in Portuguese Estado da India"; and "Re-writing the History of the Society of Jesus in India: Questions of Facts and Relevance."

Jesuits in India: In Historical Perspective (Macau, 1992), a book of papers presented at a seminar under the same theme and which he has co-edited with me, contains incisive articles on "Why Cuncolim Martyrs? An Historical Re-Assessment", "Marques de Pombal and the Jesuits of Goa", "Racial Tensions of the Society of Jesus in India before 1759", and "Records on Jesuits in Goa Archives". *Discoveries, Missionary Expansion and Asian Cultures* (New Delhi, 1994), edited by Teotonio de Souza, analyses colonial strategems and the colonial legacy.

One can have information on the Suppression in 1759 from José Bacelar e Oliveira's "Arrest, Spoliation and Exile of the Goa Jesuits according to Father Caeiro's *De Exilio*". Worth reading is the original *Jesuitas do Brasil e da India na perseguição do Marques de Pombal: século XVIII* (The Jesuits of Brasil and India during the time of the persecution of the Marquis of Pombal - eighteenth century), by José Caeiro.

Jesuit Presence in Indian History, edited by Anand Amaladass, is a collection of essays describing Jesuit activities in India, particularly in southern India on the occasion of the one hundred and fiftieth anniversary of the new Madurai Mission of the Society of Jesus. The general mood was in the words of one contributor "to celebrate the return of the Society to India" (p. 7). An insightful article by Teotonio de Souza suggested a new view-point for Jesuit historiography taking into account the people and their economic exploitations. Chiranjivi J. Nirmal's "Some Issues in Jesuit Historiography" (pp. 41-48) pointed to the need and ramifications of a 'subaltern' level at recording Jesuit history and communicating it.

Josef Schütte's *Valignano's Mission Principles for Japan*, is an informative study on the second Jesuit Visitor of the Goa Province. It deals much with the Japan mission yet the first of the two volumes has much of consequence to Goa. He describes well the near-abrasive manner of

Valignano's activities and his determination to continue in the face of much opposition from his Portuguese colleagues.

Francisco Rodrigues' *A Companhia de Jesus em Portugal e nas Missões: Esboço Historico - Superiores - Colégios 1540-1934*, has a lot of information on the Provinces of Goa and Malabar respectively. It contains lists of Generals, Visitors and Provincials which are generally correct.

William F. Rea's *The Economics of the Zambezi Missions (1580-1759)* has been a seminal work for an economic study of the Jesuit missions in Zambezia. He has probed well the material basis of the success of the missions though the study tends to highlight one-sidedly the Jesuit ingenuity against the locals. As Mozambique and the Sena formed part of the Goa Province, the work contains precious references to the investments of those regions in Goa.

Further afield, a study by Prof. Dauril Alden, a specialist in Portuguese Brazil at the University of Washington, (though not a Jesuit) on the South American Jesuit possessions, is along similar lines. We eagerly await his findings, and one of his several articles ("Sugar Planters by necessity, not choice: The role of the Jesuits in the cane sugar industry of colonial Brazil") indicates the type of tabular analysis he has excelled in. Stanford University Press (USA) is soon to publish his *The Making of an Enterprise: The Society of Jesus in Portugal, her Empire, and Beyond, 1540-1750*. At the James Ford Bell Lectures (May 1992), he spoke on "The Making of an Elite Enterprise: The Jesuits in the Portuguese Assistancy, 16th to 18th centuries".

Other Writers on the Jesuits

These writings fall into the two broad categories of praise and of condemnation of the Jesuits and their works. In the introduction to his edited work *The Livro da Seita dos Indios Orientais (Brit. Mus. Ms. Sloane 1820) of Father Jacobo Fenicio, S.J.*, Jarl Charpentier singles out the Order for its pioneership in modern scientific research.

J. Cummins in *Jesuit and Friar in the Spanish Expansion to the East* discusses the antagonisms between the two main religious Orders in the East, and the fallout of this for the evangelical enterprise. His analysis here and in an earlier article "The Suppression of the Jesuits, 1773" shows his admiration for the Order while pointing out to some of its flaws. The Count of Linhares both admired and hated the Jesuits. Anthony Disney brings this out forcefully basing himself on primary sources in his "The Viceroy

Count of Linhares at Goa, 1629-1635."

There has always been a lively interest in the Jesuit missions to the Mughal Court. One can read with interest Francis Goldie's *The First Christian Mission to the Great Moghul*; C. H. Payne, *Jahangir and the Jesuits*; and Edward Maclagan, *The Jesuits and the Great Moghul*. Father Felix produced a scholarly article on "Mughal Farmans, Parwanahs and Sanads issued in favour of the Jesuit missionaries," in *Journal of the Punjab Historical Society*.

Arnulf Camps' *Jerome Xavier SJ and the Muslims of the Moghul Empire* has a very interesting analysis of the usefulness of the Jesuit missions at the Mughal Court. It delves deeper into the third mission, and on the literary merits of the Jesuits during their stay there. Michael N. Pearson in his recent *The New Cambridge History of India: The Portuguese in India* mentions that the vast Mughal chronicles of the period contain only very scattered and rather deflating mentions of the Jesuits or of the Portuguese. When they do appear, they are not seen as at all unusual (p. 125). This comes in contrast to the general Jesuit assertion of the uniqueness of the Order's presence in the Mughal empire.

Tikiri Abeyasinghe has some pointed comments on the Jesuit bias in their writings in "History as Polemics and Propaganda: Some aspects of Fernão de Queiroz' *Conquista*." He echoes Prof. Boxer who thought the Eurocentric-minded work of Queiroz was a massive and ill-digested work.

Two useful articles I consulted in *Studia* were Jean Aubin's "Le Orçamento do Estado da India de Antonio de Abreu (1574)" and Adelino de Almeida Calado's "A Companhia de Jesus na India em meados do século XVII." Both contain budgetary details and enable us to get an idea of the State support to the works of the Society of Jesus, as well as the overall financial status of the Jesuits at the time.

Prof. Boxer with his thoroughness for detail and literary charm has written extensively on the Jesuits, and on the whole very sympathetically too. His *The Christian Century for Japan 1549-1650* is an authoritative work as is his *The Great Ship from Amacon*. In his *The Church Militant and the Iberian Expansion 1440-1770*, he provides a quick survey and assessment of the relative performance of the different religious Orders in the Portuguese empire. While praising the dedicated hard work and excellence of the Jesuit functioning, he also makes his point that the Jesuits were involved in slavery, colour discrimination, large-scale trading and had a capacity to irritate the other religious Orders by their "complacent arrogance" (p. 71). It explained, he believes, that the dissolution of the Society in 1759-73 aroused little protest and outspoken indignation in the

Roman Church as a whole (*Ibid*).

For a list of Jesuit properties at the time of their suppression, one could consult Francisco X. da Costa's edited work *Legados Pios que oneram os bens situados nos concelhos das Ilhas, Bardez, Salcette e Mormugão do distrito de Goa pelo Chantre Francisco Xavier Vaz* (Pious Obligations connected with the properties in the talukas of Ilhas, Bardez, Salcete and Mormugão). The more authoritative list, however, is available in the *Boletim do Governo* (Bulletin of the Government), 1862, nn. 3-11, pp. 18, 23-5, 30-1, 33-5, 41-2, 52-4, 64-6, 75-7, 85-6. They appear under the sections *Relação das Fazendas* (List of Properties).

Travel Accounts

Most of the travellers to Goa in the sixteenth-eighteenth centuries described their contacts with the Jesuits which ranged from favourable to condemnatory. One can find their comments in *Travels in India by Jean-Baptiste Tavernier Baron of Aubonne*, *Viagem de Francisco Pyrard de Laval*, *Early Travels in India (1583-1619)*, John Fryer's *A New Account of East India and Persia*, Niccolao Manucci's *Storia do Mogor or Moghul India 1653-1708*, *The First Englishmen in India*. Ram C. Prasad's *Early English Travellers in India* describes the political schemes of the Jesuits at the Mughul Court.

Bibliographies with References to the Goa Jesuits

P. S.S. Pissurlencar's *Roteiro dos Arquivos da India Portuguesa (1955)* is the best reference to the Jesuit records at the Directorate of Archives, Archaeology and Museum, Goa. Josef Wicki and John Correia-Afonso have mentioned useful sources in their articles in *Indo-Portuguese History: Sources and Problems*. Georg Schürhammer has a very exhaustive study on Indian historians in his book *Francis Xavier: His Life, His Times*, II, India (1541-1545), pp. 606-677. The volume has much of interest for a study of the Goa Jesuits for the period he covers.

Felix Zubillaga and Walter Hanisch have a valuable work on published material of the Monumenta Historica Societatis Iesu in *Guia Manual de los documentos historicos de la Compañia de Jesus de los cien primeros volumenes, que tratan de los origenes de la Compania, de San Ignacio, sus compañeros y colaboradores, legislacion, pedagogia y missiones de Asia y America* (1971).

Published Primary Sources

There are varied references usually to Jesuit excesses *vis-a-vis* the local population in *Archivo da Relação de Goa* (Archives of the Goa High Court); *Boletim da Filmoteca Ultramarina Portuguesa*, nos. 1-44; *Diario do 3º (sic) Conde de Linhares, Vice-Rei da India*, vols. 1-2; and in *Documentação Ultramarina Portuguesa* (DUP), vols. 3, 5. Vol. 3 of *DUP* deals with the Jesuit missions in India and has letters from the Mughul court by the Jesuits posted there (pp. 3-291), while vol. 5 has references to the Marquis of Pombal's directives to the Board of Administration in Goa dealing with the confiscated goods of the Jesuits in 1759.

Pissurlencar's edited works *Assentos do Conselho do Estado* (Proceedings of the State Council), vols. 1-5, contain minutes of the State Council authorizing Jesuits to act as their envoys to the neighbouring kingdoms either in matters of trade or peace.

Primary Sources

Goa

For an economic study of the Goa Province of the Society of Jesus the bulk of the data is available at the Directorate of Archives, Archaeology and Museum, Goa. Codices 2098-2100, 2465 and 2660 under the section *Colégio de Bom Jesus* (College of Bom Jesus) contain accounts for the same for the years 1712-1791. *Colégio de S. Paulo* (College of St. Paul) has codices 651, 663, 818, 1220, 1932, 1941, 2107-13, 2359, 2364, 3026, 4515, and 7593-4 for the years 1566-1757; *Colégio de Rachol* (College of Rachol) has codices 824, 1865-6, 2048-9 for the years 1569-1757; *Convento de Bom Jesus* (Convent of Bom Jesus) has for the years 1657-1772, the codices 1958, 2097, 2114, 2116, 2118, 2465, 2493, 2529. *Jesuitas* (Jesuits) for 1664-1806 has the codices 833, 859, 864, 1209, 1945, 1960, 2041, 2549, 2552, 2557, 2570, 2475, 2484, 4514, and 7602.

The Property Inventories (*Tombos*) for the years 1518-1845 are under the codices 629, 659, 3026, 3069, 7593-4, 7598, 7600-1, 7646.

An analysis of a few of the above listed volumes will give an idea of the range of the material for an economic study:

818: *Propriedade do Colégio de S. Paulo 1707-1711* (Property of the College of St. Paul 1707-11) deals with the income from temple lands the College had. 72 folios.

838: *Contas do Administração de terras de Salcete por Manoel Lopes*

Pereira anno 1770 até 1777 (Accounts of the Administration of Salcete by Manoel Lopes Pereira 1770-77). 139 folios. Contains lists of income and expenditure of different palm-groves which once belonged to the Jesuits.

1202: *Receita e despeza dos Padres Jesuitas 1687-1740* (Income and expenditure of the Jesuit Fathers 1687-1740). 180 folios. Contains accounts of the *Casa de Bandora* (House of Bandra).

1203: *Livro da receita e despeza dos Padres Jesuitas 1693-1756* (Book of income and expenditure of the Jesuit Fathers 1693-1756). 169 folios.

1727: *Contas do Confisco 1759-70* (Accounts from the Confiscation 1759-70). 167 folios.

1728: *Contas correntes do confisco 1770* (Accounts from the Confiscation 1770). 159 pages.

1859: *Junta da Real Administração 1765* (Board of Administration 1765). 51 folios.

1865: *Livro de arrematações de coco e bate de Rachol 1759* (Book of auction of coconuts and paddy of Rachol 1759). 90 folios. 1866: *Balança geral da receita e despeza do Colégio de Rachol dos bens de raiz, moveis, penhores, escrituras de dinheiro de juros, obrigações dos devedores e embarcações que os Jesuitas possuiam 1760* (Account of income and expenditure of the Rachol College of real estate, goods, pawns, loans, obligations which the Jesuits possessed 1760). 156 folios.

1939: *Balanço da Receita do Confisco da cidade de Goa 1780 (Income from the Confiscation of Goa, 1780). 77 folios.*

1945: *Lembrança dos artigos recebidos do Reino pelos Jesuitas 1709-1742* (Account of materials received from Portugal by the Jesuits 1709-1742) is a continuation of the above volume. 128 folios.

2014: *Balanço da Junta da Administração 1765-66* (Statement of the Board of Administration 1765-66). 49 folios.

2030: *Consignações de confisco 1804* (Allotments from the Confiscation 1804). 110 pages. Contains lists of priests who received amounts under particular houses.

2031: *Balanço Geral do Confisco 1771* (Statement of the Confiscation 1771). Its 123 folios state that a sum of 2,25,819 *xs.*. 4 *tgs.* and 47 *rs.* were in a box at the start of 1770.

2039: *Receita e despeza de Juarim 1749-59* (Income and expenditure of Juarim 1749-59). 184 folios.

2041: *Receita dos bens confiscados 1759-60* (Income from the confiscated properties 1759-60). 86 folios.

2043: *Receita e despeza da casa de Quelossim 1725-43* (Income and expenditure of the House of Quelossim 1725-43). 242 folios. Has monthly details.

2048: *Livro da receita e despeza do Colégio de Santo Inacio de Rachol 1724-30* (Income and expenditure of the College of St. Ignatius of Rachol 1724-30). 219 folios.

2049: *Despeza começada em Setembro 1747* (Expenses started from September 1747). 376 folios.

2074: *Despeza da Junta da Real Administração 1765* (Expenses of the Board of Administration 1765). 133 folios.

2088: *Receita e despeza dos Jesuitas 1684-92* (Income and expenses of the Jesuits 1684-92). 242 folios.

2089: *Receita e despeza dos Padres Jesuitas 1706-55* (Income and expenditure of the Jesuit Fathers 1706-55). 40 folios.

2090: *Receita e despeza dos Jesuitas 1692-1707* (Income and expenditure of the Jesuits 1692-1707). 242 folios. Useful for its prices of commodities the Jesuits used and the wages they paid their workers.

2091: *Receita e despeza dos Jesuitas 1720-62* (Income and expenditure of the Jesuits 1720-62). 188 pages.

2092: *Livro das Receitas e Despezas dos Jesuitas 1707-23* (Book of income and expenditure of the Jesuits 1707-23). 63 folios.

2098: *Receita e despeza do Colégio de Bom Jesus 1724* (Income and expenditure of the College of Bom Jesus 1724). 248 folios.

2118: *Inventario da sacristia de Bom Jesus* (Inventory of the sacristy of Bom Jesus). The 137 folios containing the varied articles give an idea of the wealth of the church and the possible means employed by the Jesuits to gather them.

2475: *Maço de papéis da arrecadação do produto dos bens de Jesuitas 1772* (Bundle of papers of auction of the belongings of the Jesuits, 1772). 122 pages.

2480: *Arrematações do Confisco das Ilhas 1771-1800* (Auctions from the Confiscated goods on the Islands 1771-1800). 47 folios.

2484: *Caderno de pagamento aos Padres Jesuitas que se achavão reclusos no colégio de Populo dos religiosos de S. Agostinho 1759-60* (Book of payments to the Jesuits who were detained at the College of Populo of the Augustinians 1759-60) gives the daily expenses for the Jesuits, and the number of those in detention. 98 folios.

2525: *Balanço Geral da receita do confisco da cidade de Goa 1773* (Statement of income from the Confiscation of Goa 1773). 98 folios.

2549: *Bens confiscados aos Jesuitas 1770-1785* (Belongings confiscated from the Jesuits 1770-1785), contains the money received and the expenses and manner of their disposal by the Board of Administration. 17 folios.

2552: *Jesuitas contra a communidade de Colva* (The Jesuits against the village community of Colva), contains the Jesuit petitions to the Crown at the injustices they were victims of.

2557: *Livro da receita e despeza feita para varios fins pelos Padres Jesuitas desde Fevereiro de 1753 a Setembro de 1759* (Book of income and expenditure for various needs of the Jesuit Fathers from Feb 1753 to Sep 1759).

2559: *Bens da Casa Professa 1760-1772* (Belongings of the Professed House 1760-1772). 146 folios with many unnumbered pages. Volumes such as these are useful to help gauge the extent of the property of the Jesuits. Needless to say they were prepared by the State officials and a comparison can be made of audit accounts by the Jesuits as against those by the State.

2570: *Livro de registo de efeitos remetidos e recebidos do Reino pelos Jesuitas 1664-1708* (Register of materials sent and received from Portugal by the Jesuits 1664-1708) is a useful source to discover the materials and their expenses of the imports by the Jesuits of Goa from Portugal. 90 folios.

4514: *Bens dos Jesuitas 1772* (Goods of the Jesuits 1772). 70 folios.

7600: Tombo de Cottubana de Assolná, Ambelim e Velim 1705-1769 (Land leases of Assolná, Ambelim and Velim 1705-1769). The 276 folios are an important register of the land given on lease to various holders in the villages, the rate of interest and penalties to be incurred.

7602: *Bens da Companhia de Jesus 1758-59* (Properties of the Society of Jesus 1758-59) tabulate the money at the time of the suppression. Running into 135 folios, it contains details of the pawns, title-deeds, obligations and real estate of the former Jesuit houses.

7993: *Penhores do confisco 1783-84* (Pawns from the Confiscation 1783-84). 35 folios. An evaluation of the pawned articles with people who bought them and the prices involved.

England

The British Museum Manuscripts Section has material listed under additional manuscripts (*Add. Mss.*). The following sample will give an idea of the possible use of documentation for Goa.

Codex 1685: Is a martyrology of the sixteenth and seventeenth century Portuguese missionaries.

Codices 6878-9: Relate to the church at Goa and contain a letter of King Sebastian issued in favour of the Jesuits of India in 1572.

Codices 9852-5, 9860: Discuss the Portuguese missions in the East Indies, the Malabar Province, and the Japan mission.

Codices 10,351, 10,359, 10,125, 11,280 deal with the grammars and vocabularies the Jesuits wrote for their work.

Codex 15,197 has a list of Catholics.

The India Office Library, London, has two volumes of interest:

Home Miscellaneous Series, no. 36: A memorial of the Portuguese envoy Visconde de Monte Arcada.

Pombal collection and letters from the Viceroy's translation, vol. 525: A true account of the war by the English against the Portuguese on the island of Bombay.

Portugal

Arquivo Nacional da Torre do Tombo, Lisbon.

Cartório dos Jesuitas, maço (Bundle) 86 contains a libel suit against the Jesuits in Velim, Ambelim and Assolná.

Maço 87 has some documents on St. Paul's, the controversy of the above three-mentioned villages, and the island in the River of Rachol which the Jesuits owned.

Aquivo Historico Ultramarino, Lisbon

Maços da India, nos. 1-93 have material for an economic study of the Goa Jesuits. It contains many of the accusations the villagers in Goa made against the religious on their money and land acquisitions. There are references for other Orders too.

Spain

Biblioteca Nacional, Madrid.

The Mss. I checked were mainly for the missions of China and Japan (nos. 1373, 2361, 2588, 12,930, 20,140, 18,727).

Ms. 1190 is titled *Fortalezas y cidades dela India de Portugal por Antonio Bocarro siglo XVII* (Forts and cities of Portuguese India by Antonio Bocarro, 17th century).

Archivo Historico Nacional, Madrid.

Legajo (Bundle) 249: *Cartas al Padre Ignacio José Gonzalez, Procurador General de Indias, escritas por varios padres, desde al Puerto de Santa Maria, Cadiz y outros lugares sobre los colégios de las provincias de Indias* (Letters to Fr. Ignacio José Gonzalez, Procurator General of the Indies, written by various Fathers from Puerto de Santa Maria, Cadiz and other places on the colleges and provinces of the Indies).

270, nos. 48-241: *Cartas de Santo Francisco Xavier, Cartas las Padres de Provincia de Goa* (Letter of Saint Francis Xavier, Letters of the Fathers of the Province of Goa). Contains a letter from the King seeking information from the Governors on converts and their religions.

271, nos. 1-57: *Cartas al P. Miguel de Amaral, Visitador de Provincia de Goa 1708-09* (Letters to Fr. Miguel de Amaral, Visitor of the Province of Goa 1708-09). Nos. 58-140 have information on the Portuguese and the Spanish Jesuits in Japan and China.

272: *Obras literarias, relaciones historicos, describrimentos del Gran Catayo* (Literary works, and matters on the history and discovery of China).

Archivo General de Simancas, Simancas

Legajo 393, 410, 710-49 (no. 373), 2629, 5035, 6964, 6968-9, contain documents for a history of the Jesuits in South America. 710-49 has information on the transport to Italy of the Jesuits expelled from Spain, the Indies and the Philippines, 6968 on the Jesuits in England, and 6969 on the Jesuit money in English banks.

Italy

Biblioteca Nazionale Centrale Vittorio Emmanuele II, Rome.

Fondo Gesuitico (Jesuit Sources)

No. 1014: *Controversi rituali sulle missioni dei Gesuiti nell' India, sec. XVII* (Controversy on the rituals of the Jesuit missions in India, 17th century).

No. 1364 (3): *Catalogus Episcoporum ex Societatis Iesu in India Oriental 1554-1694* (Catalogue of Bishops of the Society of Jesus in India 1554-1694).

Archivum Romanum Societatis Iesu, Rome

Nos. 22, 23, 27, 34 (1), and 60 entitled *Fundationes Goanae, Fundationes Malabariae, Goana Catalogi Triennales, et Malabar* (Foundations for Goa, for Malabar, the Triennial Catalogues for Goa, and Malabar).

GLOSSARY

adolim: a measure equivalent to 2 seers
aguila: an aromatic wood
almude: a measure equal to 16.8 litres
alvará: a decree issued by either King, Viceroy or government official and valid for a term of one year without royal confirmation
armada: fleet of warships
arrátel: a pound weight
arroba: fourteen and a half kilogrammes
bangaçaleiro: licensed wholesale stockist
bargantim: a small vessel of sails and oars
bazaruco: copper coin equivalent to one-twentieth of a *bargany* which was one-ninth of a *pardau*
boi: palanquin-bearer
boticário: apothecary, pharmacist
cáfila: convoy by sea
camara geral: general assembly of the village communities at the taluka level
canarins: native Christians of Goa (with a pejorative connotation)
cartapácio: manuscript notes
caçabé: Arabic word for seat of the province in India
Casa da India: India House in Lisbon which was the loading and unloading point for goods from Asia
chardo: one of the high castes of Goa
collecta: tax on the import of foodstuffs introduced in 1623 for financing the equipment of galleons to escort grain-bringing vessels from Kanara
confisco: confiscation
confraria: a body for overseeing the religious cult
congrua: royal stipend to clerics
conselho: council
Conselho do Estado: the State Council
Conselho da Fazenda: the Revenue Council
corja: a quantity of twenty items
cottubana: land on permanent lease

cruzado: a Portuguese coin originally of gold in value equal to 400 *rs*. Also valued at about two and a half shillings in the first half of the eighteenth century
curumbi: people belonging to the agricultural caste on the west coast of India (*kunbi*)
daimyo: a Japanese warlord
dom: from the Latin *dominus* (lord).
ducat: its relative value to a *real* was 1:11, while that of a *real* to a *pardau* was 8:1
emphiteusis: a land grant
Estado da India: the Portuguese State of India
fabrica: administrative body of church properties and finances
fazenda: a plantation or an estate
Fazenda Real: the Royal Treasury
finta: tax that the individual Jesuit houses had to pay their Province for the common expenses. It was 4 % of the income of the houses
foral: register of land rights
Fr. Provincial: the head of a religious order who has authority over all the houses of that order in a certain area or province
ganvkar: member of the village community
hacienda: estate with dwelling house or factory
juiz dos feitos: Crown attorney
khandis: measure equivalent to twenty maunds or 480 lbs. wt. (the equivalence of *khandis* was different at different places in India. Also the various European nations had varied equivalences in India)
larim: silver coin equal to 90 *rs*. of Goa
leal: a silver coin also called *bazaruco*. 75 *bazarucos* formed one *tanga*
mahajan : banker or merchant. Also member of a Hindu temple confraternity
manchua : a vessel of three masts and up to 40 tons
manioc: flour made from cassava
matical: a measure of gold dust that fitted into a length of a duck's feather six centimetres long and closed at the end with beeswax
mestiço: person of mixed blood
mezinha : medicine
moradores : temporary residents in a village with no ownership rights
muda: rice fardle
mundkar: bonded labourers generally resident in palm-groves
nachni: *eleusine coracona* (a cereal much used by the *kunbi* caste people to prepare bread and a kind of gruel)

nem: village council's unanimous decision

Novitiate: a two-year period of training on entrance into the Society of Jesus

oitava : a weight measure equivalent to about an ounce

Ouvidor Geral de Crime: Criminal Judge

Padroado Real: Portuguese Crown patronage of religious missions

pagoda : gold coin equal to the gold *pardau* (also referred to as *varaha or hon*)

para : a measure of 20 litres

pardau: a gold coin of 360 *rs*. or a silver coin of 300 *rs*

pataxo : a pinnace of about 150 tons

pedras cordiais: lit. cordial stones. Special medicinal stones prepared by Bro. Antonio Gaspar at the College of St. Paul's (Goa) and an antidote essentially for diseases of the heart

pico, picul: measure equivalent to 100 *catis* or 60 kilos

pipa : barrel

prazo : landed estate in the Zambezi missions

procurator: person in charge of the finances of the Province. He was also the domestic liaison agent for foreign missionaries procuring clothing, books, funds for them

Propaganda Fide: Roman Congregation which directs and promotes the Catholic faith in mission lands.

Provedor dos Defuntos: Purveyor for matters connected with the Dead

Province of the North: Portuguese fortresses and possessions in Daman, Diu and Bassein

real: the lowest denomination of currency in Goa, plural *reis*

samurai: Japanese army officer, military retainer of the daimyos

sanguiçel: a small war vessel

saguates: gifts

scholastic: Jesuit in period of training for the priesthood

socius: assistant

tael: one-sixteenth of a *cati*

tanga branca: had a value of 96 *rs*. in Tiswadi, and 150 in Bardez and Salcete

testamenteiro: executor of wills

thanadar: a native police chief

topaz: an equivalent of *mestiço*. In South India the term was also applied to a native Christian who could speak Portuguese and act as an interpreter

Vedor da Fazenda: Revenue Officer

vintem : Indo-Portuguese base metal coin equal to 12 *rs*.

APPENDICES

APPENDIX I

Chronology

1540: The Society of Jesus establishes itself in Europe.
1542: Francis Xavier and companions land in the city of Goa.
1546: The Province of Portugal comes into existence. Francis Xavier goes to the Moluccas.
1549: The Province of Goa begins its activities.
1550: Printing press comes to India.
1552: Xavier dies on the island of Sancian.
1555: Melchior Nunez Barreto becomes the first Jesuit to enter China.
1557: Jesuits come to Ethiopia.
1560: Jesuit mission at Monomotapa.
1567: First Provincial Church Council at Goa.
1568: Fr. Gonçalo Alvarez appointed the Visitor to India.
1574: Fr. Alessandro Valignano takes over as the next Visitor of the East India Jesuit Missions.
1580: The First Mughal Mission commences with Fr. Rodolfo Acquaviva as head.
1581: The Vice-Province of Japan separates from Goa.
1583: Martyrdom of Fr. Acquaviva and companions at Cuncolim, in Goa
1586: Work begins on the Professed House.
1590: The Second Mughal Mission with Frs. Duarte Leitão, Cristobal de la Vega and Bro. Estevão Ribeiro.
1595: Fr. Jerome Xavier heads the Third Mughul Mission.
1601: The separate Province of Malabar.
1601: Fr. Matteo Ricci enters Peking.
1611: Japan forms an independent Province.
1623: The Vice-Province of China comes into being.
1739: Maratha attack on Salcete.
1741: Jesuits in the entire Portuguese Assistancy number 1,754.
1759: Suppression of the Jesuits in the Portuguese possessions.

APPENDIX 2

Government in the Society of Jesus

- SUPERIOR GENERAL
  - VISITOR
    - PROVINCIAL OF INDIA
      - RECTORS
      - SUPERIORS
      - PROCURATORS
    - PROVINCIAL OF JAPAN
    - PROVINCIAL OF MALABAR
    - V-PROVINCIAL OF CHINA
  - FATHER ASSISTANT

Delegates of each Province elected the Superior-General at a General Congregation in Rome. The Regional Assistants, who formed his advisory council, advised him on all matters, but had no direct authority over the Fr. Visitor or any other office-holders. The General appointed the Visitor.

The Visitor for India had the job of visiting the entire India Province to gauge a picture of the spiritual and material state of the houses and its members. He had to correct abuses and had to inform Fr. General on issues that needed immediate attention.

The Fr. Provincial who held office at Goa for a usual period of five years, could not absent himself from there for a lengthy period of time.

APPENDIX 3

The Goa Province

St. Paul's, Professed House, Seminary of Santa Fé, Novitiate of Chorão, Royal Hospital, College of St. Roque.

Colleges of Margão and Rachol, of Bassein, Thane, Chaul, Daman, Diu, and the Seminary of Bassein.

Bassein parishes of Dongrim, Guirol, Our Lady of Grace, Poncer, Purim, St. Michael, and St. Thomas.

Goa parishes of Chorão, S. André, Santa Ana.

Residences of Bandra, Cambay, Surat, Thane, Tarapur, Corlem.

Salcete parishes of Belem, Benaulim, Betalbatim, Carmona, Chinchinim, Chiquitim, Cuncolim, Colva, Cortalim, Curtorim, Deusne, Loutolim, Majorda, Margão, Mormugão, Navelim, Orlim, Sancoale, Seraulim, Varca, Velção, Verna.

Kanara parishes of Siandor and Pedrure.

Mughal missions at Agra, Kabul, Delhi, Fatehpur, Lahore, Patna, Quetta, Kachur, Sambar, Tibet, Kashmir (Cachemir), Chaprang, Ladakh, Lhasa, Mana and Rodoa.

49 houses in the Deccan, one each at Ormuz, Muscat and Socotro, 15 at Mozambique, 2 at Madagascar, and 39 at Ethiopia.

Source: Carrez, Ludovicus, *Atlas Geographicus Societatis Iesu*, Paris, Georgium Colombier Typographum, 1900, p. 42.

APPENDIX 4

Frs. Provincial of the Province of Goa

Francisco Xavier, Superior	1542-52
Gaspar Barzeus, Vice-Provincial (V-P)	1552-53
Belchior Nunes, V-P	1553-54
Balthazar Dias, V-P	1554-56
Antonio de Quadros, V-P	1556
Gonçalo da Silveira	1556-59
Antonio de Quadros	1559-72
Francisco Rodrigues, V-P	1572-73
Manuel Teixeira, V-P	1573-74
Rui Vicente	1574-83
Alessandro Valignano	1583-87
Pedro Martins	1587-92
Francisco Cabral	1592-97
Nuno Rodrigues	1597-1602
Albert Laercio, V-P	1602
Manuel da Veiga	1602-05
Gaspar Fernandes	1605-09
Francisco Vieira	1609-15
Jacome Medeiros	1615-20
Luis Cardoso	1620-23
Francisco Vergara	1623-26
Valentim de Carvalho	1626-29
Francisco Garcia, V-P	1629-30
Antonio de Andrade	1630-33
Alvaro Tavares	1633-36
Manuel de Almeida	1636-39
Manuel Barradas	1640-43
Domingos Pereira	1643-45
Manuel de Mendonça	1645-48
Tomas de Barros	1648-51
Jeronimo Frois	1651-54
Jeronimo Lobo, V-P	1654-55
Manuel de Souza	1655-56
Antonio de Almeida	1656-59

Miguel de Almeida	1659-62
Estanislau Malpica	1662-65
Diogo Cardoso	1665-67
Antonio Botelho	1667-70
Simão Ferreira	1670-73
Antonio de Matos	1673-74
Bento Ferreira	1674-77
Fernão de Queiroz	1677-80
João da Maia	1680-81
Gregorio Rodrigues	1681-82
Simão Martins	1682-85
Gaspar Afonso	1685-88
Manuel Rodrigues	1688-91
Manuel do Vale	1691-93
Manuel Rodrigues	1693-94
Xavier de Almeida	1694-98
Manuel Barbosa	1698-1700
Antonio de Barros	1700-01
André Gomes	1701-04
Manuel de Carvalho	1704-07
Manuel Saraiva	1707-12
Antonio de Azevedo	1712-14
Inácio de Almeida	1714-17
João Morato	1717-21
João de Olivares	1721-25
Francisco Furtado	1725-27
João Morato	1727-28
Henrique Pereira	1728-31
João Monteiro	1731-33
João Marques	1733-37
Antonio Brandolini, Visitor & V-P	1737-42
André Pereira	1742-45
Valentim de Gouveia	1745-48
Antonio Ferreira	1748
João de Castro	1748-52
Antonio Rodrigues	1752-56
Luis Lopes	1756-60

Frs. Visitor

Gonçalo Alvares	1568-73
Alessandro Valignano	1574-95
Nicolau Pimenta	1595-1613
André Palmeiro	1618-26
Alvaro Tavares	1636-37
Manuel de Almeida	1639-42
Francisco Barreto	1660-64
Alexandre Ciceri	1682-85
Miguel de Amaral	1704-09
Antonio Broglia Brandolini	1737-42

Source: Francisco Rodrigues, *A Companhia de Jesus em Portugal e nas missões*, Porto, Apostolado da Imprensa, 1935, pp. 24-25, 33.

APPENDIX 5

Jesuit Churches

Assolná :	Our Lady of Martyrs (1616)
Rachol:	Our Lady of Snows (1576)
Loutolim:	São Salvador (1581)
Colva:	Our Lady of Mercy (1635)
Verna:	Holy Cross (1568)
Cortalim:	St. Philip and St. Tiago (16th c.)
Mormugão:	S. André (1570)
Velsão:	Our Lady of Assumption (1635)
Orlim:	St. Michael the Archangel (1568)
Margão:	Holy Spirit (1564)
Majordá:	Our Lady Mother of God (1588)
Cansaulim:	St. Thomas
Betalbatim:	Our Lady of Remedies (1635)
Carmona:	Our Lady of Help
Chandor:	Our Lady of Belem (1645)
Chicalim:	St. Francis Xavier (1625)
Chinchinim:	Our Lady of Hope (1590)
Benaulim:	St. John the Baptist (1581)
Cuncolim:	Our Lady of Health (17th c.)
Curtorim:	St. Alex (1597)
Navelim:	Our Lady of the Rosary (1597)
S. Tomé:	S. Tomé (16th c.)
Sancoale:	Our Lady of Health (17th c.)
Seraulim:	Our Lady of Pilar (1635)

APPENDIX 6

Stipends

Stipends for 1542-49	(in *pardaus*)
Japan:	600
Malacca:	600
Daman:	432
Bassein:	400
Quilon:	555, 3 *tgs.*, 20 *rs.*
Cochin:	1,500
Goa:	2,833
Rents of Chorão	919
Rents from temples	1,500
Saguates (gifts)	2,000
Wine (in *pipas*)	5
Olive (in quarters)	1
Gold *pardaus*	100

Governor Antonio Moniz Barreto donated 80,000 *cruzados*, 250 gold *pardaus* and 12 *khandis* of rice.

Besides, amounts were paid to Provincials of Goa and Malabar Provinces (in *xs.*)	50
Father of Christians (in *rs.*)	30,000
St. Paul's (in *rs.*)	890,000
The Church of Margão (in *rs.*)	128,640
Churches of Cortalim, Orlim, Mormugão and Santa Cruz: (in *rs.*)	57,600
Poor of Church of Margão (in *rs.*)	90,000
Churches of Margão, Orlim, Mormugão and Verna: (in *rs.*)	2,760,300
Each priest annually (in *rs.*)	42,000
For the poor children from Customs-House at Diu (*pardaus*)	100

Sources: *DI*, I (1540-49), pp. 481-483; *DRI*, 2, pp. 94-95, 12 Mar 1611; 14, doc. 43, 28 Mar 1620; 15, doc. 225, 11 Feb 1622, pp. 358-359; Aubin, Jean, "Le Orçamento do Estado da India de Antonio de Abreu (1574)," *Studia*, no. 4, 1959, pp. 203, 213, 236-242.

APPENDIX 7

St. Paul's: Income and Expenses 1585-88

Rents of temples of Goa, Chorão, Divar, Jua (*xs.*):	2,800
Other rents (*rs.*)	8,00,000
Bandra, Curlem, Sarja, Morim (*rs.*)	6,58,800
Bombay villages (annual rent in *rs.*)	1,350,000
Rice from Bhatkal (*khandis*)	100
Wine	100
Olive (in quarters)	1
Rents of Chorão (in *rs.*)	5,13,060
Rents of Bassein villages (in *rs.*)	6,00,000
Presents of neighbouring Kings originally given to the Crown.	
Income (*rs.*)	34,38,060
Expenses: (*rs.*)	33,18,000
Novitiate	6,00,000
Seminary	4,80,000
Chorão Church	60,000
Bandra and Kurla Churches	2,10,000
Serra Church	1,80,000
Medicines	2,40,000
Poor	1,50,000
For 80 Jesuits, 50 servants	13,98,000

King Philip had asked Viceroy D. Duarte de Menezes on 10 January 1587 to give the gifts to the Jesuits instead of money. The latter brought a law suit against the heirs of Viceroy, D. Luis de Ataide who had not honoured the deal.

Sources: DI, XIV (1585-88), pp. 462-466; XII (1580-83), pp. 398, 492; XIII (1583-85), pp. 426, 592, 692; XIV (1585-88), p. 570.

APPENDIX 8

Japan Province: Income and Expenses 1585-88

Royal grant (*cruzados*)	1,000
Rents from Ponvem and Kondoti in Bassein (*cruzados*)	500
Two houses given by Patriarch Melchior Carneiro for the Seminary of Arima (*cruzados*)	200
Contribution to the Province Fund (*cruzados*)	400
For the year 1586 (*xs.*)	17,600

Source: *DI*, XIV (1585-88), pp. 85-86, 88, 663-664.

Goa Province in 1586

Colleges and houses:	24
Jesuits:	271
Property in Bassein and Malacca yielded (*rs.*)	913,00
Crown subsidy (*rs.*)	24,00,000
Income (*rs.*)	49,70,060
Royal subsidy (*rs.*)	18,70,000
Stipend for Salcete and Bassein (*rs.*):	10,87,500

Source: *DI*, XIV (1585-88), p. 513.

APPENDIX 9

Bassein: Income 1585-88

(amounts in *pardaus*)	
Dom João and Dom Sebastião	600
Villages of Coração, Coxella and Guirindoly given by Isabel de Aguiar	400
Village of Sai donated by Dona Inez de Melo	200
Manickpur given by Inez Francisca	150
Garden in Manickpur by the same donor	140
Rice plots by the same donor	40
House rents (in *rs.*)	17,000
Total income (in *rs.*)	3,08,500
(amounts in *rs.*)	
After the death of Isabel de Aguiar	4,50,000
Village of Vellapa	60,000
Plot by Dona Ana d'Azevedo	22,000
Small plots	22,000
Legacy of Dona Lianor de Gusmão	10,000
Donation by Maria Ferreira	34,500
House at Thane	1,48,500
Dom João III	1,500
King of Cambay	3,000
Royal subsidy	1,500
Trindade parish of Ravalem, Jantarem, Asanap	300
Total income (in *rs.*)	753,300

Source: *DI* XIV (1585-88), pp. 480-485.

APPENDIX 10

Province Fund: 1585-88

Each house had to give an annual of 4% of its income.
Amount in *xs.*

College of Goa	400
Professed House	80
College of Saicete	80
Chaul	24
Thane	12
College of Bassein	60
College of Daman	40
College of Cochin	80
Quilon	28
Fishery Coast	60
College of S. Tomé	12
College of Malacca	24
Molucca	60
Macao	20
Japan	400
Total :	1,380

Source: *DI*, XIV (1585-88), p. 512.

APPENDIX 11

Salcete Parishes: Subsidies for 1626:

Our Lady of Snows (Rachol)	216-2-40
St. Philip and St. James (Cortalim)	64,960-0-00
St. Michael (Orlim)	64,960-0-00
St. Salvador (Loutolim)	64,960-0-00
St. Thomas (Cansaulim)	64,690-0-00
Mother of God (Majorda)	64,690-0-00
St. John the Baptist (Benaulim)	64,690-0-00
Our Lady of Hope (Verna)	64,690-0-00
Our Lady of Martyrs (Assolná)	64,690-0-00
St. Alex (Curtorim)	64,690-0-00
S. André (Mormugão)	64,690-0-00
Our Lady of Belem (Sarzora)	64,690-0-00
St. Francis Xavier (Chinchinim)	64,690-0-00
Holy Cross (Verna)	64,690-0-00
Our Lady of Health (Cuncolim)	64,690-0-00

Source: DAAM: *Regimento de Ordenados*, 1626, codex 3060, AH, fls. 69v-70.

APPENDIX 12

Goa Province: Income - 1698-99

(in *xs.*)	
Rachol (10 members)	17,500-0-00
Mysore Mission (8)	5,669-0-00
Sunda Mission (2)	1,305-0-00
Chorão Novitiate (22)	20,805-0-00
College of Bassein (8)	10,000-0-00
College of Daman (4)	7,660-0-00
College of Diu (4)	3,726-0-00
College of Chaul (3)	3,507-0-00
College of Thane (5)	6,321-0-00
College of Agra (2)	3,740-0-00
College of Mozambique (4)	7,000-0-00
Total	87,233-0-00
Expenses for the Roman Curia	13,140-0-00

The present codex has complaints of the Japanese Province against the Goa Province which had stopped the payment for the students of the former after the separation of these two Provinces in 1598. The accounts were signed by Fr. Jacobus Vidal on 15 November 1698. The Procurator was Fr. Ludovico Coelho.

Source: ARSI: *Jap. Sin.* 23, fls. 249-250.

APPENDIX 13

St. Paul's: Income and Expenses - 1692-1707

Income:	12,64,748 *xs.*, 3 *tgs.*, 58 *bazs.*
Expenses:	10,34,893 *xs.*, 2 *tgs.*, 22 *bazs.*
The expenses for July 1707 were (in *xs.*, *tgs.*, *bazs.*)	1,379-2-66
(some typical entries)	
Fish for the priests	162-0-14
Vegetables	13-4-71
Fruits	25-4-18
Fish for servants	19-2-60
Pork	292-4-61
Price of 2,675 eggs	25-1-68
10,861 bananas	52-2-56
13 days' work of the slaves	8-4-15

Source: DAAM: Codex 2090 (*Receita e Despeza dos Jesuitas 1692-1707*-the Income and Expenditure of the Jesuits 1692-1707), *passim*.

APPENDIX 14

Kumbarjua: Income 1667-1731

The College of Mozambique had bought the island of Kumbarjua. It had a palm-grove which yielded 570 *cruzados* annually. It had acquired some houses by 1641, and rented them out. Bartolomeu Lopes gave a legacy of 1,000 *pardaus*, followed by another of 12,000 and a third to be paid after his death. The College had owed the Goa Province 2,500 *xs*. The legacy helped in buying tne island of Kumbarjua. The income for some years (*in xs.*) were:

1667	2,500	1673	2,500
1677	3,000	1679	3,000
1689	3,000	1694	3,000
1697	7,000	1699	3,000
1706	4,000	1709	5,000
1713	5,089	1716	1,000
1731	7,990		

Source: Rea, William F., *The Economics of the Zambezi Missions: 1580-1759*, Rome, Institutum Historicum Societatis Iesu, 1976, pp. 77-80.

APPENDIX 15

College of Rachol: Income (mid-17th century)

(in *xs.*)	
1,000 title-deeds of 10 villages in Salcete given by King Sebastian	1,333
Island next to the Rachol Fort	1,500
Income on a market and a shop	200
Palm-groves in Arlim, Tonttem, Dramapur, Talaulim, Narsanali, Benaulim, Chinchinim, Varca, Ambeghola, Loutolim, Majorda, Calata, Margão	3,000

College of Bassein: Income

in *xs.*, *tgs.*, *bazs.*

Villages of Sai and Puri	629-1-6
Poncer, Anculualy and Gondoly	1,557-1-23
Gardens	394-1-23
Various estimates	502-1-00
Salt-pan	31-1-20
Alms in Puri and Maxi	1,000-0-00

Source: Almeida Calado, Adelino de, "A Companhia de Jesus na India em meados do século XVII," *Studia*, n. 40, Dec 1978, pp. 356, 359-360.

APPENDIX 16

Number of Catholics in Goa in 1718

	Foreign priests	native priests	parishioners	blacks
Ilhas	303	207	19,131	1674
Salcete	76	348	24,874	212
Bardez	172	107	19,983	267

The total number of Catholics was 20,805 for Ilhas, 25,086 for Salcete, and 20,250 for Bardez. Among the white priests there were 39 at the Sé Cathedral, 24 at the Church of the Immaculate Conceptión (Panjim), 42 at St. Peter's (Panelim), 13 at Rachol, 63 at S. André (Mormugão), 39 at Reis Magos, 26 at Nellur and 55 at Penha da França. There were 40 native clerics at Neura, 67 at Margão, 67 at Verna, and 20 at Pomburpa.

Source: AHU: India *maço* 8, doc. 99, 9 Dec 1718.

Number of Catholics in Goa in 1722

Goa	36,226
Chorão and Divar	13,052
Jua of Angediva	2,713
Salcete	71,018
Bardez	52,088
Goa Velha	6,350
Margão	6,254
Total	1,81,565

Source: BLM: Addl. Mss. 15,197 *Papeis Politicos*, Tomo 5, fls. 330-332.

APPENDIX 17

Professed House: 1724-36

Income	2,22,100-4-51
Expenses	1,45,779-2-33

Source: DAAM: Codex 2098 (*Receita e Despeza de Colégio de Bom Jesus)*

Jesuit Houses: Income

Income in *xs., tgs.,* and *rs.:*	
St. Paul's (old):	3,44,646-4-10
The Professed House:	21,16,661-3-13
St. Paul's (new):	8,40,251-5-06
The College of Rachol:	4,93,163-4-50
Malabar Province:	88,79,921-1-47
Bom Jesus:	1,65,677-3-17
China:	1,73,672-3-28
Japan:	4,30,818-1-46

Kumbarjua Properties – 1726

Land	House	Dispensaries	Coconuts
4,000	1,000	1,500	3,000
Fish	Taverns	Tile	Fruits
60	360	300	250

The figures indicate the income in *xs*. The income for the other years was higher.

Source: DAAM: *MR*, 93B, fl. 591.

APPENDIX 18

Professed House: Income (In *xs.*)

1751-52	
Income	16,854-2-35
Expenses	15,773-3-49
Balance	1,080-3-46
1751-56	
Total	1,00,850-4-54
1753-59	
Income	1,22,806-4-59
Expenses	1,16,883-1-39
Balnace	5,923-3-20

Source: DAAM: codex 2099 (*Receita e despeza do Colégio de Bom Jesus*), fls. 1-18v; *ACE*, I (1618-33), pp. 29-30, 22 Mar 1619.

APPENDIX 19

Professed House: Income and Expenses

Income	Expenses	
1,17,260-3-59	91,196-1-08	(1712-20)
1,83,898-4-51	1,34,434-1-26	(1751-59)

Source: Ferroli, D., *The Jesuits in Malabar*, II, Bangalore, King & Co., 1951, pp. 347-348.

Missions outside Goa: Expenses in 1758

Malabar	35,705-3-42
Mysore	7,238-3-13
Kittur	1,261-4-48
Raichur	2,731-0-06
Sena	2,468-0-00
Ankola	475-0-00
Paroda	531-0-00
Sivancara	531-0-30
Total	50,711-2-19

Source: AHU: India, *maço* 91, 22 March 1751.

APPENDIX 20

Goa Province: Income – 1706-55

Total: (in *xs.*)	19,48,569-1-02
Contribution for 1706 (in *xs.*)	6,496

Source: DAAM: codex 2089 (*Receita e Despeza dos Padres Jesuitas 1706-55* – the Income and Expenditure of the Jesuits 1706-55), fls. 1-40. *passim*. Each house in the Province had to send in an annual contribution (*finta*) for the common expenses.

Professed House: Income and Expenses – 1724-36

Income	2,22,100-4-51
Expenses	1,45,779-2-33
Funeral expenses of Fr. João de Olivares:	373-2-30
7,717 mangoes given to the Communidade:	116-3-46
Provisions sent to the North and South India:	2,334-0-12

Source: DAAM: codex 2098 (*Receita e Despeza do Colégio de Bom Jesus* – Income and Expenditure of the College of Bom Jesus), fls. 60v, 67v, 80v.

APPENDIX 21

Jesuit Province: Income – 1758-59

St. Paul (old)	38,088-4-49
Professed House	4,77,263-2-30
St. Paul (new)	1,01,516-4-12
Chorão	47,401-6-12
Rachol	1,97,498-3-35
Malabar	38,427-0-00
Japan	37,472-1-31
China	19,110-3-27
Diu	23,432-3-42
Daman	3,259-0-23
Total	11,07,893-1-51

Source: DAAM: codex 7602 *Bens da Companhia de Jesus* (Property of the Society of Jesus), fls. 1-135. The money came in from real estate and mortgages.

Property of Chaul in Betalbatim: 1717-1723

Income	36,939-1-18.75
Expenses	24,529-4-07.5

Source: DAAM: codex 2092 *Receita e Despeza dos Jesuitas 1707-1723* (Income and Expenditure of the Jesuits 1707-1723), *passim*

APPENDIX 22

Loans given by the Society of Jesus

They gave loans usually at either 5 or 6 per cent.
Some sample amounts (in *xs.*) were:

Province of Goa – 5%	7,000
Japan Province – 6%	7,750
College of Bahia – 12%	6,000
Japan Province – 12%	5,950
Goa Province to the Governor of Mahim, Mr. Loesl	50,000
Malabar Province to the same Governor	36,000
Goa Province – 5%	1,62,000
Japan Province – 10%	5,950
Malabar Province – 5%	4,000
Malabar Province – 6%	3,000
Malabar Province – 10%	36,000
Goa Province – 5%	6,500
Japan Province – 6%	1,250

Source: DAAM: codex 1727 (*Contas de Confisco 1759-70* – Accounts of the Confiscation), fls. 37v, 45v, 46v, 101-107v.

APPENDDIX 23

Goa Province: Income – 1759

St. Paul's:	
Amount in hand	14,208-0-55
Kumbarjua yearly income	3,609-0-21
Pawns	23,880-3-54
Professed House:	
Amount in hand	65,150-2-30
Pawns	69,665-0-00
Loans given out	43,475-0-00
Province Loans:	
Municipality of Bardez – 5%	1,00,000-0-00
Municipality of Salcete – 6%	62,000-0-00
Municipality of Salcete – 5%	33,000-0-00
Village community of Calangute – 6%	16,000-0-00
Village community of Assagão – 5%	4,000-0-00
Governor of Mahim – 10%	50,000-0-00
To others	76,806-0-00
St. Paul's (new):	78,997-0-00
Chorão:	
Income	61-043-0-46
Pawns	11,570-4-12
Rachol:	
Income	85,306-0-21
Amount given in 1746 as loan	
Municipality of Salcete at 6%	50,000-0-00
Municipality of Salcete at 5% in 1754-55	16,200-0-00

Malabar Province:	
Income from properties	2,09,496-2-08
Japan:	
Siam residence	11,338-0-58
Income from Tum Kym mission	115-2-30
Loans and pawns	5,653-0-00
Interest on loans	17,227-1-22
China:	
Loans and pawns	19,110-3-27
College of Diu:	23,432-3-42
College of Daman:	3,259-0-23

Source: DAAM: codex 7602 (*Bens da Companhia de Jesus 1758-59* – Properties of the Society of Jesus 1758-59), fls. 1-135.

APPENDIX 24

Budgets of Goa, Bardez and Salcete

Year	Income	Expenditure
1574	275 290 $380	231 795 $162
1581	263 036 $953	242 784 $701
1588	303 051 $620	259 949 $854
1607	355 530 $600	235 677 $600
1609	249 780 $000	156 627 $088
1620	326 089 $600	318 370 $600
1635	355 579 $234	334 636 $773
1749	17,51,375-4-15.5	1,66,982-4-00.5

Source: Matos, Artur T. de, "The Financial Situation of the State of India during the Philippine Period (1581-1635)," *Indo-Portuguese History: Old Issues, New Questions*, ed. Teotonio R. de Souza, New Delhi, pp. 92-93.

APPENDIX 25

Jesuits bound for Portugal: Expenses in 1760

Tobacco and medicinal expenses for them while in the various convents from 2 November 1759 to 19 November 1760, payments to the Superiors of the convents where they were at the rate of *xe* per day:	37,780-0-00
For their smoke, travel, cure and funeral expenses:	2,221-1-42
For those at the new St. Paul's including the 45 slaves attending on them, besides the two Jesuits of unstable minds:	11,985-4-30
For tobacco and medical expenses:	674-0-00
Expenses of the 127 departing Jesuits for their smoke, biscuits, meat, fish, butter, beans and other foodstuffs on their journey by boat along with seven servants and one cook:	22,994-0-10
The entire amount was:	75,655-1-22
Loans by the Government:	14,92,862-4-59
Income of the Government:	31,47,570-4-55

Source: DAAM: codex 2014 (*Balanço da Junta Administração 1765-66* – Balance Sheet of the Board of Administration), fls. 1-42.

APPENDIX 26

Jesuit Provinces: Properties

1759	
College of St. Paul's (old)	38,088-4-49
Professed House	4,77,263-2-30
College of St. Paul's (new)	1,01,516-4-12
Novitiate of Chorão	47,402-1-12
College of Rachol	1,97,498-3-35
Total	88,61,770-1-18
Province of Malabar	1,62,848-1-30
Province of Japan	37,472-1-31
Vice-Province of China	19,110-3-27

Source: DAAM: codex 7602 (*Bens da Companhia de Jesus – 1756-59*)

1765-66	
St. Paul's (old)	1,81,447-2-00
Professed House	14,84,738-1-05
St. Paul's (new)	4,01,596-0-04
Chorão	3,43,302-0-11
Rachol	79,386-2-13
Malabar	8,67,179-2-19
Japan	2,24,226-4-25
China	1,83,412-4-48
Daman	20,285-3-59
Diu	18,062-2-00
Total	41,64,826-1-37

Source: DAAM: codex 2014 (*Balanço da Junta da Administração 1765-66* – Accounts of the Board of Administration 1765-66), fls. 1-23v.

1759 4,87,216-2-45

Source: DAAM: codex 2041 (*Receita dos bens confiscados* – Income of confiscated goods), fls. 1-73. The sale of 1,577 coconuts for the College of St. Paul's (old) yielded 449-0-39 (fl. 7), and 19,680 for the College of St. Paul's (new). The sale at the rate of 1,000 for 80*xs.* netted 1,574-2-00 (fl. 10). Properties in Dramapur brought in 15,500*xs.*, Talaulim 7,136, Benaulim 4,734, and Margão (fl. 11)

1770 1,40,150-4-49

Amount recovered from sale of real estate and movable goods 3,63,121-0-01

Source: DAAM: codex 1727 (*Contas do Confisco 1759-1770)*, fls. 1-157v. The Board of Administration had 2,25,8119-4-47

1772 6,753-1-04

Source: DAAM: codex 2475 (*Papeis do arrecadação do producto dos bens dos Jesuitas 1772* – Papers relating to the auction of goods of the Jesuits, 1772), fls. 1-66, 87.

1773 7,04,146-1-40

Source: DAAM: codex 2525, fls. 1-95v. Income came from the temple properties of Chorão, Jua, Calapur, Goltim, Naroa, S. Tomé; Corlim, Carambolim, Mercurim, Murda, Morombim, Goa Velha, Majorda, Varca, Verna, Margão. The Jesuits had given a loan of 62,200*xs.* at 6% to the Municipal Council of Salcete, and another of 50,000 to that of Bardez at 5%. The Malabar Province had given a loan of 62,000 to the Communidade of Pilerne at 5%. The Province had palm-groves at Damerem, at Betim, Cunchelim, Caissua and Golombo. The sale of houses belonging to the Professed House in 1773 amounted to 5,709 and 1/2 *xs.*

1780 1,74,539-0-44

Source: DAAM: codex 1939 (*Balanço da Receita do Confisco da Cidade de Goa 1780* – State of income from the Confiscation in Goa 1780), fls. 1-77. There were fourteen palm-groves in Betalbatim belonging to Chaul. The groves of Ambelim, Velim and Assolna yielded 5,980-2-34 in 1774 (fl. 7). St. Paul's (old) netted 8,381-2-00 from its temple rents.

APPENDIX 27

Jesuit Properties

The Professed House had the palm-groves of *Velechem Batta, Nauxim, Chicalem Batta* and a plot at Bambolim; *Arecol Velo Molo (Bambolim), Ponte de Pangim* (Panjim) and three plots, and one shop of provisions. Two gardens at Santa Luzia, a place at *Rua dos Ramos* at Old Goa, and one at Kumbarjua, two parts of which were of the College of Mozambique, which administered the house, and one part of the old College of St. Paul's. The House had another plot on the same island.

Ten groves called the Mission of Tibet (*Langatem, Sonarvado, Batocarachy Xir* (all at Varca), *Ranacalem, Namoxy dos Maintos, Cambasteachy Xir, Uduguealem, Maodem, Maodem, Dugunascalem* (all at Orlim), and *Aposloagor* in Cavelossim).

The villages of Velim, Ambelim and Assolná belonged to this House, to the Novitiate at Chorão and to the Province of Malabar. They had one fallow plot at Assolná, one plot and two salt-pans at Assolná and Ambelim respectively; six fallow plots at Velim, eight plots (*pedaços*) at Velim and Ambelim, three *terreiros incultos (fallow yards) Barady* (Horta), *Paxel and Zaino* at Velim, three plots, *Baifoddda, Orela* and *Gopechem Cantem* at Assolná, and fourteen plots at Assolná and two at Ambelim. There were also two fallow plots of the palmgroves, *Ubodanddo* and *Oxvolicho Zaino* at Velim.

It had the palm-groves *Passarem Batta* and *Moroda, and* two plain tracts at Saligão. There were some small houses with a plot belonging to the same palmgrove.

There were fourteen palm-groves of Chaul, *Vessoddo, Babuxalem, Gunguna, Horta and Cera, Arcana* (all at Calata); *Mamandapor* in Mamandapur, *Imbatta, Calbatta, Furtado, Galy, Palmar Novo, Mascalem*, and *Botalem* at Betalbatim, and some small plain plots.

Source: *BG: RF*, Panjim, 10, 14, 17, Jan 1862, pp. 18, 23-25, 30-31. They are available also in *LM*, no. 164, fl. 1099.

The New College of St. Paul's had three palm-groves in Mandur, Moula and Talaulim, and *Querem* and *Pobre* at Chorão. It had *Curpavado Grande* and *Curpavado Pequeno, Faraz, Conno, Portaria, Murdy, Deulbata, Gorquealem Uddo, Pescador, Seminalem, Quencaralem, Sasdalem, Raidel* (all at Quelossim), and *Arvale, Horta* and *Tanna* at Cortalim; the island of Quelossim, the garden of the College itself, and a hand-mill at Old Goa.

Other plots were *Sancorla, Gavana, Deussuachem Xeta, Nauxim, Ducorxeta, Tanquea Xeta* (all on the same island); plain tracts at Jua, *Talcacho, Conysuavam, Vavam, Aco Dacotem, Gorconda* all in the same village), nineteen tracts at Bambolim, Goltim, Navelim, and Naroa; plots *Deussum, Cantorly, Morgurecho Aco,* and *Vavans de Massalacho,* (all at Neura), *Symorem* at Ambota, *Aclachondo* or *Perneachem Adverca* at Silapa, *Marcho Aco* of Mar Mory, and *Argumenty Grande* of Velfalim.

There was a plot *Moloy* at S. Tomé; at Corlim, there were *Quirtanacho Orgue* with parts of plots *Ofala* and *Dado* in Carambolim; and other plots in the same village, and at Gancim, Mercurim, Azossim, and Ella; besides plots *Govam Xetta, Kumbarjua, Onvola Xeta* at Cujura, plots *Murda,* and *Cavoqueire* in Grande Morombim, *Ravalnatacho Orquo, Discor Xeta, Cumbar Orquo* in the same village, and twelve other plots, *Deulanatachem Vaam, Deutrapelachi Adverca* in lower Morombim, *Raulanatacho Orquo, Dacto Devachem Vaam, Pernancho Orquo, Dequetygudem,* and *Murtachem Patem,* all in the same village. There was also income from Guadalupe, Goa Velha, and Moula.

Source: *BG: RF,* Panjim, 21 Jan 1862, pp. 33-35.

The old College of St. Paul's had four gardens of pineapples, three at S. Tomé and one at Old Goa. There was a garden named St. Xavier of the college, and a palm-grove *Damotim* at Betalbatim.

The Novitiate of Chorão: The Carmona property consisted of the palm-groves *Baimalim Dolcalem, Vessoalem, Betalbata, Nagodem, Quirbata, Marinha de Calate, Setisbetre Guialem, Culbealem, Vitolilem, Campos do Norte, Marinha de Seussua, Vagabata, Godialem, Vallo, Atalem, Emugemmanda, Ancura, Vitona, Condiantoy, Santo Xavier, Chincholealem, Dugor Morodo, Gavona, Pedemedelem, Marinha Santa*

Cruz, Xiro, Sul, Memolcalem, Vanhacamotelem, Dando, Santaxir, Santaxir, Poqucalem, Azarco, Comprido Sul, Gantagelem, and *Ambexir.*

The Province of Malabar had the palmgrove of *Our Lady of Victory* (of the Chapel of Betim), *Cassua* in Chapora, *Cantorli* at Aldona, *Golombo* at Marna, *Damerem* along with plots at Nachinola and Tivim, Conchelim at Cunchelim, *Catoca* at Aquem, shares in Neura, Golteim, Navelim, Divar, Malar and Naroa.

The Province of Japan had a palmgrove at Taleigão and plots at Taleigão, *Bandacy, Chincholem,* and *Palmar Grande.*

The Vice-Province of China had *Senquero* at Verem, and houses of the same palmgrove.

Source: *BG: RF*, Panjim, 21 Jan 1862, pp. 33-35, 21 Jan 1862, pp. 41-42, 28 Jan 1862, pp. 52-54.

The College of Rachol had the island of Rachol, and the palm-groves *Dramapor, Portaxira, Revolnata, Xetilem, Dandem, Danunguem, Ragnaxetilem* (all at Varca), and *Ramantoy, Adquirantoy, Calguealem* and *Boirealem* at Utorda; *Maduxetilem, Mobulnascalo Juem, Praia, Omanchy, Curlapeda, Samoly Oddy, Grande Maissur* and *Pequeno Maissur* (all at Benaulim), *Donculim* at Donculim, *Patrualem* and *Collegichi Sira* at Seraulim, *Bando Moto, Santa Cruz, Vanipem, Deulagana, Talaulim,* and three saltpans, *Vitupolo agor, Gorvancho agor and Govancho agor,* at Seraulim, too.

It had besides, *Chandanascalem, Mordaxalem, Colviro, Locuxinailem, Zanglantoy* and *Bordem* at Majorda, *Pomonaicalem and Deulabata* at Camorlim, *Cumbarbata, Plantmento Grande e Pequeno, Horta, Zinguinaique,* and *Santo Xavier* (all at Raia), *Foyal Baida* and *Arly* at Margão, *Carionchem Bata* at Loutolim, *Dongorim* at Majorda, and *Tambidem Odale, Chinchantoy* and *Salvador Luiz* at Calata.

There were other plots *Ambicol Grande e Pequeno* at Curtorim, *Narcaxale* at Betalbatim, *Parlapa* at Colva, three plots at Raia, *Santanascalem, Gantanachi Xir, Senhor Menino* at Sernabatim, *Dalpem* at Benaulim, *Zoisseachi Namoxi* and *Naranachi Namoxim,* at Benaulim too, a tract Assar Pão at Seraulim, and shops at Raia.

It had shares at Margão, Raia, Nagoa, Dramapur, Sarzora and Daoclim.

Other plots were *Gorvanchem Vonsura, Vengali Valio Pato* and *Someachem Vonssura* at Varca, *Santareacho Pato, Adando, Santareachy Palli*, at Varca too, *Caim Potoly, Vely Bume, Ambeachy Galy, Veranchy Congui, Chontagaly, Isanterechy Galy, Caim Patoly* in Varca, *Santarecho, Deulacho Pato Carea, Deulacho Pato* and *Toloy Cantorla*, at Loutolim.

Its other properties were *Daroly Toloy, Setodem Vicondichem Pancha, Teliachi Patte, Deussurato* and *Orli Toloy, Pandazuorn Gupinatachem paut, Virachem pancha, Toloy zuom, Dauel veno, Dumavelim* and *Santereche pancha*, all at Cortalim, and *Permancho Pato, Landapem, Zoisseachy Pately, Bandor Xetta* at Majordá.

There were *Boctancho Zuom, Devloea, Santerecho Cono, Toloy Cono, Odolea Zuvam, Vello Solavo, Dacolea Zuavelo Sovalo* and *Santalacho Conugo*, at Nagoa; *Camanacho Pato, Vanspem* and *Avontacho Galoy, Dualachem Xeta, Possuachi Galy, Volozaachy Galy, Carachy Voly, Galialy Namoxy, Telachy Conguy, Bainchy Conguy, Devalachy Conguy*, all at Sirlim, *Ananeara, Dedalem*, and *Impoty, Botechy Nomoxi, Cotorla, Dacutem Deussua, Calatem, Bosamichy, Polondy* and *Santereche pate*, all at Margão.

Yet other properties were *Tanqueachy Galy, Possuachy Namoxy, Danqueachy Namoxy, Cumbequi Xira*, at Benaulim; *Possuleanty Masavelo Congo, Contenty, Dessa Conugo, Goixetant, Devancho aco, Quirtananchy*, and *Coleachy Conghuy* at Colva; plots, *Terceiro Tanco, Bonzal, Quirtanaique* and *Gadiachy Conguy*, at Colva too, along with *Vars Zoisseachem Verodem, Boiranvanchem Verodem* and *Narananchy Galy, Quarto Lanco, Banzaly* and *Veranchy Conuguy*, and a palm-grove *Carando* at Margão.

Source: *BG:RF*, 31 Jan 1862, pp. 64-66, 4 Feb 1862, pp. 75-77.

BIBLIOGRAPHY

I. Primary Sources

A) *Archival*:

1. Directorate of Archives, Archaeology & Museum, Goa.

a. *Colégio do Bom Jesus* (College of Bom Jesus): 1712-1791.
Codices: 2098-100, 2465, 2660.
b: *Colégio de S. Paulo* (College of St. Paul): 1566-1771.
Codices: 651, 663, 818, 1220, 1932, 1942, 2107-2113, 2359, 2364, 3026, 4515, 7494.
c. *Colégio de Rachol* (College of Rachol): 1569-1757.
Codices: 824, 1865-66, 2048-49.
d. *Confisco* (Confiscation): 1771-1803.
Codices: 2030-31, 2480.
e. *Convento do Bom Jesus* (Convent of Bom Jesus): 1657-1772.
Codices: 1958, 2097, 2114, 2116, 2118, 2465, 2493, 2529.
f. *Jesuitas* (Jesuits): 1664-1806.
Codices: 833, 859, 864, 1209, 1945, 1960, 2041, 2475, 2484, 2459, 2552, 2557, 2570, 7602, 4514.
g. *Tombos* (Property Registers): 1518-1845.
Codices: 629, 659, 3026, 2069, 7493-94, 7598, 7600-01, 7646.

2. **British Museum**, London.

Additional Mss. 1685, 6878-9, 9852-5, 9860, 10,125, 10,351, 11,280, 15,197, 20,844, 1/3/146.

3. **Arquivo Nacional da Torre do Tombo**, Lisbon.

Cartorio dos Jesuitas Registry of Jesuit Records: Maço (Bundle) nos. 86-87, 90.

4. **Arquivo Historico Ultramarino**, Lisbon.

Maço (Bundle) : India, no. 1-93.

5. **Biblioteca Nacional,** Madrid.

Codices: 1190, 2361, 23733, 2588, 12,930, 18,727, 21,140.

6. **Archivo General de Simancas**, Simancas, Spain.

Legajo (Bundle) 393, 410, 710, 2629, 5035, 6964, 6968-69.

7. **Biblioteca Nazionale Centrale Vittorio** Emmanuele II, Rome:

Fondo Gesuitico (Jesuit Sources) Nos. 1014, 1247, 1249(3), 1253(28), 1255(19), 1309, 1364(3), 1374, 1384(24), 1385, 1386(5, 6, 13, 14, 17), 1463, 1549, 1567, 1620, 1669(1).

8. **Archivum Romanum Societatis Iesu,** Rome.

Provinciae Goana et Malabarica (The Goa and Malabar Provinces): Nos. 22, 23, 27, 34 (1), 60.

Fondo Gesuitico (Jesuit Sources)

627-28: Catalogi rerum seu reddituum 1736-37. Assist. Lusitaniae (Catalogue of returns of the Portuguese Assistancy 1736-37).

721-II-IX: Missioni nelle Indie Orientali; Roberto di Nobili informatio de quibusdum moribus nationis Indicae (Missions in India, the information of Roberto di Nobili about the Indian customs)

1443/9: Ordem do Seminario de Sante Fé; Confraria de Spirito Santo, Margão; Receita de Goa; Quinta da Casa Professa; clerigos bramanes (Order of the Seminary of Holy Faith; the Confraternity of Holy Spirit, Margão; Income of Goa; Farm of the Professed House; Brahmin Clergy).

B) **Published**

Abranches, Garcia, José I. (ed.). *Archivo da Relação de Goa* (Archives of the Goa High Court). Séculos XVII-XIX. Panjim: Imprensa Nacional, 1872.

Boletim da Filmoteca Ultramarina Portuguesa (nos. 1-44). Lisbon: Centro de Estudos Historicos Ultramarinos, 1954-70.

Boletim do Governo (Bulletin of the Government). Panjim: Imprensa Nacional, 1862, nos. 3-11, 18, 23-25, 30-31, 33-35, 41-42, 52-54, 64-66, 75-77, 85-86. The Jesuit properties at the time of their suppression are mentioned under the section *Relação das Fazendas (List of Properties).*

Bulhão Pato, R.A. (ed.). *Documentos Remetidos da India ou Livros das Monções* (Monsoon Correspondence). Vols. 1-4. Lisbon: Academia Real das Sciencias, 1880-1935.

Documentação Ultramarina Portuguesa (Portuguese Overseas Documentation). Vols. 1-5. Lisbon: Centro de Estudos Historicos Ultramarinos, 1960-67. (The documents deal with Portuguese activities in the Indies between the sixteenth and nineteenth centuries).

Linhares, Count of. *Diario do 3° (sic) Conde de Linhares, Vice-Rei da India.* Bks 1-2. Lisbon: Biblioteca Nacional, 1937-43.

Pissurlencar, Panduronga S.S. (ed.). *Regimentos das Fortalezas da India* (Ordinances of the Forts of India). Bastora: T. Rangel, 1951.

——. (ed.). *Assentos do Conselho do Estado* (Proceedings of the State Council). Vols. 1-4 (1618-1750). Bastora: T. Rangel, 1953-57.

Wicki, Josef, (ed.). *Documenta Indica* (Documentation on India). Vols. 1-18 (1540-1597). Rome: Institutum Historicum Societatis Iesu, 1948-88. (They contain annual letters of the Jesuit Provinces, letters from India to the Roman Curia and the replies to them, and other matters of importance for the running of the Provinces).

II. Secondary Sources

Abeyasinghe, Tikiri. "History as Polemics and Propaganda: Some Aspects of Fernão de Querioz' Conquista". *II Seminario Internacional de Historia Indo-Portuguesa* (2nd International Seminar on Indo-Portuguese History). Eds. Luis de Albuquerque & Inacio Guerrerio. Lisbon: Centro de Estudo de Historia e Cartografia Antiga, 1985, 295-299.

Alden, Dauril. "Sugar planters by Necessity, not Choice: The Role of the Jesuits in the Cane Sugar Industry of Colonial Brazil." *The Church and Society in Latin America.* Ed. Jeffrey A. Cole. Tulane University: Centre for Latin American Studies, 1984, 139-170.

——. "The making of an Elite Enterprise: The Jesuits in the Portuguese Assistancy, 16th to 18th Centuries." *The James Ford Bell Lectures* (University of Minnesota). (n. 30, 1992), 1-26.

Almeida Calado, Adelino de. "A Companhia de Jesus na India em meados do seculo XVII" (The Society of Jesus in India in the Middle of the 17th century). *Studia* (Lisbon), (no. 40, Dec 1978), 349-366.

Amaladass, Anand (ed.). *Jesuit Presence in India.* Anand: Gujarat Sahitya Prakash, 1988.

Amaro, Ana Maria. "Goa's Famous Cordial Stones." *Review of Culture* (Macau), (nos. 7-8, 1988/1989), 82-102.

Antony, Philomena. "Missionary Expansion: Cultural and Agricultural Contacts between Colonial Goa and Brazil". *Discoveries, Missionary Expansion and Asian Cultures*. Ed. Teotonio R. de Souza. New Delhi: Concept Publishing Company, 1994.

Antunes, Manuel. "O Marques de Pombal e os Jesuitas." (The Marquis of Pombal and the Jesuits) *Como Interpretar Pombal no bicentenario da sua morte?*. (How does one interpret Pombal in the bicentenary of his death?) Lisbon: Broteria, 1983, 125-146.

Arte Palmarica (Art of Palm-Cultivation) by a Father of the Society of Jesus. 9th ed. Panjim: Imprensa Nacional, 1918.

Aubin, Jean. "Le Orçamento do Estado da India de Antonio de Abreu (1574)" (Budget of the Portuguese State of India). *Studia*. (no. 4, July 1959), 169-289.

Aveling, J.C.H. *The Jesuits*. London: Blong & Briggs, 1981.

Azevedo, João Lucio de. "Os Jesuitas e a Inquisição em conflito no seculo XVII" (The Jesuits and the Inquisition in conflict in the 17th century). *Boletim da Segunda Classe da Academia das Ciencias de Lisboa*, 10 (1916), 319-345.

——. *Historia dos cristãos-novos Portugueses* (The history of the Portuguese New Christians). Lisbon, 1922.

B.N. (sic.). *The Jesuits*. Vol. 2. (*Their foundation and history*). London: Burns & Oates, 1879.

Bacelar e Oliveira, José P. "Arrest, Spoliation and Exile of the Goa Jesuits according to Father Caeiro's De Exilio." *Indo-Portuguese History: Old Issues, New Questions*. Ed. Teotonio R. de Souza. New Delhi: Concept Publishing Company, 1985, 123-132.

Baião, Antonio. *A Inquisição de Goa*. Vols. 1-2. Coimbra and Lisbon: Imprensa da Universidade Academia das Ciencias, 1930/1949.

——. *A Inquisição de Goa – Tentativa de Historia da sua origem, estabelecimento, evoluçãa e extinção* (The Inquisition of Goa – a short history of its origin, establishment, growth and end). Lisbon, 1949.

——. *Episodios Dramaticos da Inquisição Portuguesa*. Vols. 1-3 (Renascenca Portuguesa, Anuario do Rio de Janeiro, Varia). Lisbon: Seara Nova, 1972-1973.

Barbuda, Claudio L.M. de. *Instrucções com que El-Rei D. Jose mandou passar ao Estado da India no anno de 1774* (Instructions of King Joseph to the State of India in 1774). Panjim: Imprensa Nacional, 1841.

Borges, Charles J. "Christianization of the Caste System in Goa." *Goan Society through the Ages*. Ed. B.S. Shastry. Delhi: Asian Publication Services, 1987, 48-55.

——. "Jesuit Education in Goa (16th-18th centuries)." *Goa: Cultural Trends*. Ed. P.P. Shirodkar. Panjim: Directorate of Archives, Archaeology and Museum, 1988, 154-164.

—— "Foreign Jesuits and Native Resistance in Goa 1541-1759. *Essays in Goan History*. Ed. Teotonio R. de Souza. New Delhi: Concept Publishing Company, 1989, 69-80.

——. "Religious Orders and the *Estado da India* in Goa: A Balancing Act," *Goa's External Relations*. Ed. P.P. Shirodkar. Panjim: Rajhauns, 1992, 22-31.

Boxer, Charles R. *The Christian Century in Japan 1549-1650*. California: University of California Press, 1951.

——. *The Great Ship from Amacon*. Lisbon: Centro de Estudos Historicos Ultramarinos, 1959.

——. *Race Relations in the Portuguese Colonial Empire (1415-1825)*. Oxford: Clarendon Press, 1963.

——. *Francisco Vieira de Figueiredo, a Portuguese Merchant-Adventurer in South East Asia*, 1624-1667. S. Gravenhage: Martinus Nijhoff, 1967.

——. *The Portuguese Seaborne Empire: 1415-1825*. Middlesex: Pelican Books, 1973.

——. "Macao as a Religious and Commercial Entrepot in the 16th and 17th centuries." *Acta Asiatica* (Bulletin of the Institute of Eastern Culture). no. 26. Tokyo: The Toho Gakkai, 1974, 64-90.

——. *The Church Militant and Iberian Expansion 1440-1770*. Baltimore: The John Hopkins University Press, 1978.

——. *Portuguese India in the Mid-Seventeenth Century*. Delhi: Oxford University Press, 1980.

——. "A Note of the Triangular Trade between Macao, Manila and Nagasaki, 1580-1640." *Terrae Incognitae*. USA: Wayne State University Press, 1986, 51-59.

Braudel, Fernand. *Capitalism and Material Life: 1400-1800*. Glasgow: Fontana/Collins, 1977.

Broderick, James. *St. Francis Xavier 1506-1552*. London: Burns & Oates, 1952.

——. *The Origin of the Jesuits*. Chicago: Loyola University Press, 1986. Reprint.

——. *The Progress of the Jesuits (1556-79)*. Chicago: Loyola University Press, 1986. Reprint.

Caeiro, José. *Jesuitas do Brasil e da India na perseguição do Marques de Pombal: século XVIII* (The Jesuits of Brasil and India during the time of the persecution of the Marquis of Pombal – eighteenth century). Baia: Escola Tipografica Salesiana, 1936.

Camps, Arnulf. *Jerome Xavier SJ and the Muslims of the Moghul Empire: Controversial Works and Missionary Activity*. Schoneck-Barkenried: Nouvelle Revue de Science Missionaire, 1957.

Cardim, Antonio F. *Batalhas da Companhia de Jesus na sua gloriosa Provincia do Japão* (Battles of the Society of Jesus in her glorious Province of Japan). Lisbon: Imprensa Nacional, 1894.

Cary-Elwes, Columbia. *China and the Cross: Studies in Missionary History*. London: Longmans, Green and Co., 1937.

Chao, Jonathan. *A Bibliography of the History of Christianity in China*. 1970.

Charpentier, Jarl (ed.) *The Livro da seita dos Indios Orientais (Brit. Mus. Ms. Sloane 1820) of Father Jacobo Fenicio, S.J.* Uppsala: Almqvist & Wiksells Booktryckeri A.B., 1933.

Clarence-Smith, Gervase. *The Third Portuguese Empire 1825-1975: A Study in Economic Imperialism*. Manchester: Manchester University Press, 1985.

Clavell, James. *Shogun*. New York: Dell Publishing House, 1975.

Collis, Maurice. *Na Terra da Grande Imagem – Aventuras de um Religioso portugues no Oriente* (In the Land of the Great Image). Transaltion by Antonio A. Doria from the English. Porto: Civilização, 1944.

Correia-Afonso, John. *Jesuit Letters and Indian History: 1542-1773*. Bombay: Oxford University Press, 1969.

——. "Indo-American Contacts through Jesuit Missionaries". *Indica*. 14 (no. 1, Mar 1977), 29-42.

——. "Indo-Portuguese History in Jesuit Archives." *Sources of History of India*. Ed. S.P. Sen. Calcutta: Institute of Historical Studies, 1978, 530-40.

——. *Letters from the Mughal Court: The First Jesuit Mission to Akbar (1580-1583).* Anand: Gujarat Sahitya Prakash, 1980.

——. (ed.) *Indo-Portuguese History: Sources and Problems.* Bombay: Oxford University Press, 1981.

——. "Documents of the First Jesuit Mission from Goa to the Great Moghal." *II Seminario Internacional de Historia Indo-Portuguesa.* 295-299.

——. *Intrepid Itinerant – Manuel Godinho and His Journey from India to Portugal in 1963.* Bombay: Oxford University Press, 1990.

——. "The Second Jesuit Mission to Akbar (1591)." *Indica.* 28 (no. 2, Sep 1991), 73-93.

Costa, Francisco X. da (ed.) *Legados Pios que oneram os bens situados nos concelhos das Ilhas, Bardes, Salcette e Mormugão do distrito de Goa pelo Chantre Francisco Xavier Vaz* (Pious obligations connected with the properties in the talukas of Ilhas, Bardez, Salcete and Mormugão of Goa). Bastora: T. Rangel, 1960.

Cronin, Vincent. *The Wise Man from the West.* London, 1984.

Crooke, William (ed.) *Travels in India by Jean-Baptiste Tavernier Baron of Aubonne.* Vols. 1-2. Delhi: Oriental Books Reprint Corporation, 1977.

Cummins, J.S. "The Suppression of the Jesuits, 1773." *History Today.* 1973, 839-848.

——. *Jesuit and Friar in the Spanish Expansion to the East.* London: Variorum Reprints, 1986.

Cunha, J. Gerson da. *The Origin of Bombay. JBBRAS* (Bombay), 1900, Reprint. New Delhi: Asian Educational Services, 1993.

Cunha Rivara, Joaquim H. da (ed.) *Viagem de Francisco Pyrard de Laval.* Vols. 1-2. Porto: Domingos de Oliveira, 1944.

D'Abreu, Miguel Vicente. *Narração da Inquisição de Goa* escrita em Francez por Mr. Dellon (Account of the Inquistion of Goa). Panjim: Imprensa Nacional, 1866.

Danvers, Frederick C. *Report to the Secretary of State for India in Council on the Portuguese Records relating to the East Indies contained in the Archivo da Torre do Tombo and the Public Libraries at Lisbon and Evora.* London: India Office, 1892.

David, M.D. (ed.). *Asia and Christianity.* Bombay: Himalaya Publishing House, 1985.

D'Costa Anthony. "Conditions in the Goa Islands, 1510-50." *Indica.* 1 (no. 1, Mar 1964), 19-38.

——. *The Christianisation of the Goa Islands*. Bombay: Heras Institute. 1965.

De Almeida, Lopes M. (ed.). *Oriente Conquistado a Jesus Cristo pelos Padres da Companhia de Jesus da Provincia de Goa pelo Padre Francisco de Souza*. 1710. Reprint. Porto: Lello & Irmãos, 1978.

Dehergne, Joseph. *Repertoire des Jesuites de Chine de 1552 a 1800* (List of the Jesuits of China from 1552 to 1800). Rome: Institutum Historicum Societatis Iesu, 1973.

Dehergne, Joseph and Leslie, Donald D. *Juifs de Chine: A travers la correspondance inedite des Jesuites du Dixhuitieme siecle*. Rome: IHSI, 1980.

Dellon, Charles. *Histore de l'Inquistion de Goa*. Amsterdam: Louis Foubert, 1737.

——. *Voyages de Mr. Dellon avec sa relation de l'Inquisition de Goa*. Vols. 1-3. Colonia: Heritiers de Pierre Marteau, 1709.

——. *Account of the Inquisition at Goa with an appendix containing an account of the escape of Archibald Bower from the Inquisition at Macerata in Italy*. Hull: I. Wilson, 1818.

De Melo, Afonso J. "A Basilica do Bom Jesus." (The Basilica of Bom Jesus) *Boletim Eclesiaštico da Arquidiocese de Goa*. 11 (nos. 5-6, 1952), 237-257.

De Melo, Carlos M. *The Recruitment and Formation of the Native Clergy in India (16th-19th century): An Historic-Canonical Study*. Lisbon: Agencia Geral do Ultramar, 1955.

De Souza, Teotonio R. de. "Matheus de Castro Mahale: An Unsung hero." *Goa Today* (Panjim), Jan 1975, 18, 28.

——. "A Pious Hindu Commemorates in Marble the Activities of the Paulists in Kumbarjua." *Goa Today*, Feb 1977, 14, 22.

——. *Medieval Goa*. New Delhi: Concept Publishing Company, 1979.

——. "Jesuits and Trade." *The Times of India* (Bombay), 14 Jan, 1979, 8.

——. "The Voiceless in Goan Historiography: A Case for the Source-Value of Church Records in Goa." *Indo-Portuguese History: Sources and Problems*. Ed. John Correia-Afonso. 114-131.

——. "Foreign Elements in the Rural Economy of Goa during Sixteenth and Seventeenth Centuries." *Western Colonial Policy*. Ed. N.R. Ray. Calcutta, 1983, 269-284.

——. "To the Nations and Nation: The Apostle of the Indies and the Apostle of Ceylon." *Ignis* (Jesuit Ignatian Studies Journal). 14 (Mar-Aug 1985), 33-38.

——. "Jesuit Records in Portuguese on Shivaji's South Indian Campaign and its Impact on the People." *Indica*. 23 (nos. 1-2, Mar-Sep 1986), 89-100.

——. "Re-Writing the History of the Society of Jesus in India: Questions of Facts and Relevance," in *Jesuit Presence in Indian History*, 14-23.

——. "Oratorians of Goa (1682-1835)," in *Goa: Cultural Trends*. Ed. P.P. Shirodkar. Panjim: DAAM, 1988, 141-150.

——. (ed.) *Essays in Goan History*. New Delhi: Concept Publishing Company, 1989.

——. "Embassies and Surrogates: Case-Study of a Malacca Embassy to Siam in 1595." *Indica*. 26 (nos. 1-2, Mar-Sept 1989), 39-55.

——. (ed.). *Discoveries, Missionary Expansion and Asian Cultures*, New Delhi, Concept Publishing Company, 1994.

De Souza, Teotonio R. & Borges, Charles J. (eds.), *Jesuits in India: In Historical Perspective*, Macau: Instituto Cultural de Macau, 1992.

D'Mello, Ashley. "Review". *The Times of India* (Bombay), 2 August 1988, 4.

D.Sa, M. *History of the Catholic Church in India, 52-1924 A.D.*, Vols. 1-2. Bombay: B.X. Furtado & Sons, 1910-1922.

Disney, Anthony R. *The Twilight of the Pepper Empire: Portuguese Trade in Southwest India in the Early Seventeenth Century*. Cambridge (Mass.): Harvard University Press, 1978.

——. "The Portuguese Empire in India c. 1550-1650." *Indo-Portuguese History: Sources and Problems*. 148-62.

——. "The Viceroy Count of Linhares at Goa, 1629-1635." *II Seminario Internacional de Historia Indo-Portuguesa*. 303-315.

——. "T.R. de Souza, *Medieval Goa*" (book-review). *South Asia* (new series). 9 (no. 1, Jun 1986), 101-103.

——. "The World of Long-Distance Voyaging in the Seventeenth Century: The Lisbon-Goa Fleet of 1629 as a Case Study." *Studies in Maritime History*. Ed. K.S. Mathew. Pondicherry: Pondicherry University, 1990, 143-158.

D'Orsey, Alex. *Portuguese Discoveries, Dependencies and Missions in Asia and Africa*. London: W.H. Allen, 1893.

Dunne, George H. *Generations of Giants. The Story of the Jesuits in China in the Last Decades of the Ming Dynasty*. London: Burns & Oates, 1962.

Esteves Pereira, Francisco M. *O Descobrimento do Tibet pelo P. Antonio de Andrade da Companhia de Jesus, em 1624* (The Discovery of Tibet by Fr. Antonio de Andrade of the Society of Jesus in 1624). Coimbra:

Imprensa da Universidade, 1921.

Felix, Father. "Mughal Farmans, Parwanahs and Sanads Issued in Favour of Jesuit Missionaries." *Journal of the Punjab Historical Society* (Calcutta). 5 (no. 1, 1916), 1-53.

Fenning, Hugh. "Records of the Dominicans of Goa 1700-1835." *Archivum Fratrum Praedictorum*. 50 (1980), 387-410.

Fernandes, Antonio P.C. *Missionarios Jesuitas no Brasil no tempo de Pombal* (Jesuit Missionaries in Brasil during the time of Pombal). Barcellos: Bertaso, 1936.

Fernandes, Braz A. *Bandra: Its Religious and Secular History*. Bombay, 1927.

——. *Dellon and the Inquisition of Goa*. Bombay: Anglo-Lusitano, 1936.

Ferroli, Domenico. *The Jesuits in Malabar*. Vol. 1. Bangalore: The Bangalore Press, 1939.

——. *The Jesuits in Malabar*. Vol. 2. Bangalore: King & Co., 1951.

——. *The Jesuits in Mysore*. Kozhikode: Xavier Press, 1955.

Filippi, Filippo de (ed.) *An Account of Tibet. The Travels of Ippolito Desideri of Pistoia, S.J., 1712-1727*. London: George Routledge, 1937.

——. *The Nestorian Tablet and Hymn* (Translations of Chinese texts from the first period of the Church in China, 635-900). London: SPCK, s.a.

Fonseca, José N. da. *An Historical and Archaeological Sketch of the City of Goa*. Bombay: Thacker & Co., 1878.

Foster, William, (ed.). *Early Travels in India (1583-1619)*. London: Oxford University Press, 1921.

Freitas, Jordão A de. "A Inquisição em Goa, subsidios para a sua historia" (The Inquisition in Goa, material for its history). *Archivo Historico Portuguez*. 5 (1907), 216-227.

Frias, Antonio J. de. *Avreola dos Indios e Nobiliarchia Bracmana* (The Glories of the Indians and the Nobility of the Brahmins). Bombay: Livraria P.A. Fialho, 1892.

Fryer, John. *A New Account of East India and Persia*. Vols. 1-3. London, 1909.

Gallagher, J. (trans.) *China in the Sixteenth Century: The Journals of Matthew Ricci 1583-1610*. New York: Random House, s.a.

Gardini, Walter. *El Cristianismo llega a China*. Buenos Aires: Editorial Guadalupe, 1983.

Gazetteer of the Bombay Presidency, XIV *Thana* (places of interest). Bombay: Government Central Press, 1882.

Gense, James H. "First Confiscation of Jesuit Properties in Bombay." *The*

Examiner (Bombay). 10 September 1938, Sep 17, 1938.

——. *How Bombay was ceded.* Bombay: D.B. Taraporevala Sons & Co., s.a.

Gernet, Jacques. *China and the Christian Impact.* Cambridge: Cambridge University Press, 1985.

Goetstouwers, J.B. *Synopsis Historiae Societatis Jesu.* Lovani: Typis and Sancti Alphonsi, 1950.

Goldie, Francis. *The First Christian Mission to the Great Moghul.* Dublin: M.H. Gill & Sons, 1897.

Gomes-Catão, Francisco X. "Ultimos Jesuitas em Salcete no tempo de Pombal" (The last Jesuits in Salcete during the time of Pombal). *Anuario do Seminario Patriarcal de Rachol* (Annual of the Patriarchal Seminary of Rachol). 1948-49, xxxiv + xli.

——. *The Island of Chorão: A Historical Sketch.* Alwaye: Mar Louis Memorial Press, 1962.

Goldie, Francis. *The First Christian Mission to the Great Moghul.* Dublin: M.H. Gill & Son, 1897.

Gracias, F.H. *Behold All Generations* (A documented history of the origin of Christianity in Bandra and of the shrine of Our Lady of the Mount). Bombay: Examiner Press, 1964.

Gracias, Maria Fatima. "Health and Hygiene in the Portuguese Period." *Fish, Curry and Rice* (A Citizens' Report on the Goan Environment). Goa: Ecoforum. 1993, 231-232.

Gulbenkian, Roberto. "Jacome Abuna, An Armenian Bishop in Malabar (1503-1550) According to Contemporary Portuguese Sources". *Arquivos do Centro Cultural Portugues* (Paris), 4 (1972), 149-176.

Guerreiro, Fernão. *Relação Anual das coisas que fizeram os Padres da Companhia de Jesus nas suas missões* (Annual Report of the missionary deeds of the Fathers of the Society of Jesus). Vol. 1. (1600-03). Ed. Artur Viegas. Coimbra: Imprensa da Universidade, 1930.

Hambye, Eduard R. "The Moghul Court, the Portuguese and the Jesuits 1614-1617. *Journal of Indian History.* Trivandrum (Golden Jubilee Volume), 457-462.

Harney, Martin P. *Jesuits in History: The Society of Jesus through Four Centuries.* Illinois: Loyola University Press, 1962.

Hay, Malcolm. *Failure in the Far East.* Belgium: Scaldis Publishers, 1956.

Heras, Henry. *The Aravidu Dynasty of Vijayanagara.* I. Madras: B.G. Paul & Company, 1927.

——. "The Decay of the Portuguese Power in India", *Journal of the*

Bombay Historical Society. Bombay, 1928, 3-42.

——. "Three Catholic Padres at the Court of Ali Adil Shah I." *Journal of the Bombay Historical Society*., 1928, 158-163.

——. *The Conversion Policy of the Jesuits in India*. Bombay: Indian Historical Research Institute, 1933.

——. "The Jesuits in Afghanistan." *The New Review*. Calcutta: R.N. Mitra, 1935, 1-13.

Hicks, John. *A Theory of Economic History*. Bristol: Oxford University Press, 1982.

Hosten, Henry. "List of Jesuit Missionaries in Mogor (1580-1803)." *Journal of the Asiatic Society of Bengal*. 6 (no. 10, Nov 1910), 527-542.

——. "Mirza Zu-l-Qarnain, a Christian Grandee of Three Great Moghuls, with Notes on Akbar's Christian Wife and the Indian Bourbons." *Memoirs of the Asiatic Society of Bengal*. 5 (no. 4, 1916), Calcutta, 115-194.

——. (ed.) "Letters and other Papers of Fr. Ippolito Desideri, S.J., A Missionary in Tibet (1713-21)." *Journal of the Royal Asiatic Society of Bengal*. 4 (no. 24, 1938), 567-767.

——. "The Annual Relation of Father Ferdinand Guerreiro S.J. for 1607-1608." *Selections from the Journal of the Punjab Historical Society*. 3 (1982). Lahore, 75-98.

——. "The Family of Lady Juliana Dias Costa." *Selections from the Journal of the Punjab Historical Society*. 3 (1982). Lahore, 64-74.

Houpert, Joseph C. *A South Indian Mission – The Madura Catholic Mission from 1535 to 1935*. Trichinopoly, St. Joseph's, 1937.

Hoyland, J.S. (trans.). *The Commentary of Father Monserrate, S.J. on his Journey to the Court of Akbar*. 1922. Reprint. New Delhi: Asian Educational Services, 1992.

Hull, Ernest R. *Bombay Mission History with a Special Study of the Padroado Question*. Vols. 1-2. Bombay: Examiner Press, 1927 & 1930.

Humbert, John. "Catalogus Patrum et Fratrum Societatis Iesu ex India anno 11760 expulsorum" (Catalogue of the Fathers and Brothers of the Society of Jesus expelled from India in 1760). 31 (1962). Rome: AHSI, 324-359.

——. "The Goa Archives in 1963," *Indica*. 1 (no. 1, Mar 1964), 47-66.

——. "Some Answers of the Generals of the Society of Jesus to the Province of Goa. Acquaviva – Vitelleschi 1581-1645." 35(1966). Rome: AHSI, 322-346.

——. "Some Answers of the Generals of the Society of Jesus to the Province of Goa from Carrafa to Tamburini 1647-1726." 36(1967). Rome: AHSI, 72-101.

Irvine, William (trans.) *Storia do Mogor or Moghul India 1653-1708 by Niccolao Manucci*. Vols. 1-4, Calcutta, Editions India, 1965-67.

Jacobs, H. "Ambon as a Portuguese and Catholic Town, 1576-1605". *Neue Zeitschfift fur Missionswissenschaft*, 41 (n. 1, 1985), 1-17.

Kosambi, Damodar D. *An Introduction to the Study of Indian History*. Bombay: Popular Prakashan, 1975.

Latourette, Kenneth S. *A History of Christian Missions in China*. New York: Macmillan, 1929.

Leite, Serafim, *Historia da Companhia de Jesus no Brasil* (History of the Society of Jesus in Brazil). Vol. 4. Rio de Janeiro: Instituto Nacional do Livro, 1943.

Linschoten, John Huyghen van. *The Voyage of John Huyghen van Linschoten to the East Indies*. Eds. Arthur C. Burnell & P.A. Tiele. Vols. 1-2, New Delhi: Asian Educational Services, 1988. Reprint.

Ljungstedt, Andrew. *An Historical Sketch of the Portuguese Settlements in China and of the Roman Catholic Church and Mission in China*. Boston: James Munroe & Company, 1836.

Lobo, Sylvester. *A Document with the Early Revenue of Bombay*, Bombay, s.a.

Lockman, John. *Travels of the Jesuits into Various Parts of the World Compiled from Their Letters*. Vol. 1. London, 1743.

Locke, J. Courtenay (ed.) *The First Englishmen in India*. London: George Routledge, 1930.

Lopes, Felix. "Os Franciscanos no Oriente Portugues de 1584 a 1590" (The Franciscans in the Portuguese East from 1584 to 1590). *Studia*. (no. 9, 1962), 29-142.

Mackenzie, G.T. *History of Christianity in Travancore*. Trivandrum: Government Press, 1905.

Maclagan, Edward. *The Jesuits and the Great Moghul*. London: Burns Oates & Washbourne, 1932.

Marinho, P. *Galeria de Tyrannos* (O diario do P. Eckart, ou as suas prisões em Portugal desde 1755 a 1777). Porto: Fonseca, 1917.

Martires Lopes, Maria de Jesus dos. "A Inquisição de Goa na segunda metade do seculo XVIII" (The Inquisition in Goa in the second half of the 18th century), *Studia*. (no. 48, 1989), 237-282.

——. "Teaching Methods in Goa (1750-1800): Jesuits and Oratorians." *Discoveries, Missionary Expansion and Asian Cultures*. Ed. Teotonio

R. de Souza. New Delhi: Concept, 1994.

Mathew, K.S. *Portuguese Trade with India in the Sixteenth Century.* Delhi: Manohar Publishers, 1983.

Meersman, Achilles. "The Franciscans in India (From their Suppression in 1835 to the Present Day)." *NZFM,* (no. 13, 1957), 208-216.

——. *The Franciscans in Tamilnad.* Schoneck-Berkenried: Nouvelle Reuve de Science Missionaire Suisse, 1962.

——. "Notes on the Charitable Institutions the Portuguese Established in India." *ICHR.* 5 (no. 2, 1971), 95-105.

——. *The Ancient Franciscan Provinces in India 1500-1835.* Bangalore: Christian Literature Society Press, 1971.

——. *Annual Reports of the Portuguese Franciscans in India 1713-1833.* Lisbon: Centro de Estudos Historicos Ultramarinos, 1972.

——. "The Expulsion of the Jesuits from their Kittur Mission in India. *NZFM.* 28 (1972), pp. 221-24.

——. "The First Attempts to Introduce the Church in Vellore." *ICHR.* 12 (no. 1, 1978), 71-78.

Meilink-Roelofsz, M.A.P. *Asian Trade and European Influence.* The Hague: Martinus Nijhoff, 1962.

Minamiki, George. *The Chinese Rites Controversy from its Beginning to Modern Times.* Chicago: Loyola University Press, 1985.

Miranda, Luis. *The Jesuit Ratio Studiorum: An Adaptation to Secondary Schools in the Madras Presidency.* Madura: De Nobili Press, 1947.

Moraes, George M. "Astronomical Missions to the Court of Jaipur 1730-1743." *Journal of the Bombay Branch of the Royal Asiatic Society.* (no. 27, 1951), 61-65.

Morner, Magnus (ed.). *The Expulsion of the Jesuits from Latin America.* New York: Alfred A. Knopf, 1965.

Mulakara, Gervasis J. *History of the Diocese of Cochin.* Vol. 1. (European Missionaries in Cochin 1292-1558). Rome: Leberit, 1986, 124p.

Mundadan, A. Mathias. *History of Christianity in India.* Vol. 1: *From the Beginning up to the Middle of the Sixteenth Century (up to 1542).* Bangalore: Theological Publications in India, 1984.

Mountstuart, Elphinstone *The History of India.* Vol. 2, London: John Murray, 1843.

Naik, Gregory. *Jesuit Education in India* (commemorative volume of the twenty fifth anniversary of the Jesuit Educational Association of India). Anand: Gujarat Sahitya Prakash, 1987.

Nazareth, Casimiro C. de. *Mitras Lusitanas no Oriente.* Vol. 1. Lisbon: Imprensa Nacional, 1897. Vol. 2. Panjim: Artur & Viegas, 1924. Vol.

3. Bombay: Portuguese Printing Press, 1988.

Neill, Stephen. *A History of the Christian Missions*. Middlesex: Penguin Books, 1966.

——. *A History of Christianity in India. The Beginning to AD 1707.* Cambridge: Cambridge University Press, 1985.

Noonan, Laurence A. *The First Jesuit Missin in Malacca: A Study of the Use of the Portuguese Trading Centre as a Base for Christian Missionary Expansion during the Years 1545 to 1552.* Lisbon: Centro de Estudos Historicos Ultramarinos da Junta de Investigações Cientificas do Ultramar, 1974.

Noti, S. *Joseph Tieffentaller SJ – A Forgotten Geographer of India.* Bombay: Nirnayasagar Press, 1906.

Panikkar, Kavalam M. *Malabar and the Portuguese.* Bombay: D.B. Taraporevala, 1929.

——. *Asia and Western Dominance*, London, 1958.

Payne, C.H. (Trans.) *Jahangir and the Jesuits.* London: George Routledge, 1926.

Pearson, Michael N. *Coastal Western India: Studies from the Portuguese Records.* New Delhi: Concept Publishing Company, 1981.

——. *The New Cambridge History of India: The Portuguese in India.* Cambridge: Cambridge University Press, 1987.

Perera, S.G. (trans. & ed.) *The Oratorian Mission in Ceylon* (Historical documents relating to the Life and Labours of the Venerable Father Joseph Vaz). nos. 1-6. Colombo: Caxton, 1936.

Perniola, V. *The Catholic Church in Sri Lanka: The Dutch Period 1658-1795.* Sri Lanka: Tisara Prakasakayo, 1983-85.

——. *The Catholic Church in Sri Lanka: The Portuguese Period 1566-1619.* Vols. 1-3. Sri Lanka: Tisara Prakasakayo, 1991.

Pissurlencar, P.S.S. *Roteiro dos Arquivos da India Portuguesa* (A guide to the Archives of Goa). Bastora: Rangel, 1955.

——. *The Portuguese and the Marathas.* Translated by P.R. Kakodkar. Bombay: State Board for Literature and Culture, 1975.

Ploeg, J.P.M. van der. *The Christians of St. Thomas in South India and Their Syriac Manuscripts.* Bangalore: Dharmaram Publications, 1983.

Polgar, Laszlo. *Bibliography of the History of the Society of Jesus.* Vol. 1 (Sources and Studies for the History of the Jesuits). Rome: Jesuit Historical Institute, 1967.

——. *Bibliographie sur L'Histoire de la Compagnie de Jesus 1901-1980.* Vol. 1 (*Toute la Compagnie*). Rome: Institutum Historicum Societatis Iesu, 1981.

Prasad, Ram. C. *Early English Travellers in India*. Delhi: Motilal Banarsidass, 1980.

Priolkar, Anant K. *The Goa Inquistion* – Being a Quartercentenary Commemoration Study of the Inquisition in India. Bombay: A.K. Priolkar, 1961.

Qaisar, A. Jan. "Depiction of the Jesuit Priests and the Portughese (sic) in Mughal Paintings." *Revista de Cultura*. 13-14 (1991), 317-327.

Queyroz, Fernão de. *The Temporal and Spiritual Conquest of Ceylon*. Bks. 1-6. Translation by S.G. Pereira from the Portuguese. Colombo: A.C. Richards, 1930.

Silva, Severine. *History of Christianity in Canara*. Vols. 1-2. Karwar: S. Silva, 1957/1961.

Rajamanickam, S. *The First Oriental Scholar*. Tirunelveli: De Nobili Research Institute, 1972.

——. "The Old Madurai Mission – A Chronological Table." *ICHR*. 21 (no. 2, Dec 1987), 130-133.

Rea, William F. *The Economics of the Zambezi Missions: 1580-1759*. Rome: IHSI, 1976.

Renick, M.S. "Akbar's First Embassy to Goa: Its Diplomatic and Religious Aspects." *Indica*. 7 (no. 1, Mar 1970), 33-47.

Ricci, Matteo. *The True Meaning of the Lord of Heaven*. St. Louis: The Institute of Jesuit Sources, 1985.

Rocha, Leopoldo Da. *As Confrarias de Goa (Séculos XVI-XX)* (The Religious Confraternities of Goa in 16 – 20th Centuries). Lisbon: Centro de Estudos Historicos Ultramarinos, 1973.

Rodrigues, Francisco. *Jesuitas Portugueses Astronomos na China 1583-1805* (The Portuguese Astronomer-Jesuits in China 1583-1805). Porto: Porto Medico, 1925.

——. *A Companhia de Jesus em Portugal e nas missões* (The Society of Jesus in Portugal and in the missions). Porto: Apostolado da Imprensa, 1935.

Ronan, Charles & Oh, Bonnie (eds.). *East Meets West – The Jesuits in China, 1582-1773*. Chicago: Loyola University Press, 1988.

Rowbotham, Arnold H. *Missionary and Mandarin: Jesuits at the Court of China*. Berkeley: University of California Press, 1942.

Saldanha, Mariano, *Doutrina Crista em lingua concani por Tomas Estevão, S.J. Impressa em Rachol (Goa) em 1622*. (Christian Doctrine in Konkani by Thomas Stephens, S.J. Printed in Rachol in 1622). 2nd ed. Lisbon: Agencia Geral das Colonias, 1945.

——. "A Primeira Imprensa em Goa" (The First Printing Press in Goa). *Boletim do Instituto Vasco da Gama* (Panjim). (no. 73, 1956), 80-137.

Santos, Angel, *Jeronimo Javier, S.J. Apostol del Gran Mogol* (Jeronimo Xavier, Apostle of the Grand Moghul). Pamplona: Principe de Viana, 1962.

——. *Las Misiones Bajo el Patronato Portugues* (The Missions under the Portuguese Patronage). Madrid: Eapsa, 1977.

Scammell, Geoffrey V., *The World Encompassed: The First European Maritime Empires c. 800-1650*. London: Methuen & Company, 1981.

Scholberg, Henry. *Bibliography of Goa and the Portuguese in India* (with the collaboration of Archana A. Kakodkar and Carmo Azevedo). New Delhi: Promilla & Company, 1982.

Schurhammer, Georg. "Armenian Bishops in Malabar?." *Arquivos do Centro Cultural Portugues* (Paris). 1972, 141-148.

——. *Francis Xavier: His Life, His Times*. Vols. 1-4, Translation by M.J. Costelloe from the German. Rome: The Jesuit Historical Institute, 1973-1982.

Schutte, Josef F. *Valignano's Mission Principles for Japan*. Vol. I (Parts 1-2). Anand: Gujarat Sahitya Prakash, 1980/1985.

Sergio, Antonio, *Breve Interpretação da Historia de Portugal* (A Short Interpretation of the History of Portugal). Lisbon: Livraria Sa da Costa, 1979.

Shastry, B.S. (ed.) *Goan Society through the Ages*. Delhi: Asian Publication Services, 1987.

Shirodkar, P.P. (ed.) *Goa: Cultural Trends*: Panjim: Directorate of Archives, Archaeology and Museum, 1988.

Silva Rego, Antonio da (ed.) *Documentação para a historia das Missões do Padroado Portugues do Oriente* (Documentation for a history of the missions of the Portuguese Crown Patronage in the East). Vols. 1-12. Lisbon: Agencia Geral das Colonias/do Ultramar, 1947-58.

Simoes, Manuel, "Camilo, Pombal e os Jesuitas." *Como Interpretar Pombal no bicentenario da sua morte?*. Lisbon: Broteria, 1983, 147-164.

Smith, D.H. *Chinese Religions from 1000 BC to the Present Day*. New York: Rinehart & Winston, 1968.

Souza, Francisco de. *Oriente Conquistado a Jesu Christo pelos Padres da Companhia de Jesus da Provincia de Goa*. (The Conquest of the East to Jesus Christ by the Fathers of the Society of Jesus of the Province of Goa). Vol. 1. Bombay: Examiner Press, 1881.

Souza, George Bryan. *The Survival of Empire: Portuguese Trade and Society in China and the South China Sea, 1630-1754.* Cambridge: Cambridge University Press, 1986.

Sta Maria, Bernard. *My People My Country* (The Story of Malacca Portuguese Community). Malacca: Portuguese Development Centre, 1982.

Steensgaard, Niels. *The Asian Trade Revolution of the Seventeenth Century: The East India Companies and the Decline of the Caravan Trade.* Chicago: University of Chicago Press, 1974.

Subrahmanyam, Sanjay. *The Portuguese Empire in Asia 1500-1700: A Political and Economic History.* London: Longman, 1993.

Tawney, R.H. *Religion and the Rise of Capitalism.* Middlesex: Penguin Books, 1937.

Teixeira, Manuel. *The Portuguese Missions in Malacca and Singapore (1511-1958).* Vols. 1-2 (Malacca), Vol. 3 (Singapore). Macau: Instituto Cultural de Macau, 1987.

Thekkedath, Joseph. *History of Christianity in India. From the Middle of the Sixteenth Century to the End of the Seventeenth Century.* Vol. 2. Bangalore: Theological Publications of India, 1982.

Thekedathu, Joseph. *The Troubled Days of Francis Garcia SJ Archbishop of Cranganore (1641-59).* Rome: Universita Gregoriana, 1972.

Thomaz, Luis Filipe. "The Indian Merchant Communities in Malacca under the Portuguese Rule," in *Indo-Portuguese History: Old Issues, New Questions*, 58-72.

Trindade, Frei Paulo da. *Conquista Espiritual do Oriente* (The Spiritual Conquest of the East). Ed. F. Felix Lopes. Vols. 1-3. Lisbon: Centro de Estudos Historicos Ultramarinos, 1962-67.

Ursis, Sabatino de. *P. Matheus Ricci S.J.* Rome: Enrico Voghera, 1910.

Velez, Manuela Blanco. "Notas sobre o poder temporal da Companhia de Jesus na India (seculo XVII). *Studia.* 49 (1989), 195-214.

Velinkar, Joseph. "Francisco Aranha, Builder of Salcete Churches." *Indica.* 17 (no. 2, Sep 1980), 139-145.

——. "Jesuit Educational Style in Sixteenth Century Goa." *Indica.* 21 (no. 1, Mar 1984), 17-27.

Viljoen, Stephan. *Economic Systems in World History.* London: Longman Group, 1974.

Wallerstein, Immanuel. *The Modern World-System. Capitalist Agriculture and the Origins of the European World Economy in the Sixteenth Century.* Vol. 1. Florida: Academic Press, 1974.

Weber, Max. *The Religion of China: Confucianism and Taoism.* Glencoe: Free Press, 1951.

Weld, Alfred. *The Suppression of the Society of Jesus*. London: Burns & Oates, 1877.

Wessels, Cornelius, *Early Jesuit Travellers in Central Asia 1603-1721*. The Hague: Martinus Nijhoff, 1924.

Wheeler, J.T. *European Travellers in India*. Calcutta: 1956.

Whitehead, James G. et al (eds.). *China and Christianity. Historical and Future Encounters*. Notre Dame: University Press, 1979.

Wicki, Josef (ed.). *Primeira Parte da Historia dos Religiosos da Companhia de Jesus composta pello Pe. Sebastiam Gonçalves* (The First Part of the History of the Religious of the Society of Jesus composed by Fr. Sebastian Gonçalves). Vol. 1. Coimbra: Atlantida, 1957.

——. "Der Bericht des Jesuiten Provinzials von Goa an die Kinigliche Akademie der Portugiesischen Geschichte." (The Information of the Jesuit Provincials of Goa of the Portuguese Royal Academy of History). *AHSI*. 39 (1970), 102-1166.

——. "Die Anfange der Missionsprokur der Jesuiten in Lissabon bis 1580," (The Beginnings of the Jesuit Mission Office in Lisbon from 1580). *AHSI*. 40 (1971), 246-322.

——. "Dois Compendios das Ordens dos Padres Gerais e Congregações Provinciais da Provincia dos Jesuitas de Goa, feitos em 1664" (Two volumes containing orders of the General Superiors and the Provincial Congregations of the Jesuit Province of Goa). *Studia*. (nos. 43-44, Jan-Dec 1980), 343-532.

Wills, John E. *Embassies and Illusions: Dutch and Portuguese Envoys to K'ang-hsi, 1667-1687*. Cambridge (Mass.): Harvard University, 1984.

Witek, John W. *Controversial Ideas in China and in Europe: A Biography of Jean-François Foucquet, S.J. (1665-1741)*. Rome: AHSI, 1982.

Xavier, Felippe N. *Bosquejo Historico das Communidades* (An Historical Sketch of the Village Communities). Bastora: T. Rangel, 1852.

Yule, Henry & Burnell, A.C. *Hobson-Jobson*. Ed. William Crooke. Delhi: Rupa, 1986.

Zubillaga, Felix. "El Procurador de la Companhia de Jesus en la Corta de Espana (1570)" (The Procurator of the Society of Jesus in the Spanish Court in 1570). *AHSI*. 16 (1947), 1-55.

——. "El Procurador de las Indias Occidentales" (The Procurator of the West Indies). *AHSI*. 22 (1953), 367-417.

——. "La Provincia Jesuitica de Nueva Espana su Fundamento Economico: Siglo XVI," (The economic foundations of the Jesuit Province of New Spain: 16th century). *AHSI*. 38 (1969), 3-1169.

Zubillaga, Felix & Hanisch, Walter. *Guia Manual*. Rome: IHSI, 1971.

MAPS

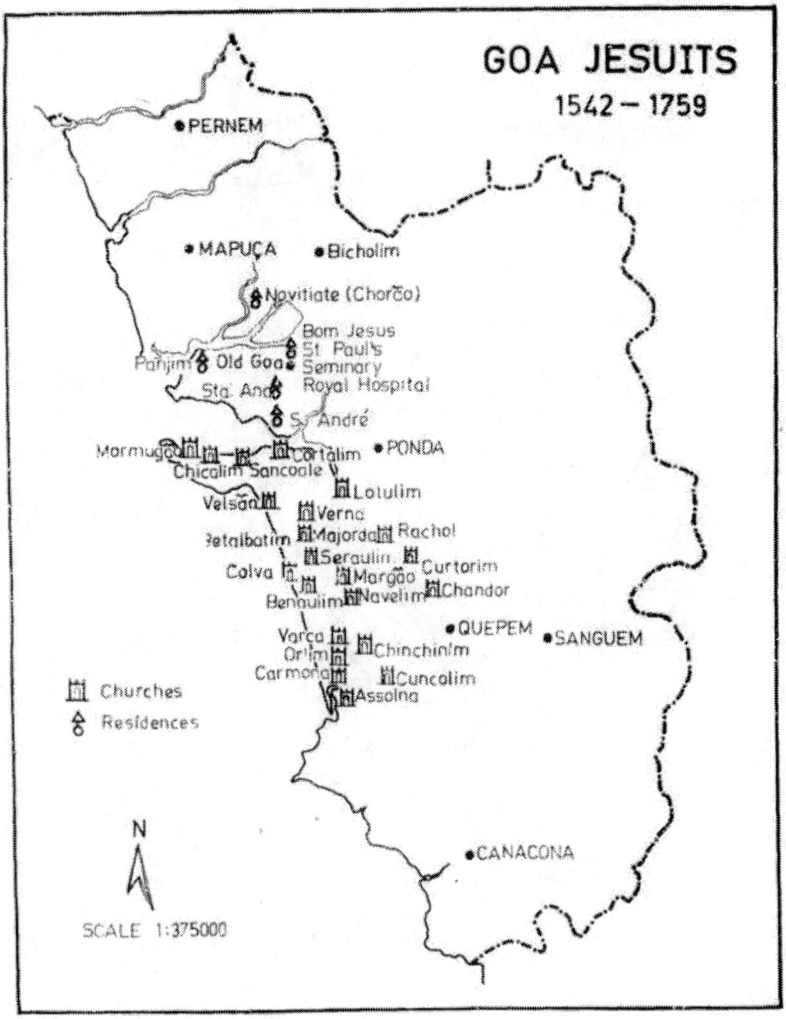

MAP 1 : Goa Jesuits 1542-1759

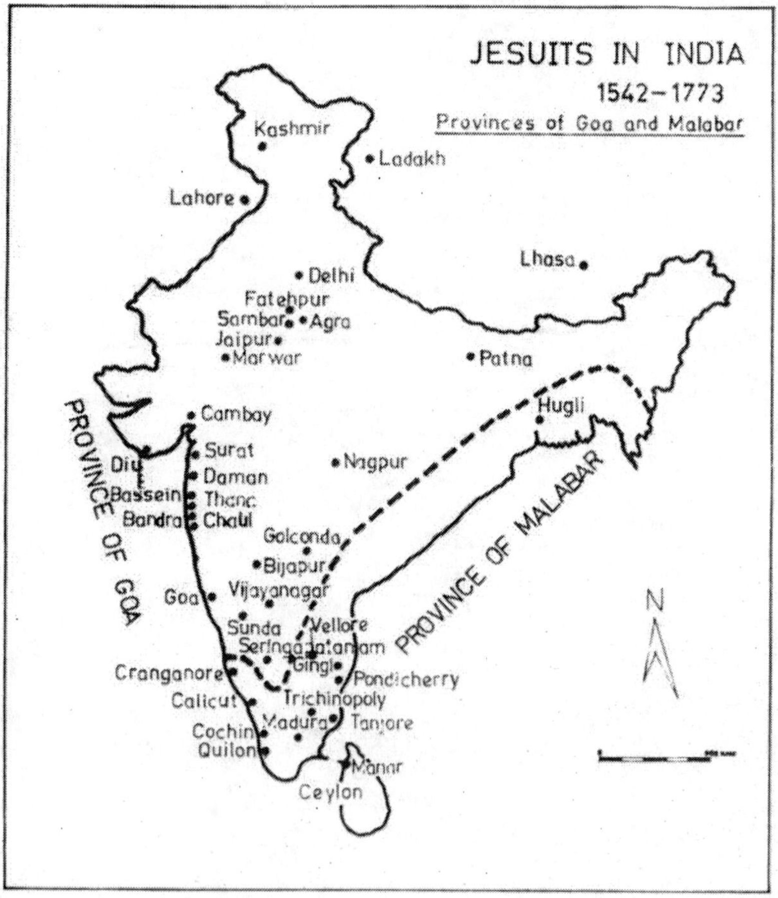

MAP 2 : Jesuits in India, 1542-1773: (Provinces of Goa and Malabar)

MAP 3 : Manuel Godinho Eredia (1615)
Source: Portugaliae Monumenta Cartographia. Lisbon : Imprensa Nacional, 1987, IV, p. 53.

INDEX